Book II

PHYSICAL SCIENCE ACTIVITIES FOR GRADES 2–8

Science Curriculum Activities Library

MARVIN N. TOLMAN
JAMES O. MORTON

illustrated by Carolyn Quinton

Parker Publishing Company, Inc.
West Nyack, New York

10 9 8 7 6

Library of Congress Catalog Card Number: 86-61402

ISBN 0-13-669797-6

Printed in the United States of America

ABOUT THE AUTHORS

DR. MARVIN N. TOLMAN

Trained as an educator at Utah State University, Marvin N. Tolman began his career as a teaching principal in rural southeastern Utah. The next eleven years were spent teaching grades one through six in schools in San Juan and Utah counties and earning graduate degrees.

Currently associate professor of elementary education, Dr. Tolman has been teaching graduate and undergraduate classes at Brigham Young University since 1975. Subject areas of his courses include math methods, science methods, and computer literacy for teachers. He has served as a consultant to school districts, has taught workshops in many parts of the United States, and published several articles in professional journals. Dr. Tolman is one of two authors of *What Research Says to the Teacher: The Computer and Education*, published in 1984 by the National Education Association, and a coauthor of *Computers in Education*, published by Prentice-Hall, 1986.

Dr. Tolman now lives in Spanish Fork, Utah, with his wife, Judy, and their five children.

DR. JAMES O. MORTON

For more than thirty years, James O. Morton, Ed.D., Teachers College, Columbia University, has taught students of all ages. He began his career as an elementary school teacher in the Salt Lake City, Utah, public schools, where he served later as a principal and as curriculum director. For one year Dr. Morton was a visiting lecturer in education at Queens College, New York City. He also served as an instructor on the summer faculty of Teachers College, Columbia University. For fifteen years Dr. Morton was an associate professor of science education at the University of Utah.

Dr. Morton has served as a national consultant in the development of science curriculum from early childhood through university graduate programs in all geographical areas of the United States. His publications have appeared in scientific and professional journals.

Dr. Morton currently works as a writer and science consultant and lives with his wife, Lornel, in Klamath Falls, Oregon.

ABOUT THE *LIBRARY*

The *Science Curriculum Activities Library* provides elementary teachers with over 475 science activities that give students hands-on experience in various areas. To be used in conjunction with your regular science texts, the *Library* includes three books, each providing activities exploring a different field:

- Life Sciences
- Physical Sciences
- Earth Sciences

In most public schools today, emphasis is on the fundamental skills of language arts and mathematics. The teaching of science has often been relegated to a supplementary place in the curriculum. What may be overlooked is that a strong science program with a discovery/inquiry approach can enrich the development of mathematics, as well as other academic content areas. The activities in the *Library* develop these skills. Most activities call for verbal responses, with questions that encourage analyzing, synthesizing, and inferring instead of answering yes or no.

Development of thinking and reasoning skills and to understanding content are the main goals of the *Library*'s science activities. Learning how to learn and how to apply the various tools of learning are more useful in a person's life than is the acquisition of large numbers of scientific facts. Through these process skills, students are encouraged to explore, invent, and create. The learning of scientific facts is a byproduct of this effort, and increased insight and retention of facts learned are virtually assured.

HOW TO USE BOOK II: PHYSICAL SCIENCES

Book II consists of over 170 easy-to-use, hands-on activities in the following areas of physical sciences:

- Nature of Matter
- Energy
- Light
- Sound
- Simple Machines
- Magnetism
- Static Electricity
- Current Electricity

Teacher Qualifications

You need not be a scientist to conduct an effective and exciting science program at the elementary level. Interest, creativity, enthusiasm, and willingness to get involved and try something new will go a long way. Two of the most critical qualities of the elementary teacher as a scientist are (1) commitment to helping students acquire learning skills and (2) recognition of the value of science and its implications for the acquisition of such skills.

Capitalize on Interest

It is expected that some areas will be of greater interest to both you and your students, so these interests should be considered when you select science topics. Since these materials are both nongraded and nonsequential, areas of greatest interest and need can be emphasized. As you gain experience with using the activities, your skill is guiding students toward appropriate discoveries and insights will increase.

Organizing for an Activity-centered Approach

Trends of the past have encouraged teachers to modify a traditional textbook approach by using an activity-based program, supplemented by the use of textbooks and other materials. We favor this approach, so the following activities encourage hands-on discovery. Valuable learning skills are developed through this direct experience.

One of the advantages of this approach is the elimination of a need for every student to have the same book at the same time, freeing a substantial portion of the textbook money for purchasing a variety of materials and references, including other textbooks, trade books, audio and video tapes, models, and other visuals. References should be acquired that lend themselves developmentally to a variety of approaches, subject matter emphases, and levels of reading difficulty.

Starter Ideas

Section 1, "Starter Ideas," should be used first. The sequence of other sections may be adjusted according to interest, availability of materials, time of year, or other factors. Some sections use concepts developed in other parts of the book. When this occurs, the activities are cross-referenced so concepts can be drawn from other sections as needed.

Starter Ideas are placed at the beginning of the book to achieve several specific goals:

- To assist in selecting topics for study.
- To provide a wide variety of interesting and exciting hands-on activities from many areas of science. As students investigate these Starter Ideas, they should be motivated to try additional activities in related sections of the book.
- To introduce teachers and students to the discovery/inquiry approach. When you have experienced several of these activities, they will spend time on the other sections more efficiently.
- To be used for those occasions when only a short period of time is available and a high-interest independent activity is needed.

Unique Features

The following points should be kept in mind while using this book:

1. It places the student in the center of the discovery/inquiry approach to hands-on learning.
2. The main goals are problem solving and the development of critical-thinking skills. Content is a spinoff, but is possibly learned with greater insight than if it were the main objective.
3. It attempts to prepare teachers for inquiry-based instruction and sharpen their guidance and questioning techniques.
4. Most materials recommended for use are readily available in the school or at home.
5. Activities are intended to be open and flexible and to encourage the extension of skills through the use of as many outside resources as possible: (a) The use of parents, aides, and resource people of all kinds is recommended throughout; (b) the library, media center, and other school resources, as well as a classroom reading center related to the area of study, are essential in teaching most of the sections; and (c) educational television programs and videocassettes can often enrich the science program.
6. With the exception of the activities labeled "teacher demonstration" or "whole-class activity," students are encouraged to work individually, in pairs, or in small groups. The teacher gathers and organizes the materials, arranges the learning setting, and serves as a resource person. In many instances, the materials listed on an index card with the

procedure are all students will need in order to perform the activities. Ideas are given in "To the Teacher" at the beginning of each section and in "Teacher Information" at the end of each activity to help you develop your content background and your questioning and guidance skills.

7. Full-page activity sheets, such as "Record of Measurements I" and "Measuring with a Movable Pulley," are offered throughout this book. These sheets can easily be reproduced and kept on hand.

At the end of the book are a bibliography, sources of free and inexpensive materials, and a list of science supply houses. This information will help you organize your program so that each activity is used to its fullest potential.

Format of Activities

Each activity in this book includes the following information:

- *Activity Number*: Activities are numbered sequentially throughout the book for each reference.
- *Activity Title*: The title of each activity is in the form of a question that can be answered by completing the activity and that requires more than a simple yes or no answer.
- *Special Instructions*: Some activities are intended to be used as teacher demonstrations or whole-group activities, or require close supervision for safety reasons, so these special instructions are noted.
- *Materials*: Each activity lists the materials needed. The materials used are easily acquired, but, when necessary, special instructions or sources have been given.
- *Procedure*: The steps for the students to follow are given in easy-to-understand language.
- *Teacher Instructions*: Suggested teaching tips and background information follow the procedure. This information supplements that given in "To the Teacher."

Use of Metric Measures

Most linear measures used are given in metric units followed by standard units in parentheses. This is done to encourage use of the metric system. Other measures, such as capacity, are given in standard units.

Grade Level

The activities in this book are intended to be nongraded. Many activities in each section can be adapted for use with young children, yet most sections provide challenge for the more talented in the middle and upper elementary grades.

Final Note

Remember, the discovery/inquiry approach used in *Physical Sciences* emphasizes verbal responses and discussion. With the exception of recording results, activities do not require extensive writing. Discovering the excitement of science and developing new techniques for critical thinking and problem solving should be the major goals of your science program.

Marvin N. Tolman
James O. Morton

ACKNOWLEDGMENTS

Mentioning the names of all individuals who contributed to the *Science Curriculum Activities Library* would require an additional volume. The authors are greatly indebted to the following:

- Teams of graduate students at the University of Utah for initial assistance and testing of design and methodology.
- Teachers and students of all levels, from early childhood through postdoctoral, who taught us while they thought we were teaching them.
- School districts throughout the United States who cooperated by supporting and evaluating ideas and methods used in this book.
- Friends who provided special facilities so we could have the freedom to work and create: Drs. Richard and Virginia Ratcliff and family, Mike and Sue Grinvalds and family, and Sally Gross.
- Special consultants who made significant contributions to the development, quality, and accuracy of the manuscript: Lornel T. Morton (illustrating, typing, and editing); Sue P. Grinvalds (illustrating); Gregory L. Tolman (illustrating); Bonnie R. Newman (consultant); Kathryn L. J. Ardt (consultant); Vera A. Christensen (media); and Denise Swift (typing)
- Dr. James E. Baird, chairman of the Department of Elementary Education at Brigham Young University, for his encouragement and support, and for running interference to protect precious writing time.
- Finally, the last names of the authors, Tolman and Morton, are correct. However, the first names could well be changed to Judy and Lornel, for without their love, support, encouragement, patience, and acceptance these books could not have been written.

CONTENTS

About the Library .... *iv*

How to Use Book II: Physical Sciences .... *v*

Concept/Skills Index .... *xvii*

Section 1 STARTER IDEAS *1*

To the Teacher • *2*
Activity 1: How Can You Get Salt Out of Pepper? • *3*
Activity 2: What Can You Learn from an Egg? • *4*
Activity 3: How Can You Tell if Water Is Hot or Cold without Touching It? • *5*
Activity 4: How Does a Camera See the World? • *6*
Activity 5: How Can a Water Drop Make Things Larger? • *8*
Activity 6: How Can Water Make a Coin Appear? • *9*
Activity 7: What Do Bears Know That People Don't? • *10*
Activity 8: Can You Find The Coin? • *11*
Activity 9: How Can You Make a Glass Disappear? • *12*
Activity 10: How Can a Thread Help Carry Your Voice? • *13*
Activity 11: How Well Does Sound Travel through Solids? • *14*
Activity 12: What Happens When You Burn a Candle at Both Ends? • *15*
Activity 13: How Can the Depth of a Bathyscaph Be Controlled? • *16*

Section 2 NATURE OF MATTER *17*

To the Teacher • *18*
Activity 14: What Are Solids, Liquids, and Gases? • *19*
Activity 15: What Are Mixtures and Solutions? • *21*
Activity 16: Is Dissolving Solids a Physical Change or a Chemical Change? • *22*
Activity 17: What Is Rust? • *23*
Activity 18: How Can Chemical Changes Help You Write a Secret Message? • *24*
Activity 19: How Dry Can You Wring a Wet Sponge? • *25*
Activity 20: What Is Condensation? • *27*
Activity 21: What Is the Shape of a Drop of Water? • *28*

Activity 22: How Does Temperature Affect the Speed of Molecules? • *29*
Activity 23: How Does Temperature Affect Solubility? • *30*
Activity 24: How Can Perfume Get into a Sealed Balloon? • *31*
Activity 25: How Can You Cause Molecules to Move through solids? • *32*
Activity 26: What Is Viscosity? • *33*
Activity 27: How Can a Blown-Out Candle Relight Itself? • *34*
Activity 28: How Can You Remove the Flame from a Candle without Putting It Out? • *35*
Activity 29: How Can You Make One Type of Fire Extinguisher? • *37*
Activity 30: How Can You Make a Ball Bounce by Itself? • *38*
Activity 31: What Is Polyethylene? • *39*
Activity 32: How Does a Hydrometer Work? • *40*
Activity 33: How Can You Make Large Sugar Crystals from Tiny Ones? • *42*

Section 3 ENERGY. 43

To the Teacher • *44*
Activity 34: How Is Work Measured? • *45*
Activity 35: How Much Energy Is Stored in a Bow? • *46*
Activity 36: How Can You Get the Most Energy from the Sun? • *47*
Activity 37: What Other Type of Energy Accompanies Light from the Sun? • *48*
Activity 38: How Do Molecules Behave When Heated? • *50*
Activity 39: What Happens to Solids as They Are Heated and Cooled? • *51*
Activity 40: What Happens to Liquids as They Are Heated and Cooled? • *52*
Activity 41: What Happens to Gases as They Are Heated and Cooled? • *53*
Activity 42: How Does a Nail Change as It Is Driven into a Board? • *54*
Activity 43: How Can the Energy of Sound Cause Something to Move? • *55*
Activity 44: How Can Magnetism Do Work? • *56*
Activity 45: How Does Gravity Affect Heavy and Light Objects? • *57*
Activity 46: What Is Center of Gravity? • *58*
Activity 47: Where Is Your Center of Gravity? • *59*
Activity 48: What Is Centrifugal Force? • *60*
Activity 49: What Is Inertia? • *62*

Activity 50: How Do Potential Energy and Kinetic Energy Compare? • *63*
Activity 51: How Much Horsepower Do You Have? • *64*

Section 4 LIGHT *65*

To the Teacher • *66*
Activity 52: Why Do Shadows Change in Size? • *67*
Activity 53: What Can You Make with a Shadow? • *68*
Activity 54: What Path Does Light Follow? • *70*
Activity 55: How Does Color Affect Energy Absorbed from Light? • *71*
Activity 56: What Happened to the Pencil? • *73*
Activity 57: Can You Find the Coin? • *74*
Activity 58: How Can a Postage Stamp Hide under Clear Glass? • *75*
Activity 59: What Makes Light Bend? • *76*
Activity 60: How Does Water Affect Light Travel? • *77*
Activity 61: How Can You Make a Lens from a Drop of Water? • *78*
Activity 62: How Are Convex and Concave Lenses Different? • *79*
Activity 63: How Can You Measure the Magnifying Power of a Lens? • *80*
Activity 64: How Does a Lens Affect Light Travel? • *81*
Activity 65: What Color Is White? • *82*
Activity 66: What Does a Prism Do to Light? • *85*
Activity 67: How Can You Make a Prism? • *86*
Activity 68: What Affects the Quality of Reflection? • *87*
Activity 69: What Is the Difference between Reflected Light and Source Light? • *88*
Activity 70: What Is Reflected Light? • *89*
Activity 71: How Is Light Reflection Like the Bounce of a Ball? • *90*
Activity 72: How Many Images Can You See? • *92*
Activity 73: How Well Can You Control the Reflection of Light? • *94*
Activity 74: How Does a Periscope Work? • *96*
Activity 75: How Can You Pour Light? • *97*
Activity 76: How Can You Make a Glass Disappear? • *99*
Activity 77: What Is Color? • *100*

Section 5 SOUND *103*

To the Teacher • *104*
Activity 78: What Is Sound? • *105*
Activity 79: What Are Some Things Sounds Tell Us? • *106*

Activity 80: How Well Can You Match Sounds? • *107*
Activity 81: How Are Sounds Made? • *108*
Activity 82: What Causes Sound? • *109*
Activity 83: How Do We Produce Sounds? • *111*
Activity 84: Can Sounds Be Shaped? • *112*
Activity 85: How Can Sounds Be Produced? (Part I) • *113*
Activity 86: How Can Sounds Be Produced? (Part II) • *114*
Activity 87: How Can Sounds Be Produced? (Part III) • *115*
Activity 88: How Can Sounds Be Produced? (Part IV) • *116*
Activity 89: How Can You See Sound? • *117*
Activity 90: How Can You See Your Voice? • *118*
Activity 91: How Does Sound Travel? (Part I) • *119*
Activity 92: How Does Sound Travel? (Part II) • *120*
Activity 93: How Does Sound Travel? (Part III) • *121*
Activity 94: How Does Sound Travel? (Part IV) • *122*
Activity 95: How Fast Does Sound Travel? • *123*
Activity 96: How Can Sound Be Controlled? • *124*
Activity 97: What Happens to Sound When There Are Fewer Molecules? • *126*
Activity 98: What Is a Tuning Fork? • *127*
Activity 99: Can You Make A Goblet Sing? • *128*
Activity 100: How Can Sounds Be Heard More Clearly? • *129*
Activity 101: What Are Some Ways to Use Sound? • *130*
Activity 102: Can You Think of Words That Sound Like the Object They Describe? • *132*
Activity 103: Can You Invent or Make a Musical Instrument? • *133*

Section 6 SIMPLE MACHINES *137*

To the Teacher • *138*
Activity 104: What Happens When You Rub Your Hands Together? • *139*
Activity 105: How Do Lubricants Affect Friction? • *141*
Activity 106: How Do Starting Friction and Sliding Friction Compare? • *142*
Activity 107: How Does Rolling Friction Compare with Sliding Friction? • *144*
Activity 108: What Is the Advantage of a First-Class Lever? • *145*
Activity 109: What Type of Simple Machine Is the Teeter-Totter? • *147*
Activity 110: How Can a Lever Be Used to Lift Heavy Things? • *148*
Activity 111: How Can You Predict the Effort Required to Lift a Load with a First-Class Lever? • *149*

Activity 112: What Do We Lose as We Gain Force with a Lever? • *152*
Activity 113: How Is a Second-Class Lever Different from a First-Class Lever? • *155*
Activity 114: What Do You Gain and What Do You Lose by Using a Second-Class Lever? • *157*
Activity 115: What Is a Third-Class Lever? • *160*
Activity 116: What Is Gained and What Is Lost by Using a Third-Class Lever? • *162*
Activity 117: What Is the Wheel-and-Axle? • *165*
Activity 118: What Type of Simple Machine Is the Pencil Sharpener? • *167*
Activity 119: What Is a Fixed Pulley? • *169*
Activity 120: What Is a Movable Pulley? • *172*
Activity 121: What Can Be Gained by Combining Fixed and Movable Pulleys? • *176*
Activity 122: What Is an Inclined Plane? • *179*
Activity 123: What Is a Wedge? • *183*
Activity 124: What Is a Screw? • *185*
Activity 125: What Kind of Simple Machine Is the Screwdriver? • *187*

Section 7 MAGNETISM *189*

To the Teacher • *190*
Activity 126: Which Rock Is Different? • *191*
Activity 127: Where Did the First Metal Magnet Come From? • *192*
Activity 128: What Will a Magnet Pick Up? • *193*
Activity 129: What Do Magnets Look Like? • *194*
Activity 130: How Do Magnets Get Their Names? • *195*
Activity 131: Which Magnet Is Strongest? • *196*
Activity 132: Through Which Substances Can Magnetism Pass? • *197*
Activity 133: What Part of a Magnet Has the Strongest Pull? • *199*
Activity 134: What Is a Special Property of Magnetism? • *200*
Activity 135: How Can You See a Magnetic Field? • *201*
Activity 136: What Happens When a Magnet Can Turn Freely? • *202*
Activity 137: What Is a Compass? • *203*
Activity 138: How Can You Make a Compass? • *204*
Activity 139: What Are the Earth's Magnetic Poles? • *205*
Activity 140: How Do Materials Become Magnetized? • *207*
Activity 141: How Can You Find the Poles of a Lodestone? • *209*

Section 8 STATIC ELECTRICITY *211*

To the Teacher • *212*
Activity 142: What Is the Kissing Balloon? • *213*
Activity 143: How Does Rubbing with Wool Affect Plastic Strips? • *215*
Activity 144: What Changes the Way Balloons React to Each Other? • *216*
Activity 145: What Will Puffed Rice Do to a Comb? • *217*
Activity 146: How Can You Make Paper Dance? • *218*
Activity 147: Why Does Paper Leap for a Balloon? • *219*
Activity 148: What Does Puffed Rice Run Away From? • *220*
Activity 149: How Can You Make Salt and Pepper Dance Together? • *221*
Activity 150: How Can You Make a String Dance? • *222*
Activity 151: How Can You Make a Spark with Your Finger? • *223*
Activity 152: How Can You Make an Electroscope? • *224*

Section 9 CURRENT ELECTRICITY *227*

To the Teacher • *228*
Activity 153: What Is a Circuit? • *229*
Activity 154: What Is a Short Circuit? • *230*
Activity 155: Can You Make a Switch? • *231*
Activity 156: How Can You Make a Series Circuit? • *233*
Activity 157: How Can You Make a Parallel Circuit? • *235*
Activity 158: What Materials Will Conduct Electricity? • *236*
Activity 159: What Is Resistance? • *237*
Activity 160: How Does Electric Current Affect a Compass? • *238*
Activity 161: What Happens When Electric Current Flows through a Wire? • *239*
Activity 162: What Is an Electromagnet? • *240*
Activity 163: What Is a Way to Change the Strength of an Electromagnet? • *241*
Activity 164: What Is Another Way to Change the Strength of an Electromagnet? • *242*
Activity 165: What Happens When Current Flowing through a Wire Changes Direction? • *244*
Activity 166: How Does the Direction of the Flow of Current Affect an Electromagnet? • *245*
Activity 167: How Can You Tell if Electric Current Is Flowing Through a Wire? • *247*
Activity 168: How Is Electricity Produced by Chemical Means? • *249*

Activity 169: How Does a Dry-Cell or Flashlight Battery Work? • *251*
Activity 170: How Can Electricity Be Produced by a Lemon? • *253*
Activity 171: How Can Mechanical Energy Produce Electricity? • *254*
Activity 172: What Is a New, Important Source of Electric Power? • *256*
Activity 173: How Can Electricity Help Us Communicate? • *258*

Bibliography *260*

Sources of Free and Inexpensive Materials *261*

Science Supply Houses *263*

CONCEPTS/SKILLS INDEX FOR BOOK II: PHYSICAL SCIENCES

The following concepts/skills index represents the scientific concepts or "Big Ideas" included in this book. The recommended age and grade levels at which the Big Ideas are introduced or developed in greater depth in each section are broken down this way:

preK: ages 3–5 (early childhood)
K–3: ages 5–8 (kindergarten-primary)
4–8: ages 9–14 (upper grades)

Each concept has been stated in simple but scientifically accurate tterms, followed by the numbers of recommended activities that introduce or reinforce the concept.

In some sections, background concepts necessary to an understanding of observed behavior cannot be "discovered" by hands-on experiences or activities at the elementary school level. When these Big Ideas are introduced, the activity column of the index will list "Teacher-student/demonstration/discussion." In these situations, strategies for presenting the necessary background information will be found in "To the Teacher" at the beginning of the section and "Teacher Information" after each activity.

As worded, the concepts/skills in this index are intended for teacher use to give an overview of each section. They are *not* intended to be used as an evaluation of student knowledge.

Throughout the book, a hands-on, activity-centered approach is emphasized. The scientific process skills of observing, classifying, communicating, measuring, inferring, and experimenting are intended to be the major outcomes of this program. Content acquisition and development in science and other subject areas will be major concomitant learning. In attempting to recommend age or grade levels at which concepts should be introduced, we recognize that a great variation will exist because of individual differences in students, which only you can determine.

Remember, a positive attitude toward science and "sciencing" on the part of both teachers and students is the major purpose of this book and will determine its effectiveness.

NATURE OF MATTER

Big Idea	*Suggested Grade Level*	*Activities*
There are three states of matter: solid, liquid, and gas.	preK–8	14
A mixture consists of two or more substances that retain their separate identities when mixed together.	preK–8	15

NATURE OF MATTER (continued)

Big Idea	*Suggested Grade Level*	*Activities*
A solution results when a substance is placed in a liquid and seems to become a part of the liquid, yet no chemical change has taken place.	preK–8	15, 16
Solids can dissolve in liquids and undergo a physical change without a chemical change.	preK–8	15, 16
Chemical changes from different matter. For instance, when iron oxidizes, iron oxide (rust) is formed. It is no longer iron.	K–8	17
When a substance burns or scorches, a chemical change takes place.	4–8	18, 27
Water changes states as it goes through evaporation, condensation, and freezing.	preK–8	19, 20
Water molecules attract each other. The unbalanced attraction of the top layer of water molecules is called surface tension.	K–8	21
The movement of molecules speeds up as temperature increases.	4–8	22, 23
Rate of solubility increases as temperature increases.	4–8	22, 23
Space exists between molecules of substances, even solids. Some gas molecules are small enough to permeate some solids.	4–8	24, 25
A liquid's resistance to flow is called viscosity.	K–8	26

ENERGY

Big Idea	*Suggested Grade Level*	*Activities*
Energy comes in many forms including heat, light, gravity, electricity, magnetism, and sound.	4–8	37, 42, 43, 44, 45
Potential energy is the ability to do work.	4–8	50
Kinetic energy is energy of motion.	4–8	50

ENERGY (continued)

Big Idea	Suggested Grade Level	Activities
Potential energy can be either mechanical energy or chemical energy.	4–8	50
Work is defined as moving a force over a distance and is measured in foot-pounds.	4–8	34, 35
Dark-colored objects absorb heat faster than do light-colored objects.	K–8	36
Increased heat causes molecules to move faster, expanding the substance that is heated.	K–8	38, 39, 40, 41
Centrifugal force is the force that tends to impel an object outward from a center of rotation.	4–8	48
Inertia is resistance to change.	4–8	49

LIGHT

Big Idea	Suggested Grade Level	Activities
A shadow is an area of decreased light, compared with surrounding area, due to blockage of the light by some object.	preK–8	52, 53
Shadows change in size according to the distance between the object and the light source and the distance between the object and the surface onto which the shadow is cast.	preK–8	52, 53
Light travels in straight lines. Its direction can be changed by reflection or refraction, but the new path continues to be straight.	K–8	54
Color is determined by reflection and absorption of light.	4–8	55
Refraction is the bending of light as it passes at an angle from one transparent medium to another. This is due to the reduction in the speed of light as the medium increases in density. Light travels more slowly through water than through air and more slowly through glass than through water.	preK–8	56, 57, 58, 59, 64, 76

LIGHT (continued)

Big Idea	*Suggested Grade Level*	*Activities*
Convex lenses cause light to converge, or bend inward.	K–8	60, 61, 63
Concave lenses cause light to diverse, or bend outward.	4–8	62
Light can be converted to other forms of energy, such as heat energy and electrical energy.	4–8	69
When sunlight passes through prisms, the wave length of each color of light is bent to a different degree, forming a continuous color spectrum.	K–8	65, 66, 77
Light can be reflected.	K–8	68, 70, 71, 72
Source light is different from reflected light.	K–8	69
Reflected light can be controlled.	4–8	73, 74, 75

SOUND

Big Idea	*Suggested Grade Level*	*Activities*
Sound is usually all around us, even when it seems quiet.	preK–8	78
We get much information from our sense of hearing.	preK–8	79
Sounds differ in pitch and loudness. We can tell these differences by careful listening.	preK–8	80
Sounds are produced by the vibration of matter.	K–8	81, 98, 99
The pitch of the sound can be changed by the rate or frequency of the vibration.	K–8	82
Our vocal chords help us to make different sounds by changing the pitch.	K–8	83
Our throat, mouth, teeth, and lips help us to talk by "shaping" sounds into words.	K–8	84
Air can vibrate to produce sound.	K–8	85
Solids can vibrate to produce sound.	K–8	86

SOUND (continued)

Big Idea	Suggested Grade Level	Activities
Air and solids can vibrate together to produce and change sound.	K–8	87, 88
Vibrations can be made visible.	K–8	89, 90
Sound travels through substances by causing a wave motion in its molecules.	4–8	91
Sound travels best when the molecules are tightly packed.	4–8	92, 93, 94, 97
Compared to many forms of energy, sound travels slowly.	4–8	95
Sound can be intensified and directed.	K–8	96, 100, 101
Some words imitate sounds.	K–8	102
You can create your own musical instruments.	K–8	103

SIMPLE MACHINES

Big Idea	Suggested Grade Level	Activities
All machines consist of the following six simple machines, or combinations thereof:		
a. The lever is a bar that rests on a fulcrum and is acted upon by forces applied to its effort arm and its load arm.	preK–8	108, 109, 110, 111, 112, 113, 114, 115, 116
b. The wheel-and-axle is a form of spinning lever. The wheel and axle are attached to each other, forming a single unit.	4–8	117, 118, 125
c. The pulley is a wheel that turns around an axle.	4–8	119, 120, 121
d. An inclined plane is a slanting surface.	K–8	122, 123
e. The wedge looks like an inclined plane but is used for a different purpose.	4–8	123
f. The screw is an inclined plane that winds around and in a spiral.	4–8	124

SIMPLE MACHINES (continued)

Big Idea	*Suggested Grade Level*	*Activities*
Friction plays an important role in the operation of machines:		
a. Friction is a force that causes two objects to resist movement over each other.	K–8	106
b. Friction is created when two things rub against each other. No surface is completely free of bumps and hollows. The rougher the surface, the more friction created as these bumps and hollows slide past each other.	preK–8	104
c. Making the surfaces smoother and applying lubrication are ways of reducing friction.	preK–8	105, 107
d. Friction can be reduced with rollers.	preK–8	107
e. Friction is sometimes undesirable, as when it wears out bicycle tires, clothing, and moving parts of machines.	K–8	Teacher-student/ demonstration/ discussion
f. Friction is sometimes helpful, such as when it keeps our feet from sliding on the sidewalk and causes a match to strike.	K–8	Teacher-student/ demonstration/ discussion
Work is measured as force times distance:		
a. Although machines can make work easier, they do not save work. For any advantage gained, there is a tradeoff. For instance, when a barrel of oil that two men cannot lift is rolled up a ramp (inclined plane) to a loading dock, less force is needed than to lift the barrel but the distance the barrel must be moved is greater.	4–8	122, 123 (Teacher-student/demonstration/ discussion)

SIMPLE MACHINES (continued)

Big Idea	*Suggested Grade Level*	*Activities*
b. Because of friction, a machine always puts out less work than was put into it. In the above example, a greater amount of total work is performed by using the ramp than if the barrel could be lifted directly.	4–8	Teacher-student/ demonstration/ discussion
Mechanical advantage is an increase in force or in speed and distance produced by a machine:		
a. Some machines give us a mechanical advantage of force.	4–8	111, 112, 113, 114 (Teacher-student/ demonstration/ discussion)
b. Some machines give us a mechanical advantage of speed and distance.	4–8	115, 116
c. No machine can increase force and at the same time increase speed and distance.	4–8	Teacher-student/ demonstration/ discussion

MAGNETISM

Big Idea	*Suggested Grade Level*	*Activities*
There are natural magnets.	preK–8	126
You can make other magnets with a natural magnet.	K–8	127
Magnets will pick up or attract some materials.	preK–8	128
Magnets can be different in their size, color, and shape.	preK–8	129
Magnets often get their names from their shapes or what they do.	K–8	129, 130
Magnets can be of different strengths.	K–8	131
Magnets can attract through different substances.	K–8	132
Magnets are strongest at their ends or poles.	K–8	133
Magnets have a north-seeking and a south-seeking pole.	4–8	134

MAGNETISM (continued)

Big Idea	Suggested Grade Level	Activities
Magnets have invisible magnetic fields.	4–8	135
The earth behaves like a large magnet. It has a north-seeking and a south-seeking pole.	4–8	136, 139
When a bar magnet is permitted to turn freely, the north-seeking pole will be attracted to the earth's North Pole.	4–8	136
A compass is a magnet.	K–8	137
A compass can be made from a magnetized needle or bar magnet.	K–8	138
Scientists believe that magnetic materials are made up of groups or domains of atoms. When the domains line up in the same direction, the material becomes magnetized.	4–8	140
Lodestones have poles, just as other magnets do.	4–8	141

STATIC ELECTRICITY

Big Idea	Suggested Grade Level	Activities
Static electricity does not move. It is static (stationary). When electricity moves, it is called current electricity.	4–8	Teacher-student/ demonstration/ discussion
Static electricity (or an electrostatic charge) is produced by friction when two unlike materials are rubbed together:	K–8	142, 143, 145 147
a. All matter is made up of tiny particles called atoms. Atoms are composed of even tinier particles called protons, neutrons, and electrons.	4–8	Teacher-student/ demonstration/ discussion
b. The protons and neutrons form the center (nucleus) of the atom and cannot be removed from the atom by rubbing.	4–8	Teacher-student/ demonstration/ discussion

STATIC ELECTRICITY (continued)

Big Idea	*Suggested Grade Level*	*Activities*
c. Electrons are lighter than protons and neutrons and move rapidly around the nucleus.	4–8	Teacher-student/ demonstration/ discussion
d. Each proton has a positive charge, each electron has a negative charge, and each neutron is neutral.	4–8	Teacher-student/ demonstration/ discussion
e. Ordinarily, each atom has the same number of protons (positive charges) and electrons (negative charges). The atom, under these conditions, is said to be neutral.	4–8	Teacher-student/ demonstration/ discussion
f. When two materials are rubbed together, electrons pass from one material to the other.	K–8	142, 143
Some materials release electrons more easily than do other materials. Glass, fur, and wool, for example, give up electrons rather easily when rubbed by plastic or rubber.	K–8	142, 143, 152
When an object gives up electrons, it loses some of its negative charges and is left with more positively charged particles (protons) than negatively charged particles (electrons). In this case, we say the object is positive. (It has a positive electrostatic charge.)	4–8	Teacher-student/ demonstration/ discussion
When an object gains extra electrons (negatively charged particles), we say the object is negative. (It has a negative electrostatic charge.)	4–8	Teacher-student/ demonstration/ discussion
When two charged objects approach each other, they either attract or repel each other:	K–8	144, 149, 152
a. Like charges (both objects positive or both negative) repel each other.	K–8	144, 148, 152
b. Unlike charges (one positive, one negative) attract each other.	4–8	144, 145, 149, 150

STATIC ELECTRICITY (continued)

Big Idea	*Suggested Grade Level*	*Activities*
When two neutral objects approach each other, they neither attract nor repel. The response is neutral.	K–8	Teacher-student/ demonstration/ discussion
When a charged object approaches a neutral object, the neutral object takes on a charge opposite that of the charged object and the two objects then attract each other:	4–8	142, 145, 147, 150
a. If a neutral object is brought near a negatively charged object, the electrons on the surface of the neutral object are repelled, thus leaving an induced positive charge on the surface of the neutral object. We say the neutral object has been charged by induction.	4–8	142, 145
b. On the other hand, if a neutral object is brought near a positively charged object, electrons near the surface of the neutral object tend to be drawn nearer the surface of the neutral object, creating an induced negative charge at the surface of the neutral object. The neutral object with its induced negative charge, is then attracted to the positively charged object.	4–8	142, 145
c. An object that has been charged by induction has neither lost nor gained electrons. Some of its electrons have simply been shifted nearer to or farther from the surface. When this object is removed from the charged object, the electrons resume their normal balanced position.	4–8	142, 143, 145

STATIC ELECTRICITY (continued)

Big Idea	Suggested Grade Level	Activities
When a negatively charged object touches a positively charged object, electrons are transferred and both objects become neutral or more nearly neutral.	4–8	143, 144
When a charged object touches a neutral object, electrons are transferred. The charged object loses some of its charge and the neutral object becomes charged to some degree.	K–8	143, 144
If the charge is great enough, this transfer of electrons can take place without the two objects touching, such as when lightning occurs. In this case, such a tremendous charge of static electricity is built up that a huge spark is produced as the electrons leap suddenly between clouds or between cloud and ground in nature's effort to neutralize the charge.	4–8	Teacher-student/ demonstration/ discussion
a. The lightning itself is current electricity.	4–8	151
b. Lightning strikes in various ways (cloud to ground; ground to cloud; cloud to cloud; within a cloud), depending on the location of the surplus of electrons. Remember, electrons move; protons do not.	4–8	Teacher-student/ demonstration/ discussion

CURRENT ELECTRICITY

Big Idea	Suggested Grade Level	Activities
Electricity is caused by moving electrons.	4–8	153
A complete circuit consists of a source of electrical energy, a path of low resistance through which the electricity can travel, and something to resist or use electrical energy.	K–8	154

CURRENT ELECTRICITY (continued)

Big Idea	*Suggested Grade Level*	*Activities*
Electric current can flow through some materials and not others. It flows easily through conductors such as copper wire. Resistors, such as iron or tungsten wire, will conduct electric current but create friction that produces heat and/or light.	K–8	158, 159
Materials that will not conduct electricity are called insulators. Examples are glass and rubber.	K–8	158, 159
A switch can be used to open and close a circuit and control the flow of electricity.	K–8	155
Short circuits are usually dangerous because they provide an easy path without resistance for the current. Excessive heat and fires are often caused by short circuits.	K–8	154
Electricity produced by chemical means (batteries) flows in one direction from the negative to the positive terminals of the power source. In order for electric current to flow, there must be an unbroken path from the negative to the positive terminals.	4–8	154, 165
Circuits can be wired so that electric current flows in a single path through one or more resistors. This is called series wiring and any break in the path will stop the flow of current in the circuit.	4–8	156
Circuits can be wired so each resistor has a separate unbroken path to and from the power source. This is called a parallel circuit.	4–8	157
When electric current flows through a wire, a magnetic field is formed around it.	4–8	160, 161
When the wire is coiled, the magnetic field becomes stronger.	4–8	162

CURRENT ELECTRICITY (continued)

Big Idea	*Suggested Grade Level*	*Activities*
A soft iron core inside a coil of wire becomes magnetized when the current flows through the wire. This is called an electromagnet.	4–8	162
Electromagnets can be made stronger by increasing the number of coils of wire.	4–8	163
Electromagnets can be made stronger by increasing the current in the circuit.	4–8	164
Electromagnets can be turned on and off.	4–8	162
Electromagnets have poles.	4–8	165
The poles of an electromagnet can be reversed by reversing the direction of the flow of current through the wire.	4–8	165, 166
Electric current can be produced by submerging different elements, such as copper and zinc, in an acid or salt solution.	4–8	167, 168, 169, 170
Electric current can be produced by mechanical means.	4–8	171
When a conductor, such as copper wire, is moved through a strong magnetic field, current is caused to flow within the wire.	4–8	171
If the wire is coiled, or the magnetic field is made stronger, the current produced in the wire will increase.	4–8	167, 171
Current produced in this manner does not flow in one direction, but instead alternates back and forth within the wire.	4–8	171
Electricity produced by mechanical means has made electricity plentiful and relatively inexpensive.	4–8	171
Generators use some other form of energy (water or steam pressure) to produce electrical energy.	4–8	171

CURRENT ELECTRICITY (continued)

Big Idea	*Suggested Grade Level*	*Activities*
Scientists are investigating new sources for the production of electricity. The solar (light) cell is one of the most promising.	K–8	172
Thermocouples, windmills, and even ocean tides are being studied as possible sources of energy to produce electricity.	K–8	172
The telegraph was the first example of people's use of electricity for communication.	K–8	173

Section 1

STARTER IDEAS

TO THE TEACHER

The following section is a challenge to you. The ideas presented here have been collected over a period of many years from the bright, creative minds of thousands of scientists, teachers, students, and children of all ages. Within your mind are creative ideas that these Starter Ideas will stimulate. The challenge is an invitation to explore, inquire, invent, and create.

In these simple, easy, inexpensive activities you will find your special invitation for creative inquiry. With few exceptions, the sections of this book do not build in a sequential way, so you can begin almost anywhere and explore forward or backward.

Starter Ideas are single-concept ideas that range far and wide in the unlimited areas we often try to cover in science. (One dictionary definition of *cover* is *to conceal.* We hope you will not try to conceal these ideas but will instead uncover, explore, and develop them.) Starter Ideas are intended to start your exploration in the exciting world of the sciences.

Try the ideas at random. When you find something you and your students like, there will usually be a reference to the section of the book where you can explore it in greater depth. If you or your students become bored or don't like an area, think of ways to add interest or move to another science topic. You need not feel you must do everything just because you enjoy something about it. As educators, we know young people do best the things they enjoy most. Your best teaching is done for the same reason. If you find something you don't understand, look for new creative ways to learn and develop the concept. New interests will blossom as you explore new horizons and student interest is likely to increase along with yours.

If there is one "must" everyone in our society needs to understand, it is that we have unlimited wants and limited fragile natural resources. It is important that we use what we have wisely. We must also understand that science, especially the new technology, must remain our servant, not become our master.

Whatever you choose, an activity is in Starter Ideas to help you get started. The purpose is to explore and inquire creatively, and through these explorations, to develop every facet of your students' ability to learn.

In this section there is really nothing you have to do but explore, enjoy, and create. Somewhere in the next few pages you will find the place to begin your exciting journey in science.

There is an ancient Chinese saying: "A journey of a thousand miles begins with a single step." It is our hope that Starter Ideas will provide that first step.

ACTIVITY 1: How Can You Get Salt Out of Pepper?

MATERIALS NEEDED

- Plastic bag
- ½ cup salt
- 1 teaspoon pepper

PROCEDURE

1. This bag has salt and pepper in it. Your problem is to get the pepper out of the salt.
2. How might you do it?
3. Test your ideas.

TEACHER INFORMATION

This activity is intended to help children learn to conduct and evaluate problem-solving procedures. There is no "right" answer but some procedures may be more effective or efficient than others. For example, picking the pepper out is slow and tedious. Dissolving the salt in water and straining the solution through a cloth is more efficient. Encourage the children to think of and try as many ways as possible. This could introduce a discussion of the way science and technology have combined to find easier and more efficient ways to do things.

ACTIVITY 2: What Can You Learn from an Egg?

MATERIALS NEEDED

- Hard-boiled egg
- Raw egg
- Water glass
- Salt

PROCEDURE

1. One of these eggs is raw and the other hard-boiled. Can you tell which is the hard-boiled egg?
2. Peel the hard-boiled egg.
3. Put it in a glass of water.
4. Add salt, a tablespoon at a time, until something happens to the egg. What happened?
5. What can you say about this?

TEACHER INFORMATION

When the peeled egg is put in the untreated water, it will sink to the bottom of the glass. As salt is added to the water, the egg will rise and float on top. This is because salt increases the density of the water until the egg is able to float.

Floating an egg in brine solution is the method some people use to tell when the brine is just right for pickling.

Hard-boiled eggs spin better than raw ones. If you spin a raw egg, stop it and let it go, and it will begin to spin again. Because of inertia, the outside of the egg stops but the inside continues to move. Sometimes you can hear or feel the inside of a raw egg if you shake it.

ACTIVITY 3: How Can You Tell If Water Is Hot or Cold Without Touching It?

MATERIALS NEEDED

- Two water glasses
- Food coloring
- Hot and cold water
- Medicine dropper

PROCEDURE

1. Get a glass of very cold water and one of hot water (not boiling).
2. Put a drop of food coloring in each glass.
3. What happened?
4. If you wanted something to dissolve rapidly in water, which temperature would you choose?

TEACHER INFORMATION

A drop of food coloring will mix much more rapidly in hot water than in cold water. This is because, as materials are heated, the molecules in them move more rapidly. The rapid movement of the molecules "stirs" the water and causes the food coloring to mix at a faster rate.

Water does not compress, but it will expand and contract due to changes in temperature. Other common liquids behave in the same way. Have you ever noticed gasoline leaking from an automobile gas tank on a hot day? Gasoline is usually stored below ground where it is cool. If the owner completely fills the tank on a hot day, the gasoline will expand as it warms and some might run out.

ACTIVITY 4: How Does a Camera See the World?

(Teacher Demonstration)

MATERIALS NEEDED

- Pinhole camera
- Candle
- Match

PROCEDURE

1. Darken the room.
2. Light the candle.
3. Point the pinhole in the box toward the candle.
4. Look at the image on the tissue paper at the back of the box. What do you observe about the image of the candle flame?
5. What can you say about this?

TEACHER INFORMATION

As the light from the candle passes through the pinhole, the image is inverted because light travels in a straight line (Figures 4-1, 4-2, and 4-3).

The human eye also receives images upside down on the retina, but the brain somehow turns them right side up again before we "see" them. CAUTION: **Close supervision of candle flame is required. This should be a teacher-demonstration activity.**

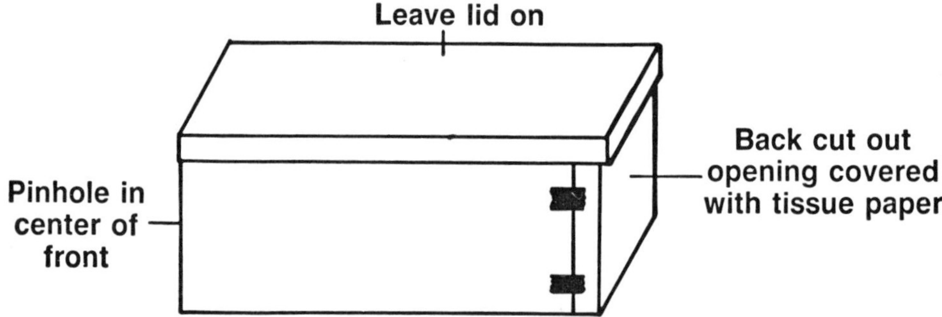

FIGURE 4-1. Shoe box with pinhole and tissue paper.

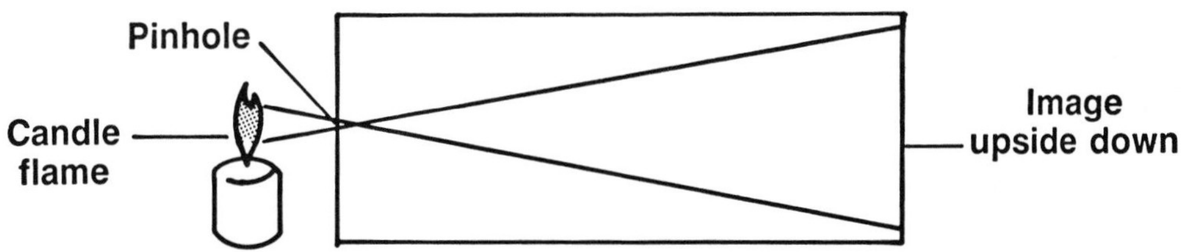

FIGURE 4-2. Diagram of candlelight going through pinhole camera.

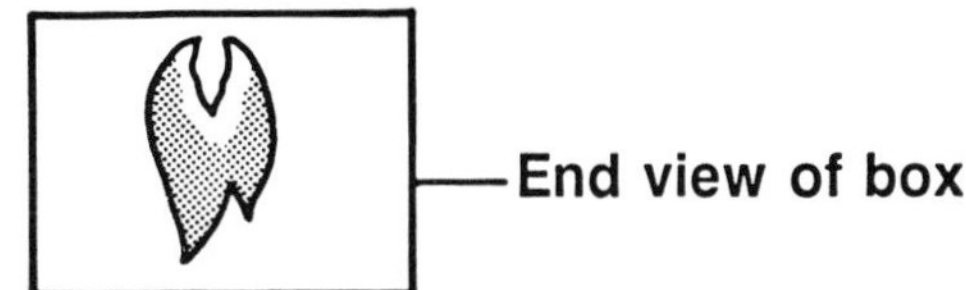

FIGURE 4-3. End view of box.

ACTIVITY 5: How Can a Water Drop Make Things Larger?

MATERIALS NEEDED

- Thin copper wire 6 in. to 8 in. long
- 8-cm. (3-in.) long nail
- Water

PROCEDURE

1. Make a small loop in the end of the wire. You may want to wrap it around the nail to make it the correct size.
2. Capture a drop of water in the loop.
3. Use the drop of water in the loop to look at print in a book. What happened? What can you say about this?
4. Gently tap the wire. Try to get most of the water drop out of the loop (a little must remain all across it).
5. Look at the print again. What happened? What can you say about this?

TEACHER INFORMATION

This activity can be used to introduce refraction of light. Light travels at different speeds through different media. Thus, light bends as it travels through one medium (such as air) into another (such as water). The water drop acts as a convex lens and makes objects appear larger. The thin film in the loop works as a concave lens and makes things appear smaller.

For younger children, you may want to put a drop of water on printed paper. The print will be magnified.

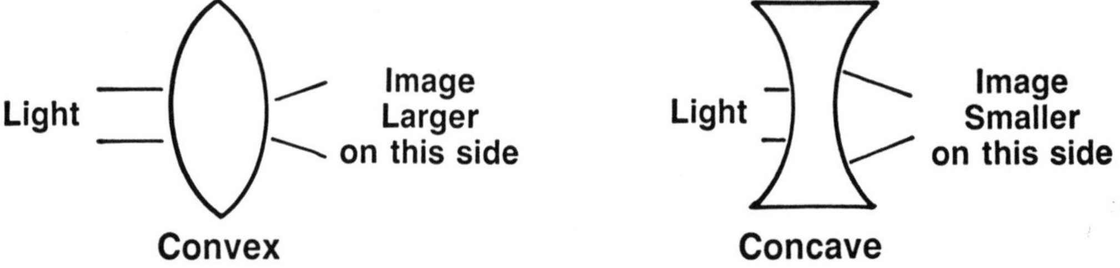

FIGURE 5-1. Convex and concave lenses.

ACTIVITY 6: How Can Water Make a Coin Appear?

MATERIALS NEEDED

- Opaque bowl
- Coin
- Water

PROCEDURE

1. Put the coin in the bowl. Mark the spot so you're sure it doesn't move.
2. Put the bowl on the table and crouch down until you can no longer see the coin. (Don't go down too far—just until you can no longer see the coin!)
3. Have a friend slowly pour water in the bowl. What happened?
4. What can you say about this?

TEACHER INFORMATION

Light travels in what appears to be a straight line in air, but when it goes through water, it is bent by refraction, as it travels more slowly through water than through air. As water is poured into the bowl, the light will bend and more of the bottom of the bowl will be exposed. The coin will appear. (See also Activity 57.)

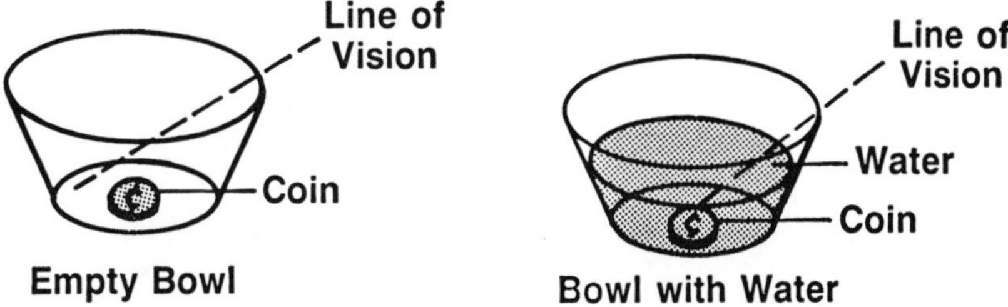

FIGURE 6-1. Bowl and coin showing how water bends light.

ACTIVITY 7: What Do Bears Know That People Don't?

MATERIALS NEEDED

- 8-ounce water glass
- Pencil
- Water

PROCEDURE

1. Use an 8-ounce glass about two-thirds full of water.
2. Put a pencil in the glass (slanted, not straight up). Observe the pencil at, above, and below the water level.
3. What can you say about this?
4. Why do you think this might be called, "What do bears know that people don't?" Think of a bear trying to catch a fish it sees in the water.

TEACHER INFORMATION

When the pencil (a ruler also works well) is put in the glass of water, it appears to bend as it enters the water. This is because the light is bent as it travels through the water. Actually, the pencil is not where it appears to be under the water. Bears seem to learn this and use it when fishing. They know where the fish is even though it isn't exactly where it appears to be.

Children may also notice that the pencil appears bigger under the water. This is because the curved surface of the glass and the water in it act as a convex lens. (See also Activity 56.)

ACTIVITY 8: How Can You Change a Stocking Without Putting It On?

MATERIALS NEEDED

- Sheer nylon stocking
- Clear lightweight plastic (fresh vegetable bag from grocery store)
- Smooth wall, blackboard or cork board
- Cool, dry day

PROCEDURE

1. Holding it by the top, place the nylon stocking against the wall.
2. Use the plastic to rub and smooth the stocking against the wall. It is best to rub with long strokes in one direction from top to toe. Do this about 20 times.
3. Release your hold on the top of the stocking. What happened?
4. Keeping an arm's length away from the stocking, grasp at the top and slowly pull it away from the wall. Be sure nothing comes near it.
5. Still holding it at arm's length, do you observe any difference in the stocking?
6. Slowly bring the stocking toward you. What happened? Can you explain why this happened?

TEACHER INFORMATION

This is an introductory idea including induction, attraction, and repulsion of like and unlike static charges. Be sure the nylon you use has been washed thoroughly in clear water so any anticling treatment has been removed.

At first the nylon will hang limply against the wall. As the plastic is rubbed on the nylon it will remove electrons from the stocking giving it a positive charge. By the time the stocking has been stroked 20 times it should smooth out and cling to the wall without support. This is caused by a form of induction explained in the section" on Static Electricity".

When the stocking is pulled away from the wall and held at arm's length it will fill out in all directions as if an invisible leg were inside. This is because the entire stocking has a positive charge and like charges repel or push away from each other.

Similar interesting and challenging activities may be found in Section 8, "Static Electricity."

ACTIVITY 9: How Can You Make a Glass Disappear?

MATERIALS NEEDED

- Two large glass jars
- Two small jars or drinking glasses
- Water
- Cooking oil

PROCEDURE

1. Place the two small jars inside the large jars.
2. Fill one pair of jars with water.
3. Can you see the small jar?
4. Fill the other pair of jars with cooking oil.
5. Can you see the small jar?
6. Explain your observations.

TEACHER INFORMATION

As light passes from one transparent material to another (such as air, water, and glass), the light is bent at the boundary between the two materials. This happens because of the differing speeds at which the materials transmit light. Light moves at about the same speed through petroleum products (including cooking oil) as it does through glass. Therefore, as light passes between glass and oil it doesn't bend at the boundaries, leaving the boundaries invisible. (This activity is repeated in Section 4, "Light.")

ACTIVITY 10: How Can a Thread Help Carry Your Voice?

MATERIALS NEEDED

- Two paper cups
- Toothpick
- Cotton thread, about 4 m. (4 yds.) long

PROCEDURE

1. Use the toothpick or your pencil to punch a small hole in the center of the bottom of each cup.
2. Push one end of the thread through the hole of each cup.
3. Break the toothpick in half and tie each end of the thread to one piece of toothpick so the thread cannot pull out of the hole in the cup.
4. Keep the thread tight and be sure it doesn't touch anything.
5. Put the cup to your ear and have your friend talk into his or hers. Now you talk and have your friend listen. Now whisper.
6. What happened? What happens when you touch the thread? Explain why you think this happens. Make a set of telephones at home and show to your family.

TEACHER INFORMATION

This is a very inexpensive way to provide a telephone for each student in your class to take home and tell about. The telephone works in a very simple way. Sound waves cause the bottom of the first cup to vibrate. These vibrations, in turn, cause the thread to vibrate. The vibrating thread causes the bottom of the other cup and the air inside to vibrate. The sounds you hear are a result of these vibrations; the air in the second cup strikes your eardrum in nearly the same way it struck the bottom of the first cup as your partner spoke into it.

Use heavy cotton thread. Polyester is easier to find, but it tangles easily. Dental floss is an excellent substitute, but more expensive.

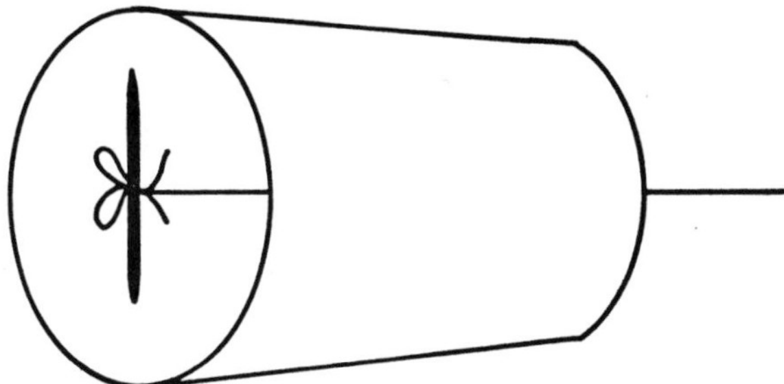

FIGURE 10-1. Paper cup with toothpick and thread.

ACTIVITY 11: How Well Does Sound Travel Through Solids?

MATERIALS NEEDED

- Metal coat hanger
- Two heavy cotton strings 50 cm. (20 in.) in length

PROCEDURE

1. Tie two strings to the coat hanger as shown in Figure 11-1.
2. While holding the strings, bump the coat hanger against a desk or other solid hard object.
3. Wrap the end of each string around one of your index fingers.
4. Put your index fingers in your ears.
5. Bump the hanger against the desk again.
6. Compare the first sound with the one you just heard.
7. What can you say about how sound travels through solids (the string)?

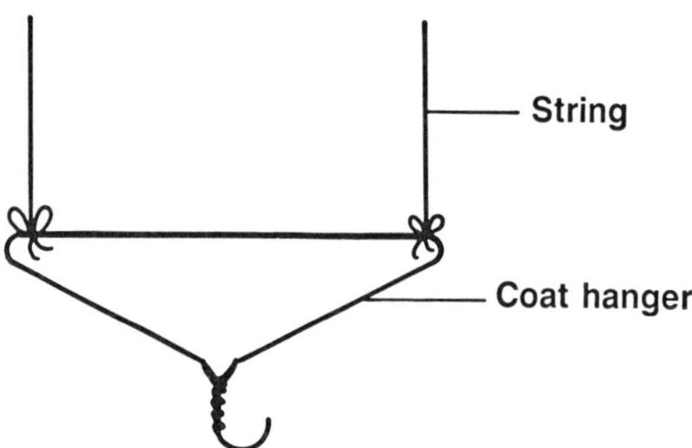

FIGURE 11-1. Coat hanger with two strings.

TEACHER INFORMATION

When the hanger is first bumped against the desk, it will make a soft, metallic sound. When the fingers are placed in the ears, the hanger will make a loud, clear sound. This is because sound travels better through solids than through air.

You might also use two tablespoons instead of a coat hanger. Try other solid materials, too.

(See also Activity 92.)

ACTIVITY 12: What Happens When You Burn a Candle at Both Ends?

(Teacher demonstration)

MATERIALS NEEDED

- Candle or long taper
- Match
- Toothpicks
- Water glasses

PROCEDURE

1. Prepare a candle so the wick may be lighted at both ends.
2. Stick round toothpicks into the candle and balance it on the water glasses as shown in the illustration. It doesn't have to balance perfectly.
3. Light both ends of the candle. Observe for several minutes. What happened? What can you say about this?

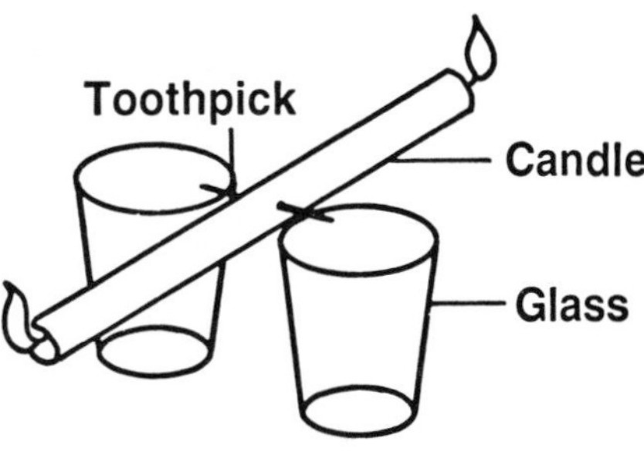

FIGURE 12-1. Candle burning at both ends, balanced between glasses.

TEACHER INFORMATION

CAUTION: Activities with fire or heat should be done only under close adult supervision. This activity should be a teacher demonstration.

When the candle is lighted at both ends, the end tilting downward will burn more wax away and become lighter. After it tilts up, the angle of the lower candle end will be such that it will burn more wax away. As this process continues to reverse, the candle will begin rocking, often quite vigorously.

ACTIVITY 13: How Can the Depth of a Bathyscaph Be Controlled?

MATERIALS NEEDED

- Deep pan (or bucket) of water
- Small glass bottle with tight-fitting lid
- Plastic tubing
- Wax

PROCEDURE

1. Make two holes in the lid. One should be just large enough to insert the tube through it and the other can be much smaller.
2. Insert one end of the tubing through the larger hole in the lid and press wax on the lid around the tubing to seal it from leakage of water or air.
3. Fill the jar about half full of water and put the lid on tight.
4. Place the jar in the bucket of water.
5. Hold the lid-end of the jar under water. Put the end of the tube in your mouth and adjust the amount of water in the jar by blowing or drawing on the end of the tube until the jar floats just beneath the surface of the water.
6. Now draw on the tube very slightly to allow a little more water to enter the jar. What happened to the jar?
7. Blow and draw on the tube to change the amount of water in the jar. What happens to the jar?
8. How could this idea be used in a bathyscaph designed to study the ocean at different depths?

TEACHER INFORMATION

A vessel in water can be caused to float at different depths by altering the density of the vessel. Density can be increased by displacing a chamber of air (or a portion of it) with water, or decreased by displacing the water with air. This is one way the depth of an underwater vessel can be adjusted.

Section 2

NATURE OF MATTER

TO THE TEACHER

Everything around us is matter of one form or another. The air we breathe, the food we eat, the books we read, our bodies—all of these things are made of various types of chemicals and substances. The topic of this section is very broad and is related to many other science topics. No attempt has been made to be comprehensive in coverage, but only to expose students to a few of the basic properties and relationships of matter. Activities have been selected that involve materials and supplies common to the school or the home in preference to those requiring sophisticated equipment.

It is recommended that after a study of the nature of matter, opportunities be sought to apply the general concepts learned while studying other science topics. For example, in a study of weather, air, or water, the principles of evaporation and condensation are essential. The effect of temperature change on expansion and contraction is another idea common to weather, air, water, and the topic of this section. In a study of plants, animals, or the human body, the nature of matter has many applications.

ACTIVITY 14: What Are Solids, Liquids, and Gases?

MATERIALS NEEDED

- Charcoal briquette or small piece of coal
- Hammer
- Block of wood
- Ice cube
- Dish
- Paper towel
- Paper and pencil

PROCEDURE

1. Put the ice cube in the dish and place the block of wood and the dish on a table.
2. Place the paper towel over the block of wood and the charcoal on the paper towel. The purpose of the wood is to provide a pounding block.

FIGURE 14-1. Dish with ice, wood, paper towel, and briquette.

3. Examine and describe the charcoal and the ice cube. How are they alike? How are they different? Tell whether you think each is a solid, liquid, or gas.
4. Crush the piece of charcoal with the hammer. Be sure it is on the paper towel and the wood block when you do. Pound lightly with the hammer so the pieces don't scatter. For additional safety, you can put the briquette in a plastic bag (such as a sandwich bag) before pounding.
5. Examine the charcoal again. In what ways is it the same as it was before? How is it different? Is it a solid, liquid, or gas?
6. Let the ice cube remain in the dish. Examine and describe it after a few minutes, after an hour, and after a day. Each time, decide whether it is a solid, a liquid, or a gas.

7. After the last observation, again compare the charcoal with the ice cube. How did they respond differently when they were left undisturbed? Why do you think this happened?
8. Make a list of solids, a list of liquids, and a list of gases.

TEACHER INFORMATION

All matter is either solid, liquid, or gas. Charcoal remains a solid even when powdered. Water has the unusual property of being easily changed to any of the three states. The solid and liquid states are easily observed. Point out that when water becomes a gas it is invisible. In many substances, including wood and charcoal, certain elements combine with oxygen, when burned, and produce a gaseous substance, except for a small amount of ash left behind in solid form. As gases form during burning, visible solid and liquid particles are often suspended in the gases. We call this smoke.

ACTIVITY 15: What Are Mixtures and Solutions?

MATERIALS NEEDED

- Two glass jars
- Spoons (or stirrers)
- Sugar
- Water
- Marbles or small rocks
- Paper clips
- Toothpicks
- Bits of paper
- Paper and pencil

PROCEDURE

1. Fill each jar about half full of water.
2. Put the marbles, paper clips, toothpicks, and bits of paper in one jar and a spoonful of sugar in the other jar.
3. Stir both jars and observe what happens to the materials in the water.
4. Compare the results in the two jars. One is a mixture and the other is a solution.
5. Try other substances in water, such as sand, powdered milk, or powdered chocolate. Make a list of those you think produce a mixture and those that produce a solution. Explain the differences you observe.

TEACHER INFORMATION

A mixture consists of two or more substances that retain their separate identities when mixed together. Solutions result when the substance placed in a liquid seems to become part of the liquid. A solution is really a special kind of mixture—one in which the particles are all molecular in size.

Materials listed can easily be substituted or supplemented with other soluble and nonsoluble materials.

ACTIVITY 16: Is the Dissolving of Solids a Physical Change or a Chemical Change?

MATERIALS NEEDED

- Tumbler
- Sugar (or salt)
- Paper and pencil
- Water
- Stirrer

PROCEDURE

1. Put about two teaspoons of sugar in a tumbler of water and stir until the sugar is completely dissolved.
2. Put the tumbler where it can remain undisturbed while the water evaporates.
3. Check the tumbler twice each day. If you notice anything different about it, record your observations.
4. When the water has completely evaporated, record your observations of the tumbler. Do you think the dissolving of the sugar in the water was a physical change or a chemical change? Why do you think as you do? Support your answer with your observations.

TEACHER INFORMATION

A physical change usually alters only the state of matter, such as from a solid to a liquid or from a liquid to a gas. Physical changes are frequently reversible. For example, water can be obtained by condensing it out of the air or by melting an ice cube. Chemical changes involve changes in molecular structure and are not reversible. As the water in this activity evaporates, crystals of sugar appear. They will be massed together and will not look the same, but a taste will reveal that it is sugar.

You might also burn a bit of sugar for students to compare. After the burned substance has cooled, let someone taste it and determine whether the sugar underwent a physical change or a chemical change. It will no longer taste like sugar, except to the extent that unburned sugar crystals remain. This represents a chemical change. The sugar has been oxidized through heat, leaving a carbon residue.

ACTIVITY 17: What Is Rust?

MATERIALS NEEDED

- Two small identical jars
- Two small identical dishes
- Paper and pencil
- Steel wool
- Water

PROCEDURE

1. Put a small wad of steel wool into one of the jars. Push it clear to the bottom. Pack it just tightly enough that it will stay at the bottom of the jar when the jar is turned upside down.
2. Put about 2 cm. (¾ in.) of water in each of the two dishes. Be sure you put the same amount in each one.
3. Turn the two jars upside down and stand one in each of the dishes. One jar should have steel wool in the bottom and one should be empty.

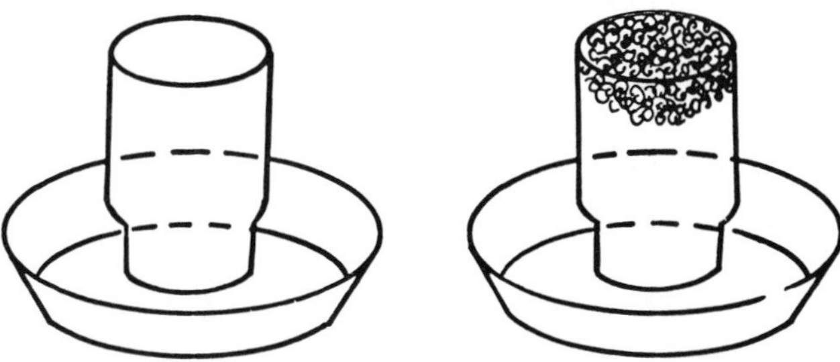

FIGURE 17-1. Two dishes with inverted jars. One has steel wool.

4. Examine each day for one week and record your observations, noting such things as water level and appearance of the steel wool.
5. At the end of one week, study the recorded day-by-day observations and explain the noted changes.

TEACHER INFORMATION

As steel wool is exposed to moist air over a period of time, the moisture serves as a medium to bring oxygen molecules in the air in close contact with molecules of iron in the steel wool. Oxygen molecules and iron molecules combine to make iron oxide. This process uses up some of the oxygen in the air inside the jar, reducing the amount of gas (air) in the jar. This, in turn, reduces the air pressure inside the jar, thus the atmospheric pressure outside the jar is greater than the pressure inside the jar, and water is forced into the jar. Student observations should include the rising water level inside the jar containing steel wool as well as the rust color forming on the steel wool itself.

ACTIVITY 18: How Can Chemical Changes Help You Write a Secret Message?

MATERIALS NEEDED

- Small jar
- Milk (only a few drops)
- Toothpick
- White paper
- Lamp with light bulb

PROCEDURE

1. Dip the toothpick into the milk and use it as a pen to write a message on the paper. Let the milk dry.
2. What happens to your message as the milk dries?
3. Hold the paper close to a burning light bulb. What happens as the paper absorbs heat from the light bulb? What can you say about this?

TEACHER INFORMATION

As the milk dries, the residue blends in with the white paper and becomes invisible. When heat is applied, a chemical reaction takes place in the milk residue, turning it dark and making it easily visible against the white paper.

Students could try the same activity using lemon juice instead of milk as their "ink".

ACTIVITY 19: How Dry Can You Wring a Wet Sponge?

MATERIALS NEEDED

- Meter stick (or yardstick)
- Sponge
- Paper and pencil
- String
- Water

PROCEDURE

1. Wet the sponge, then wring all the water you can out of it.
2. Tie the sponge to one end of the meter stick.
3. Tie a string near the middle of the meter stick, then suspend it by tying it to something overhead. Slide the string on the meter stick to cause it to hang level as in Figure 19-1.

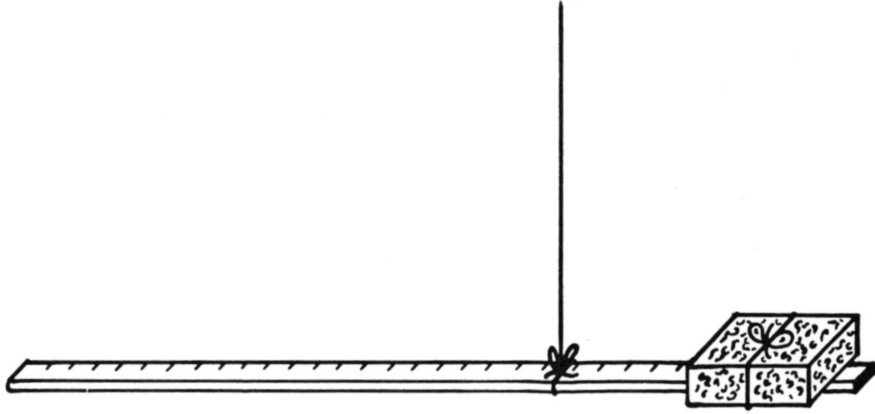

FIGURE 19-1. Balanced meter stick.

4. Record the time and draw a picture of the setup as it appeared when you made it.
5. Every 15 minutes for two hours, record the time and draw a picture of the setup.
6. What happened to the meter stick during the two hours? Explain why you think this happened. How can you find out if you were right?

TEACHER INFORMATION

The sponge cannot be wrung completely dry. As it sits for the two-hour period, much if not all of the remaining moisture will evaporate. As the water evaporates, the sponge becomes lighter and the system will no longer be balanced. The process of drawing the position of the setup several times will make students aware of the change as it is taking place. Students will probably want to feel the sponge. This should be avoided until the end of the investigation because of the risk of sliding the string on the stick and nullifying the results.

ACTIVITY 20: What Is Condensation?

(Teacher-supervised activity)

MATERIALS NEEDED

- Metal pan (or beaker)
- Water
- Sheet of glass or hand mirror (preferably cold)
- Heat source

PROCEDURE

1. Put about 1 cm. (½ in.) of water in the pan.
2. Heat the water until it boils.
3. Hold the sheet of glass over the boiling water.
4. Observe the glass carefully. What do you see forming on the bottom of the glass? Explain why you think this happens.

TEACHER INFORMATION

As water is heated, the rate of evaporation is increased. The sheet of glass or mirror held over the escaping water vapor cools the vapor and causes it to condense into liquid form, as shown by the drops of water forming on the bottom. This process will be speeded up if the mirror or sheet of glass is cooled first, but this can be dangerous because of the risk of breaking the glass.

Similar evidence of condensation can be observed by placing a pitcher (or other container) of ice water out on a table. Water vapor in the air is cooled by the pitcher and drops of water form on its surface.

ACTIVITY 21: What Is the Shape of a Drop of Water?

MATERIALS NEEDED

- Waxed paper
- Water
- Medicine dropper
- Pencil

PROCEDURE

1. Draw some water into the dropper.
2. Put several drops on the waxed paper, keeping each separate from the others. Hold the dropper about 1 cm. (½ in.) above the waxed paper as you squeeze lightly on the bulb.
3. Examine the drops of water. What is their shape? How do they compare in size?
4. Put the point of your pencil into a drop of water, observing carefully to see how it responds. What did the drop of water do at the surface? Do the water molecules seem to be more attracted to the pencil lead or to each other?
5. Push one of the drops around with your pencil point, observing its behavior.
6. Push two drops together—then three or four. What did they do?
7. What can you say about the attraction of water molecules for each other? For the pencil lead? For the waxed paper?
8. If you could put a drop of water out in space where there is no gravity, what do you think it would look like? What shape would it have?

TEACHER INFORMATION

Water molecules attract each other. The attraction of like molecules for each other is called *cohesion.* Within the liquid the force of this attraction is balanced, as each molecule is attracted by other molecules all the way around. The top layer of molecules has an unbalanced attraction, as they are pulled downward and sideways but not up. This unbalanced attraction of the top layer of water molecules is called *surface tension.* The roundness of the drops on the waxed paper is an indication of surface tension. When several drops are put together they flatten out more, because of the increased effect of gravity. A drop of water in the absence of gravity would take on the shape of a perfect sphere.

The surface tension of water forms a bond strong enough to float a razor blade or paper clip laid carefully on the water. When detergent is added to the water, the surface tension is broken and the floating object will sink.

Many other substances have surface tension. It has been suggested that better ball bearings could be formed in space than in factories on earth because a drop of molten steel would naturally form a perfect sphere. A drop of water out in space would evaporate almost instantly.

ACTIVITY 22: How Does Temperature Affect the Speed of Molecules?

MATERIALS NEEDED

- Two tumblers
- Food coloring
- Paper and pencil
- Two eye droppers
- Hot and cold water

PROCEDURE

1. Put very cold water in one tumbler and hot water in the other. Fill each about half full.
2. Draw four or five drops of food coloring into each of the two eye droppers. Put as near the same amount in each as possible.
3. Hold a dropper over each tumbler and squeeze to empty the contents of both at exactly the same time.
4. Compare the movement of the color in the two containers. In which tumbler did the color spread more rapidly?
5. If you have time, try different colors and different water temperatures. Record your observations.

TEACHER INFORMATION

As temperatures increase, molecules move faster. The food coloring should diffuse noticeably more rapidly in the hot water than in the cold water. In this experiment, water temperature is the variable. You might have students try the same experiment with color as the variable. For instance, use two tumblers of cold water and put red in one and green (or blue) in the other.

You might also consider having students use a stopwatch and a thermometer and record the actual time required for maximum diffusion (equal color throughout, as judged by the students).

ACTIVITY 23: How Does Temperature Affect Solubility?

MATERIALS NEEDED

- Two tumblers (equal size)
- Cold water
- Hot water (or a heat source)
- Two spoons (or other stirring instruments)
- Measuring spoons
- Sugar
- Marker

PROCEDURE

1. Be sure the tumblers are equal size.
2. Make a mark on each tumbler about a fourth of the way down from the top. The mark should be at exactly the same point on each tumbler.
3. Using cold water for one tumbler and hot water (very hot) for the other, fill each exactly to the mark.
4. Using a measuring spoon (teaspoon is about right) put one level spoonful of sugar in each tumbler.
5. Stir the water in each tumbler until the sugar has completely dissolved in the water.
6. Add another level spoonful of sugar and again stir until completely dissolved.
7. Continue doing this, counting the spoonfuls of sugar added to each tumbler. Stop adding sugar when you can no longer make it completely dissolve in the water.
8. Which dissolved more sugar, the cold water or the hot water? How much more? Why do you think this was so?

TEACHER INFORMATION

Hot water molecules move more rapidly than cold water molecules. The dissolving sugar molecules are therefore dispersed more completely throughout the liquid and a greater amount of sugar is dissolved in the hot water.

Students might also try dropping a sugar cube into a tumbler of hot water and a tumbler of cold water. Without stirring, time each to see how long it takes to completely dissolve the sugar. Another interesting investigation is to put equal amounts of sugar into equal amounts of water, then stir one but not the other. Again, check and record the time required to dissolve.

ACTIVITY 24: How Can Perfume Get into a Sealed Balloon?

MATERIALS NEEDED

- Two balloons
- Two small bowls
- Perfume
- Water
- String

PROCEDURE

1. Put one-half cup of water in each of the two bowls.
2. Mix several drops of perfume into the water of one bowl.
3. Blow up both balloons and tie them. Use a string with a bow knot so they can be untied later.
4. Place one balloon in each bowl. Wedge them into the bowl if you can, to produce an air-tight seal.
5. Leave the materials undisturbed for at least two hours.
6. After at least two hours, take the balloons to another room where the perfume in the bowl cannot be smelled.
7. Untie the balloon that was on the nonperfume bowl. Let the air out slowly and smell it.
8. Untie the balloon that was on the perfume bowl. Let the air out slowly and smell it.
9. What did you notice about the air in the balloons? What can you say about this?

TEACHER INFORMATION

Molecules in the perfume are small enough to permeate the balloon. When the air is let out of the balloon after a two-hour period, the smell of perfume in the air of the balloon should be evident.

ACTIVITY 25: How Can You Cause Molecules to Move Through Solids?

MATERIALS NEEDED

- Balloon
- String
- Marker
- Paper and pencil

PROCEDURE

1. Blow up a balloon and tie it.
2. Measure the size of the balloon by wrapping the string around it at the largest point and marking the string. Record the length of string required to go around the balloon.
3 Place the balloon where it will not be disturbed and where the temperature will remain quite constant.
4. For three days, measure the balloon twice a day with the same string and mark the string to indicate the length required to go around the balloon. Each time you measure, record the length of string required.
5. At the end of three days, describe your observations. Try to explain any changes you noted.

TEACHER INFORMATION

You might check to see that the balloon is tied tightly so air cannot leak through the opening. You can do this by submerging it in water to check for air bubbles. As the balloon sits, air molecules actually permeate the balloon walls and it will lose air slowly even though air is not escaping by any observable means. For the duration of this activity the air temperature should remain as constant as possible. If air temperature changes, the balloon will expand or contract (in warmer and cooler air, respectively), and will nullify the results.

ACTIVITY 26: What Is Viscosity?

MATERIALS NEEDED

- Four tall olive jars with lids (or other jars with small diameters)
- Four marbles (different colors)
- Corn syrup
- Mineral oil
- Vegetable oil
- Water
- Paper and pencil

PROCEDURE

1. Be sure all four jars are the same size.
2. Place a marble in each jar.
3. Fill each jar with one of the liquids and put the lid on it. There should be no air under the lid.
4. When all lids are tightly in place, get someone to help you turn all four jars upside down at once. Observe the marbles.
5. Record which marble sank to the bottom first, second, third, and fourth. Repeat and compare the results with your first record.
6. Test other liquids and compare with these.
7. Discuss your findings with your friends or your teacher.

TEACHER INFORMATION

Other liquids can be substituted for those listed above, but they should vary in viscosity (thickness). The marbles will sink more slowly in liquids with greater viscosity. Viscosity is *resistance to flow.* If olive jars or other tall, thin jars are not available, baby food jars can be used. Try to get the larger size, for height. Test tubes work very well, if they are available. They must have stoppers, of course.

The activity can even be done in open bowls. Put the liquids in separate bowls and a spoon in each bowl. Students should take a spoonful of the liquid and pour it back into the same bowl, observing how fast it pours out of the spoon. This doesn't have quite the interest or accuracy of the marble activity, but it will work.

ACTIVITY 27: How Can a Blown-out Candle Relight Itself?

(Teacher-supervised activity)

MATERIALS NEEDED

- Two candles
- Metal pan
- Match

PROCEDURE

1. For this activity, keep the candles over the pan and be sure you have a supervisor with you.
2. Light both candles.
3. Hold the two candles horizontally with one flame about an inch above the other.

FIGURE 27-1. Two candles, one above the other, both burning.

4. Holding both candles steady, blow out the lower flame and observe for a few seconds.
5. What happened? Can you explain why?

TEACHER INFORMATION

Wax, in solid form, does not burn. Heat changes wax to a vapor, which burns when combined with oxygen in the air. When a candle flame is blown out, hot gases continue to rise for a short time. These gases can ignite and act as a wick if another flame is close by and in their path. The flame will burn down the gases and relight the lower candle.

ACTIVITY 28: How Can You Remove the Flame from a Candle Without Putting It Out?

MATERIALS NEEDED

- Glass jar with lid
- Birthday candle
- Tablespoon
- 30 cm. (1 ft.) of pliable wire
- Baking soda
- Vinegar
- Match

PROCEDURE

1. Put two tablespoons of vinegar and one tablespoon of baking soda in the bottom of the jar. Bubbles will form.
2. Set the lid upside down on the jar, to cover the jar without sealing it.
3. Let the jar sit until the bubbling has nearly stopped.
4. While you are waiting for the bubbles to stop, form a holder for the candle from the wire.
5. Place the candle in your wire holder and light the candle.
6. Remove the cover from the jar and slowly lower the candle into the jar until the top of the wick is about an inch below the rim of the jar, then bring the candle back up.
7. Try it again. Explain what happens.

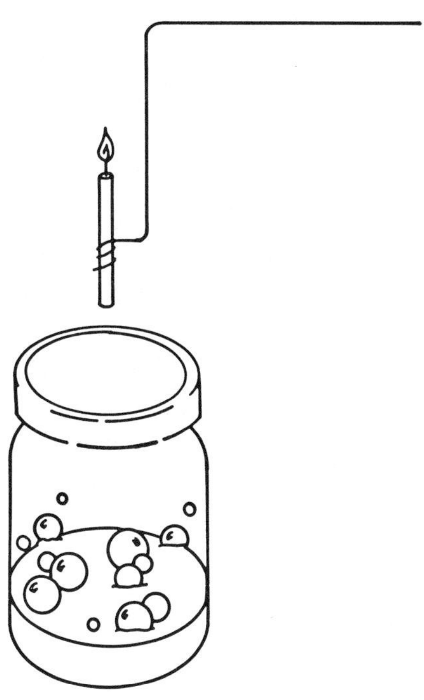

FIGURE 28-1. Candle lowered by wire into jar.

TEACHER INFORMATION

Combining vinegar and baking soda forms carbon dioxide, which is heavier than air and therefore drives the air out of the jar, leaving the jar filled with carbon dioxide. As the flame is lowered below the rim of the jar, it is starved for oxygen and the candle actually burns out. Gases continue to rise from the candle for a short time, however, and the flame sits on top of the layer of carbon dioxide, burning the rising gases in the presence of oxygen.

ACTIVITY 29: How Can You Make One Type of Fire Extinguisher?

(Teacher-supervised activity)

MATERIALS NEEDED

- Large soda bottle (or quart jar)
- Vinegar
- Baking soda
- Candle
- Match
- Sink or pan
- Tablespoon
- Measuring cup

PROCEDURE

1. Stand the candle in the sink or pan. Be sure there are no flammable materials nearby.
2. Put one tablespoon of baking soda into the bottle.
3. Measure about 3–4 ounces of vinegar with the measuring cup and pour it into the bottle.
4. As bubbles form, hold the bottle over the candle flame and tip it as though you were pouring water from the bottle onto the flame, but do not tip it far enough to pour out the vinegar.
5. What happened to the flame? Explain why you think this happened.

TEACHER INFORMATION

CAUTION: This activity must be carefully supervised due to the involvement of fire.

Baking soda is sodium bicarbonate. Vinegar contains acetic acid. When the two mix, carbon dioxide (CO_2) is formed. Carbon dioxide is heavier than air, so when the bottle is tipped, the CO_2 pours out. You don't see it pour because carbon dioxide is colorless. As it pours over the flame, the CO_2 deprives the flame of oxygen and the flame is extinguished. Carbon dioxide is commonly used in some fire extinguishers.

Carbon dioxide is one of the more common gases. Humans and animals produce it and breathe it into the air. Plants absorb it and, in turn, make oxygen. Carbon dioxide is put into soft drinks to give them the bubbles, or fizz. Dry ice is carbon dioxide, frozen to make it solid. If dry ice is available, have students repeat this activity, using a small piece of dry ice in the place of vinegar and baking soda. Any use of dry ice must be carefully supervised, as it can burn the skin.

ACTIVITY 30: How Can You Make a Ball Bounce by Itself?

(Teacher-supervised activity)

MATERIALS NEEDED

- Old tennis ball
- Scissors

PROCEDURE

1. With the scissors, cut the tennis ball in half to make two dish-shaped halves. You will need to start the cut by punching a hole with the point of the scissors or with a knife.
2. Trim around the edge of one of the halves until its diameter is about 5 cm. (2 in.).
3. Turn the ball dish inside out and set it on the floor or on a table. Observe for several seconds.
4. What happened? Explain why you think it behaved this way. What might you do to make it happen faster or more slowly?

TEACHER INFORMATION

After a brief observation, the "dish" should jump. Rubber molecules act like tiny springs, giving rubber the tendency to spring back to its original shape when distorted. This property gives rubber its bounce. With the inverted "dish," the restoring action of the rubber first has to overcome the resistance of the backward bend. When it reaches a certain point, though, the movement is very quick. The edges strike the surface with considerable force and the ball flips into the air.

As students ponder the last question in step 4, you might need to encourage them to try trimming a little more off the edges of the dish or taking the other half of the ball and trimming off less than they did with the first one. Trimming less will delay the action and trimming more will speed it up.

ACTIVITY 31: What Is Polyethylene?

MATERIALS NEEDED

- One polyethylene bag with tie
- One nonpolyethylene plastic bag with tie
- Sharpened pencil
- Water
- Sink or large pan

PROCEDURE

1. Check to be sure one of the bags is polyethylene. It will be indicated on the container.
2. Fill both bags with water and put ties around the tops. Keep them over a sink or large pan.
3. Stab the pencil through the nonpolyethylene bag and observe what happens.
4. Stab the pencil through the polyethylene bag.
5. Compare the results with what happened in step 3. What can you say about this?

TEACHER INFORMATION

Polyethylene has the strange property of shrinking together when it is torn. When the bag is punctured, the polyethylene shrinks and stops (or reduces) the flow of water. This property is a factor in puncture-resistant tires.

ACTIVITY 32: How Does a Hydrometer Work?

MATERIALS NEEDED

- Lipstick tube cap
- Several small nails (or screws)
- Tape (or gummed label)
- Plastic tumbler
- Water
- Salt
- A variety of liquids
- Marker
- Paper and pencil

PROCEDURE

1. Fill the tumbler about two-thirds full of water.
2. Place 8 or 10 weights (small nails or screws) in the lipstick cap.
3. Put the gummed label or a piece of tape lengthwise on the lipstick cap.
4. Place the lipstick cap, open end up, in the glass of water. Add or remove weights until the cap floats vertically with the water level about halfway up the cap.

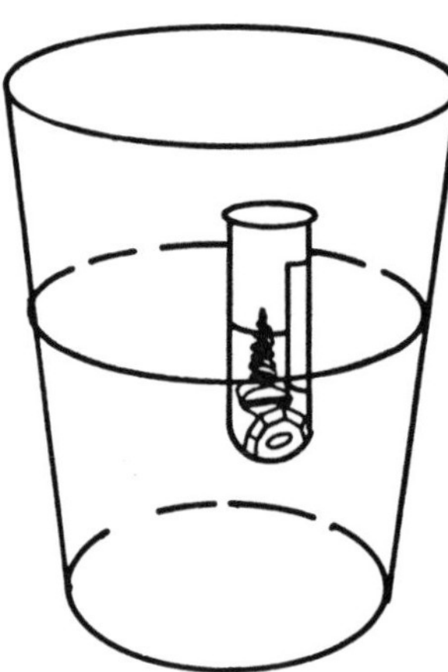

FIGURE 32-1. Lipstick cap floating vertically with nails showing.

5. Mark the water level on the cap.
6. Your cap is now a hydrometer. Hydrometers are used for measuring density of liquids, comparing them with the density of water. If the density is greater than that of water, the cap will float higher. If the density is less than that of water, the cap will sink deeper.
7. Dissolve about ¼ cup of salt in your jar of water. Without changing the number of weights in the cap, put it in the salt water. Does your hydrometer float deeper than it did in plain water or does it float higher? What does this tell you about the density of salt water?

8. Test other liquids, such as milk, vinegar, and rubbing alcohol.
9. As you test various liquids, make a list of those you think have a greater density than water and those that have a lesser density.

TEACHER INFORMATION

Any object that floats displaces an amount of liquid equal to its own weight (Archimedes principle). If the specific gravity (density) of the liquid is greater, the object floats higher, as it has to displace less liquid to equal its own weight. If the hydrometer floats deeper, it is in a liquid of lower density.

Hydrometers are used to test such liquids as antifreeze and battery acid, following the Archimedes principle.

ACTIVITY 33: How Can You Make Large Sugar Crystals from Tiny Ones?

MATERIALS NEEDED

- Drinking glass or jar
- Water
- Cotton string or thread
- Pencil
- Sugar
- Pan
- Heat source
- Stirrer or wooden spoon

PROCEDURE

1. Put a cup of water in the pan and heat it until it boils.
2. When the water begins to boil, turn off the heat, and add about 1½ cups sugar and stir.
3. If all the sugar dissolves, add a bit more and stir. Keep doing this until no more sugar will dissolve in the water.
4. Let the water cool, then pour it into a drinking glass.
5. Tie a piece of cotton thread or string to a pencil and lay the pencil across the glass, allowing the string to extend to the bottom of the glass.
6. Place the drinking glass on a shelf where it can remain undisturbed for several days.
7. Examine the glass, particularly the string, each day and write down your observations. DO NOT TOUCH THE GLASS.
8. When you observe no more changes, try to explain what happened during the days the glass remained on the shelf.

TEACHER INFORMATION

As sugar dissolves in water the grains break down into molecules so small they can't be seen even with a powerful microscope. A molecule of sugar is the smallest particle of sugar that can exist. If it were any smaller, it would cease to be sugar.

In this activity sugar crystals are dissolved into molecules, forming a supersaturated solution (containing more sugar in solution than could be dissolved at room temperature). Then as the solution cools, crystals begin coming out of solution and collecting around the string. As this happens, large sugar crystals are formed. You could call it rock candy.

Students could also try forming crystals from other substances, such as salt or powdered alum, following the same procedure.

Section 3

ENERGY

TO THE TEACHER

We use many forms of energy every day, yet we never see it. The sun's energy literally powers the earth, but it is so common we take it for granted. It is just there. Energy comes in many forms, none of which looks like "energy." It is disguised as a match stick, a lump of coal, a gallon of gasoline, or a glass of orange juice; it is never just energy. In a broad sense, energy is so much a part of us and our surroundings that it would be impossible to deal with it as a topic separate from other topics treated in this book. The sun's energy keeps us warm and gives us light. Part of the sun's energy is converted by plants into food for animals. Cattle convert some of that energy from plant form to muscle, which we eat (beefsteak, hamburger, and so forth). Energy is consumed by people in both plant and animal form. We, in turn, convert it into human flesh and bones. The sun's energy is a vital ingredient of our own bodies and of a great deal of our surroundings.

In a narrower sense, energy is sometimes defined as the capacity for performing work (*Webster's New Collegiate Dictionary*). It exists in two forms, potential energy and kinetic energy. *Potential energy* is the ability to do work. *Work* is defined as force acting through a distance. Specifically, work = Force × Distance. *Kinetic energy* is the energy of motion. A rubber band stretched out has potential energy. When it is released, its potential energy is converted to kinetic energy. A stick of dynamite has potential energy. When a small electrical charge or the right amount of heat is applied, the potential energy is converted to kinetic energy with great force.

The potential energy in dynamite is chemical energy. The potential energy in the rubber band, or in a set mousetrap, or in a raised hammer is mechanical energy.

The energy we consume in the form of meat, fruit, and vegetables isn't all used to build body cells. We use some of it to walk and talk. We even use some of this energy as we think.

Most sections of this book deal directly or indirectly with forms of energy. This section recognizes these but emphasizes additional topics, such as heat, gravity, and the relationship between energy and work.

Activities that appear complex can usually be used in the lower grades by de-emphasizing terminology and mathematical applications. With simplified explanations of the concepts, children can participate in the activities and benefit from exposure to these principles.

ACTIVITY 34: How Is Work Measured?

MATERIALS NEEDED

- One-pound weight
- Foot ruler

PROCEDURE

1. Stand the ruler on the table or the floor.
2. Raise the one-pound weight to the top of the ruler. *Note:* The amount of work you did to raise one pound a distance of one foot is called one foot-pound.
3. Raise the one-pound weight six inches. How much work did you do? How much potential energy does the weight have at that point?
4. Raise the weight two feet. How much work did you do this time? How much potential energy does the weight have?
5. Set the weight on the table. How much potential energy does it have now?
6. Slide the weight to the edge of the table. How much potential energy does it have at that position?
7. Try to determine the amount of potential energy of various objects from different positions and the amount of work required to move those objects certain distances.
8. Climb a set of stairs. How much work did you do to get to the top? What is your potential energy, assuming the possibility of falling or jumping to the bottom?

TEACHER INFORMATION

The foot-pound is a standard unit for measuring work or potential energy. Mechanics use a torque wrench to measure the degree of stress on a bolt as it is turned to hold the head or some other part of an engine. The torque wrench indicates the stress in foot-pounds, which is a measure of the work done to turn the bolt. (The metric system equivalent to foot-pounds is newton-meters, or joules, not at all in common usage in the United States.)

A durable plastic or cloth bag filled with one pound of sand or similar substance would be an excellent weight for this activity. If a hard object is used, newspaper or other material could be placed on the table or floor to muffle the sound when the weight is dropped and protect the surface from possible damage.

ACTIVITY 35: How Much Energy Is Stored in a Bow?

(Teacher-supervised activity to be done outdoors)

MATERIALS NEEDED

- Toy bow
- Toy arrow tipped with suction cup
- Spring scale
- Foot ruler
- Measuring tape

PROCEDURE

1. Do this activity outdoors. Find an isolated area.
2. Put the arrow on the bow. Hold the bow and arrow at a comfortable height and point the arrow straight ahead in a direction away from people.
3. Draw the bowstring back six inches and let it go.
4. Measure the distance the arrow traveled.
5. Attach the spring scale to the bowstring and pull the string back six inches. How many ounces or pounds of force were required to pull the string back six inches?
6. Predict the amount of force required to pull the string back one foot. Measure it with the spring scale.
7. Predict the distance the arrow will travel with the string pulled back one foot.
8. Shoot the arrow with the string pulled back one foot. Be sure the bow is held at the same height as before and still aimed straight ahead.
9. Measure the distance and compare with your predictions.
10. Predict the force required to pull the string back 1½ feet and the distance the arrow will travel. Try it and test your predictions.

TEACHER INFORMATION

Even though the arrow used in this activity is tipped with a suction cup for safety, close supervision is very important. Injury can still result if a child is hit in the face with the arrow. Young children can do the activity with less measuring and still predict the distances the arrow will travel. A ruler (or stick) could be marked at appropriate points to indicate the distance from the string to the bow. Children can indicate their predictions for distance the arrow will travel by placing a marker on the ground.

ACTIVITY 36: How Can You Get the Most Energy from the Sun?

MATERIALS NEEDED

- Three identical jars
- Paper and pencil
- Black paper
- Aluminum foil
- Tape
- Three thermometers
- Sand

PROCEDURE

1. Fill the three jars with sand.
2. Cover one jar with black paper, including the top, and tape the paper in place.
3. Cover the second jar with aluminum foil, including the top, and tape the foil in place
4. Leave the third jar uncovered.
5. Record the temperature on the thermometers. Be sure all three indicate the same temperature.
6. Insert one thermometer into the sand of each jar. With the two covered jars, puncture a hole in the top covering and insert the thermometer through the hole.
7. Place all three jars in the sunlight. All should receive the same direct sunlight.
8. Check and record the temperature of the three thermometers every fifteen minutes for about two hours.
9. How do the temperatures compare? What can you say about the effect of a black surface and a shiny surface on absorption of energy from the sun?
10. Remove the jars from the sunlight and continue to record the temperatures of the three thermometers for two more hours.
11. How do the temperature changes compare? What can you say about the effect of a black surface and a shiny surface on heat loss?

TEACHER INFORMATION

The uncovered jar of sand will provide a control to help students observe the effect of both the black and the shiny surface. The temperature of the jar with the black surface should increase noticeably faster than that of the other two. The foil will reflect heat and the temperature increase of the sand covered by it should be very slow.

Astronauts wear reflective clothing to help protect them from the direct rays of the sun.

ACTIVITY 37: What Other Type of Energy Accompanies Light from the Sun?

(Teacher-supervised activity)

MATERIALS NEEDED

- Two magnifying glasses
- One sheet of paper
- Glass bowl

PROCEDURE

1. Ask your teacher where you should do this experiment. You will need to be in bright sunlight with no wind.
2. Hold the magnifying glass between the paper and the sun so a beam of light focuses on the paper.
3. Notice that as you move the magnifying glass closer to and farther from the paper, the point of light changes in size. Notice also that it gets brighter as it gets smaller.
4. Adjust the distance between the paper and the magnifying glass to make the point of light very small and bright.
5. Pull the magnifying glass back about 1 cm. (½ in.) and watch the paper.
6. Do you see anything happening to the paper? If so what, and why do you think it is happening? What kind of energy is causing this to happen?
7. What do you think might happen if you used two magnifying glasses focused on the same spot on the paper? Try it.

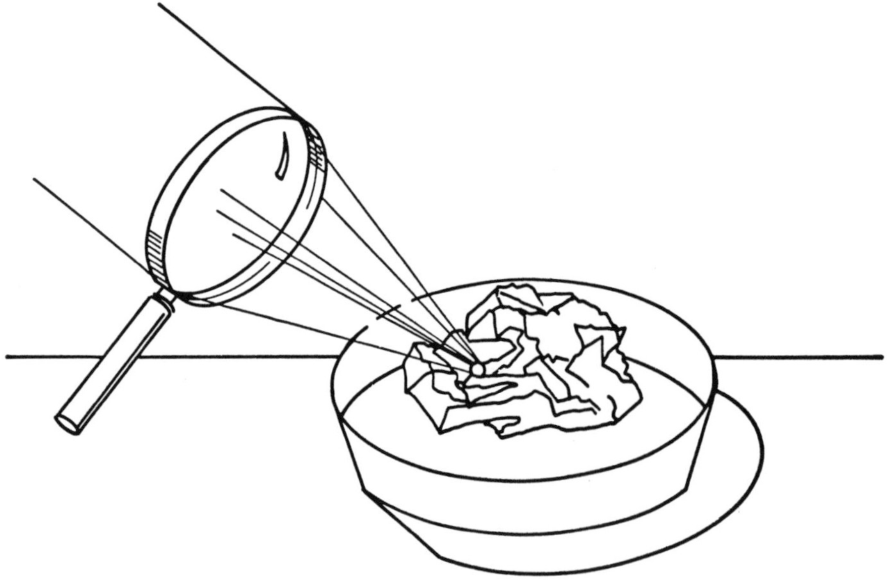

FIGURE 37-1. Magnifying glass with sheet of paper in glass bowl.

TEACHER INFORMATION

As light rays from the sun are concentrated by a magnifying glass, so are the infrared, or heat, rays. The magnifying glass can concentrate bright sunlight to such a degree that it will scorch the paper or even possibly ignite it. As illustrated in Figure 37-2, the focal distance for heat (infrared) rays is slightly longer than the focal distance for light. For this reason, step 5 suggests moving the lens back slightly after the focal point is found. You will need to adjust the distance from lens to paper slightly to find the focal point for heat—the point at which the greatest possible concentration of heat is focused on the paper.

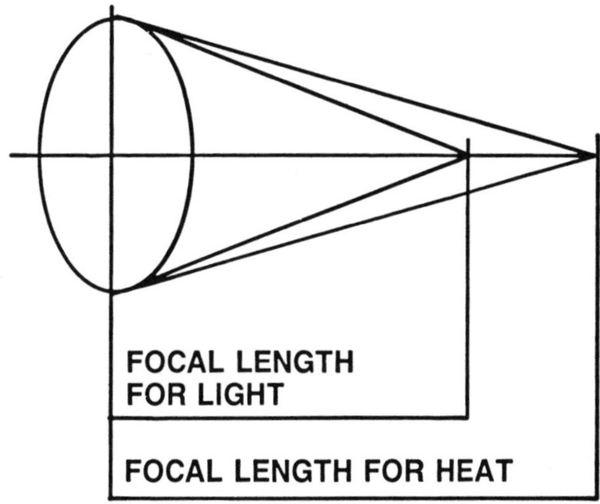

FIGURE 37-2. Focal distance for heat and light.

ACTIVITY 38: How Do Molecules Behave When Heated?

(Teacher demonstration)

MATERIALS NEEDED

- Chalk or masking tape

PROCEDURE

1. Have several students stand in a group.
2. Mark a border on the floor around the group with chalk or tape. Leave a few inches between the group and the border all the way around.
3. Ask students to move around slowly. Everyone should move constantly, but no one should move fast and there should be no pushing and shoving. They are to try to stay within the border marked on the floor.
4. Now instruct those in the group to move a bit faster. They are still to try to stay within the border.
5. Continue speeding up the movement of the group until they can no longer remain within the line marked on the floor.
6. Discuss what happened as those in the group increased their speed. Ask how this relates to the movement of molecules as temperature is increased.

TEACHER INFORMATION

As a substance increases in temperature, molecules move faster but do not increase in size. In their rapid movement they bump into each other more frequently and require more space, just as did the group of students. If the members of the group were all running at top speed, they would have required much more space.

ACTIVITY 39: What Happens to Solids As They Are Heated and Cooled?

(Teacher-supervised activity)

MATERIALS NEEDED

- Wire, about 1 m. (1 yd.) long
- Large nail or small bolt
- Candle
- Match

PROCEDURE

1. Wrap one end of the wire around the nail and anchor the other end to a support. Adjust the wire so the nail swings freely but barely misses the table or floor.
2. Light the candle and heat the wire.
3. Observe the nail. What happened?
4. Remove the candle and allow the wire to cool.
5. Observe the nail. What happened?
6. What can you say about the effect of heat on solids?

TEACHER INFORMATION

CAUTION: This activity uses open flame, necessitating close supervision.

As the wire is heated by the candle, it will expand and the nail, which was swinging freely above the surface, will drag. As it cools, the wire will contract and the nail will swing freely again. Other solids expand and contract similarly when heated and cooled.

ACTIVITY 40: What Happens to Liquids As They Are Heated and Cooled?

MATERIALS NEEDED

- Narrow-necked jar with a one-hole rubber stopper or a cork with a hole drilled through the center
- Water
- 30-cm. (12-in.) length of thin, clear plastic tubing
- Marker, rubber band, or masking tape

PROCEDURE

1. Fill the jar completely with cold water.
2. Insert the plastic tubing through the rubber stopper or cork. (You may need to use candle wax to seal between the tube and the hole in the cork.)
3. Place the stopper in the jar. As you press the stopper into place, there should be no air space beneath the stopper and water should be forced partway (not more than halfway) up the tube above the stopper.
4. Mark the tube at the water level with a marker, or by putting a rubber band or tape around it.
5. Place the jar in a window in direct sunlight.
6. Check the water level in the tube every few minutes for at least two hours.
7. What happened to the water level as the water warmed in the sunlight?
8. Remove the jar from the sunlight and place it in a cool place.
9. Again check the water level in the tube every few minutes.
10. What happened to the water level as the water cooled?
11. What can you say about the effect of temperature change on liquids?

TEACHER INFORMATION

As the jar of water warms in the sunlight, the water will expand and the water level will rise in the tube, demonstrating that as the temperature of a liquid increases the liquid expands. As the water cools it will contract, and the level of the water in the tube will drop.

If food coloring is available, have students add a few drops to the water. This makes the water level in the tube easier to see and the change is more dramatic.

This device can become a thermometer if you have students attach a card to the tube and mark the card at different temperatures, by taking temperature readings from a commercial thermometer. Water evaporation in the tube will eventually destroy the accuracy of it as a thermometer and it will need to be recalibrated.

ACTIVITY 41: What Happens to Gases As They Are Heated and Cooled?

MATERIALS NEEDED

- Narrow-necked jar with one-hole stopper
- 30-cm. (12-in.) length of thin, clear plastic tubing
- Candle wax
- Water

PROCEDURE

1. Put a small amount of water in the bottom of the jar.
2. Insert the plastic tube through the stopper. Seal around the tube with candle wax.
3. Place the stopper in the jar. The lower end of the tube must be in the water.
4. Notice the water level in the tube.
5. Place the jar in a window in direct sunlight.
6. Check the water level in the tube every three or four minutes for at least one-half hour.
7. What happened to the water level as the air warmed in the sunlight? Why?
8. Remove the jar from the sunlight and place it in a cool place.
9. Again check the water level in the tube every few minutes.
10. What happened to the water level as the air cooled? Why?
11. What can you say about the effect of temperature change on gases?

TEACHER INFORMATION

If sealing wax is available, use it instead of candle wax. Sealing wax remains pliable and provides a better seal, whereas candle wax hardens and becomes crumbly. Chewing gum will also work.

As the air in the jar warms in the sunlight, it will expand, forcing water up the tube, and very likely spilling it out the top of the tube, demonstrating that as the temperature of a gas increases, the gas expands. As the air cools, it will contract and the level of the water in the tube will drop.

If food coloring is available, add a few drops to the water to make the water level in the tube more visible. This is a type of thermometer.

ACTIVITY 42: How Does a Nail Change As It Is Driven into a Board?

(Teacher-supervised activity)

MATERIALS NEEDED

- Hammer
- Nail, at least 5 cm. (2 in.) long
- Board, at least 4 cm. (1½ in.) thick
- Pounding surface

PROCEDURE

1. Place the board on a good pounding surface such as another board, a stack of newspapers, or cement.
2. Pound the nail at least 2½ cm. (1 in.) into the board. Do not pound it all the way in.
3. As soon as you stop pounding, feel the nail. What difference do you notice in the nail?
4. Pull the nail out of the board with the hammer.
5. As soon as you get the nail out of the board, feel it again.
6. What difference do you notice in the nail by feeling it? What can you say about this?

TEACHER INFORMATION

As the nail is pounded into the board, some of the energy from the hammer is changed to heat energy due to friction between the nail and the board. As the nail is removed from the board, friction again changes some of the energy to heat. If the nail is pulled out quickly, the heat might be even more noticeable than when it was pounded in.

ACTIVITY 43: How Can the Energy of Sound Cause Something to Move?

MATERIALS NEEDED

- Two guitars

PROCEDURE

1. Stand the two guitars face to face, about 5–10 cm. (2–4 in.) apart.
2. Strum the strings of one guitar. After two or three seconds, silence the strings of the guitar you strummed by putting your hand on them.
3. Listen carefully.
4. What do you hear? How did it happen?

TEACHER INFORMATION

This activity is to show that sound can actually do work. It can make something move. Energy is transferred from one guitar to the other by sound waves and the strings of the second guitar vibrate. The two guitars should be tuned alike so the vibrating frequency is the same for the two sets of strings.

(For further ideas, see Section 5, "Sound.")

ACTIVITY 44: How Can Magnetism Do Work?

MATERIALS NEEDED

- Magnet
- Steel ball

PROCEDURE

1. Place the magnet on the table.
2. Place the steel ball on the table about 2–3 cm. (1 in.) from the end of the magnet.
3. Let go of the steel ball.
4. What happened?
5. What is work and how was work done in step 3?

TEACHER INFORMATION

Work was defined in this section's "To the Teacher" as moving something (force acting through a distance). The magnet should cause the steel ball to roll toward it. If this did not happen, try putting the steel ball a bit closer to the magnet or find a stronger magnet.

ACTIVITY 45: How Does Gravity Affect Heavy and Light Objects?

MATERIALS NEEDED

- Large book
- Small book
- Wadded paper
- Pencil
- Eraser
- Paper clip
- Paper

PROCEDURE

1. Take the large book in one hand and the small book in the other. Hold the two books at exactly the same height.
2. Drop both books at the same time. Have someone watch to see which book hits the floor first.
3. Repeat the book drop three times to be sure of your results.
4. Which book falls faster, the large one or the small one?
5. Compare the pencil and the paper in the same way. First predict which you think will fall faster.
6. Compare the various objects, two at a time. In each case predict which will fall faster, then compare with three drops to test your prediction.
7. Of all the materials you tried, which falls fastest? Most slowly?
8. Explain how the force of gravity compares with objects that are large, small, heavy, and light, according to your findings. How do the falling speeds compare?
9. Compare the falling speed of the wadded paper with that of a flat sheet of paper dropped horizontally.
10. Compare the falling speeds of two flat sheets of paper, one dropped vertically and the other, horizontally.
11. Compare the falling speed of the wad of paper with that of a flat sheet of paper dropped vertically.

TEACHER INFORMATION

The force of gravity pulls all objects to the earth at the same rate, regardless of the size or weight of the object. Air resistance can slow the rate of fall, so the flat paper, held in horizontal position, will fall more slowly. Except for the factor of air resistance, the rate of fall is equal. A rock and a feather will fall at the same speed if placed in a vacuum.

ACTIVITY 46: What Is Center of Gravity?

MATERIALS NEEDED

- Meter stick (or yardstick)
- String
- Chair
- Various books

PROCEDURE

1. Balance the meter stick on the back of the chair. It will balance at its "center of gravity," which should be at or very near the 50-cm. (18-in.) mark. The part of the chair where the meter stick rests is the *fulcrum.*
2. Get two identical books and tie a string around each one.
3. Make a loop in the other end of each string and slide the loops over opposite ends of the meter stick. Leaving the books supported at the ends of the meter stick, where is the center of gravity (where the fulcrum has to be to balance the books)?
4. Replace one of the books with a smaller book. With the books still suspended at the ends of the meter stick, where is the center of gravity?
5. Replace the other book with a larger one. Where is the center of gravity this time?
6. What can you say about the center of gravity when a large object is balanced with a small object? Consider the teeter-totter as you explain your answer.
7. Do you know what a *mobile* is? What does the idea of center of gravity have to do with mobiles?

TEACHER INFORMATION

This activity is closely related to the activities on first-class levers in Section 6, "Simple Machines." Center of gravity is the balance point of an object. The center of gravity of round objects is at the center.

Mobiles are fascinating to construct and provide excellent application of the concept of center of gravity. Encourage students to make a mobile following this activity.

ACTIVITY 47: Where Is Your Center of Gravity?

MATERIALS NEEDED

- Pencil or other small object

PROCEDURE

1. Put your pencil on the floor.
2. Standing near the pencil, pick it up without bending your legs or moving your feet.
3. Stand against the wall, with your heels touching the wall.
4. Drop your pencil on the floor near your feet.
5. Bend over and pick up your pencil without moving your feet or bending your legs.
6. What happened? Why?
7. Repeat steps 1 and 2. Notice your movements as you pick up the pencil. Explain what happened in step 5 in terms of the effect of the center of gravity.

TEACHER INFORMATION

Any time we are on our feet, whether we are walking, running, standing or bending over, we are constantly adjusting to the center of gravity in order to remain "balanced." The body makes these adjustments so automatically that we don't think about them.

Invite students to try steps 3 to 5 with family members. Replacing the pencil with a dollar bill, and offering it to the person who can pick it up without breaking the rules, will increase interest and efffort substantially. The money is as safe as if it were behind lock and key.

ACTIVITY 48: What Is Centrifugal Force?

MATERIALS NEEDED

- Small tube, about 10 cm. (4 in.) long
- String, about 1 m. (1 yd.) long
- Two pencil erasers (or other small weights)

PROCEDURE

1. Thread the string through the tube.
2. Tie one pencil eraser to each end of the string.
3. Hold the tube upright and move it around in a circular motion so the top weight swings around and around.

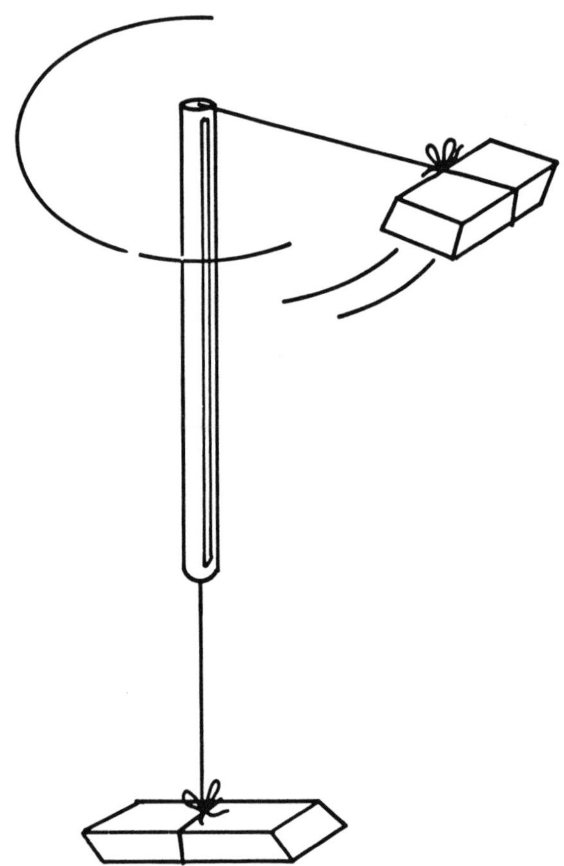

FIGURE 48-1. Tube, string, and erasers—one swinging.

4. Swing the weight around faster. Do not swing it near anyone. The tendency of the upper weight to move outward when rotating is called *centrifugal force.*
5. Change the speed of rotation, faster and slower, and observe the lower weight.
6. What happens to the lower weight as you increase and decrease the speed of rotation? What can you say about the speed of rotation and its effect on centrifugal force?

TEACHER INFORMATION

The tube used in this activity could be a cardboard tube. It could even be the barrel of a ball point pen. If a small, sturdy tube is not available, use a wooden bead out of someone's toy box. The bead needs to be large enough to hold firmly in the hand without interfering with the movement of the string passing through it.

Centrifugal force is the force that tends to impel an object outward from a center of rotation. Newton's first law of motion states that an object at rest tends to remain at rest and an object in motion tends to remain in motion at the same speed and in the same direction unles it is acted upon by an outside force. Centrifugal force results from the tendency of the object to continue moving in a straight line. If it is held back by another force it cannot do that, thus the circular motion. The force that holds it back is *centripetal force,* defined as the force that tends to impel an object toward the center of rotation.

ACTIVITY 49: What Is Inertia?

MATERIALS NEEDED

- Two chairs
- Broom
- Four lengths of cotton thread about 40–50 cm. (1½ ft.) each
- Two rocks (or other weights) about 2 lbs. each

PROCEDURE

1. Lay the broom across the backs of two chairs (or other supports).
2. Tie two pieces of thread to the broom handle, several inches apart.
3. Tie one of the rocks to each of the threads attached to the broom handle. The rocks should hang down several inches from the broom handle.
4. Tie each of the other two threads to one of the rocks. These threads should hang freely from the rocks.
5. Hold tightly to one of the lower threads and pull down slowly but firmly until a thread breaks.
6. Hold tightly to the other lower thread and jerk quickly, breaking a thread.
7. Which thread broke when you pulled slowly? Which one broke when you jerked? Explain.
8. Get some new thread and repeat the activity to verify your results.

TEACHER INFORMATION

As a lower thread is pulled slowly, the force of the pull is equal on both the upper and lower thread. In addition, the upper thread is supporting the weight of the rock (pull of gravity). Thus, the upper thread will usually break if the two threads are identical.

Newton's first law of motion states that an object at rest tends to remain at rest and an object in motion tends to remain in motion in the same direction and at the same speed unless it is acted upon by an outside force. This is sometimes referred to as the law of *inertia.* Inertia is the resistance to change referred to in Newton's first law. The rock, in this case, is an object at rest. As the lower thread is given a quick jerk in step 6, the resistance, or inertia, of the rock protects the upper thread from receiving the full impact of the downward force. Thus, greater force is applied to the lower thread than to the upper thread, and the lower thread will break.

ACTIVITY 50: How Do Potential Energy and Kinetic Energy Compare?

(For older children or teacher demonstration)

MATERIALS NEEDED

- Mousetrap
- Ball
- String
- Pencil eraser

PROCEDURE

1. Set the mousetrap. What kind of energy does it have?
2. Drop the pencil eraser on the release lever. What kind of energy was present at the moment the trap sprang shut?
3. Drop the ball and let it bounce a few times. Describe one full bounce, from the top of the bounce to the bottom and back to the top, in terms of the presence of kinetic and potential energy.
4. Tie the eraser to the string. Hold the end of the string and swing the eraser like a pendulum. Describe one full swing, back and forth, in terms of the presence of kinetic and potential energy.

TEACHER INFORMATION

This activity requires the student to distinguish between kinetic and potential energy. When the mousetrap is set, the presence of the loaded spring gives it potential energy. At the moment the spring is released, the potential energy is converted to kinetic energy, or moving energy. Great care should be taken to assure that fingers are not injured by the mousetrap.

As the ball is held above the floor, it has potential energy. The ball is released and the potential energy is converted to kinetic energy as the ball falls toward the floor. When the ball strikes the floor, it is compressed, and the kinetic energy is converted to potential energy. The potential energy in the compressed rubber propels the ball into the air, again converting the potential energy to kinetic energy. Some of the energy escapes in the form of heat as the ball meets resistance with the air and the floor. Thus, the height of the cycle decreases as the ball bounces.

The swinging pendulum passes through a cycle similar to that of the bouncing ball. All energy contained in the system is potential energy at the instant the pendulum is all the way to the top on either side of the cycle. At the moment the pendulum is at the bottom, moving neither upward nor downward, all of the energy is kinetic.

If the pendulum is at rest, it has neither potential nor kinetic energy. When in a position that gravity can cause movement when released, it has potential energy.

ACTIVITY 51: How Much Horsepower Do You Have?

(For upper grades)

MATERIALS NEEDED

- Stairs
- Stopwatch
- Paper and pencil

Note: The formula for computing horsepower was proposed by James Watt, who found that a horse could do 550 foot-pounds of work in one second. This formula is still used in determining the horsepower of automobile engines. The formula is

$$\text{Horsepower} = \frac{\text{Foot-pounds}}{\text{Seconds} \times 550.}$$

PROCEDURE

1. Measure 10 feet (vertical distance) up the stairs or ladder.
2. Have someone time you as you climb that distance as fast as you can.
3. Compute your "horsepower" by using the above formula. For "foot-pounds," multiply your weight by 10 (number of vertical feet climbed).
4. A small motorbike has about 30–50 horsepower. A medium-sized car has about 100–300 horsepower. How many horsepower do you have?

TEACHER INFORMATION

Using the formula should not be too difficult for students of the upper elementary grades. The following example assumes the student's weight to be 100 pounds and the time required to climb 10 vertical feet to be 3 seconds:

$$\text{Horsepower} = \frac{100 \times 10}{3 \times 550} = \frac{1000 \text{ foot-pounds}}{1650} = 0.61$$

Section 4

LIGHT

TO THE TEACHER

Like many other scientific phenomena, light is so common that we take it for granted. Yet without it we could not live. Plants use light from the sun to produce oxygen, which is vital to all animal life, including humans. Without plants we would have no food. Light from the sun also heats the earth, without which there could be no life at all.

The question of what light really is has evaded scientists for centuries. Yet it is as fascinating as it is elusive, and continues to be the object of many studies. We know a great deal about light because of these studies. For instance, we know that light is a form of energy that travels freely through space. We also know that in addition to the sources of natural light (the sun and the stars), light can be created in various ways. When light comes from sources that people control, it is called artificial light. We use artificial light every day in the form of fluorescent lights, incandescent lights, and candles. The laser produces a form of light that has found widespread use in industry, medicine, and communications.

Activities included in this section encourage investigation into some of the ways in which light behaves. As students participate in these activities, the teacher should encourage students to ponder the relationship of this topic to the study of the eyes and to art.

The scope of the activities in this section is limited to a few very basic concepts about light. Students investigate shadows, color, reflection, and refraction; and they are introduced to prisms and lenses. Many of these concrete activities are easily adaptable for children in the early grades. For the student whose interests extend beyond these basic investigations, many resources are available—encyclopedias, science books, and suppliers of scientific equipment.

ACTIVITY 52: Why Do Shadows Change in Size?

MATERIALS NEEDED

- Projector or flashlight
- Screen or blank wall

PROCEDURE

1. Place the projector across the room from the screen or blank wall.
2. Turn the projector on and the room lights off.
3. Stand in the light, near the screen or wall, and look at your shadow.
4. Move slowly toward the projector, watching your shadow as you move.
5. What happened to your shadow as you moved toward the projector?
6. Why do you think this happened?

TEACHER INFORMATION

Light from the projector passes through the lens and spreads out as it travels through space, forming a cone-shaped path of light with the lens at the narrow end of the cone. As an object moves toward the light source (the lens), the object blocks out a greater and greater portion of the light. Since the shadow is the area not receiving direct rays of light, the shadow increases in size as more of the light is blocked.

ACTIVITY 53: What Can You Make with a Shadow?

MATERIALS NEEDED

- Projector or flashlight
- Wall or screen

PROCEDURE

1. Using a wall or a piece of paper or cardboard as a screen, see if you can make the animal shapes shown in Figure 53-1 with shadows.
2. Try some other shapes of your own.
3. What happens to the shadow-figures as you move your hands closer to or farther from the light?
4. Where is the darkest part of the shadow? Explain why you think this is so.

FIGURE 53-1. Shadow pictures.

TEACHER INFORMATION

This activity is intended mostly for enjoyment and creativity. In reference to step 4, however, the student should notice that the shadow is darkest toward the middle. The outer edges of the figure are not shaded from the entire light bulb, as illustrated in Figure 53-2, and are therefore not as dark as the portion that is completely shaded.

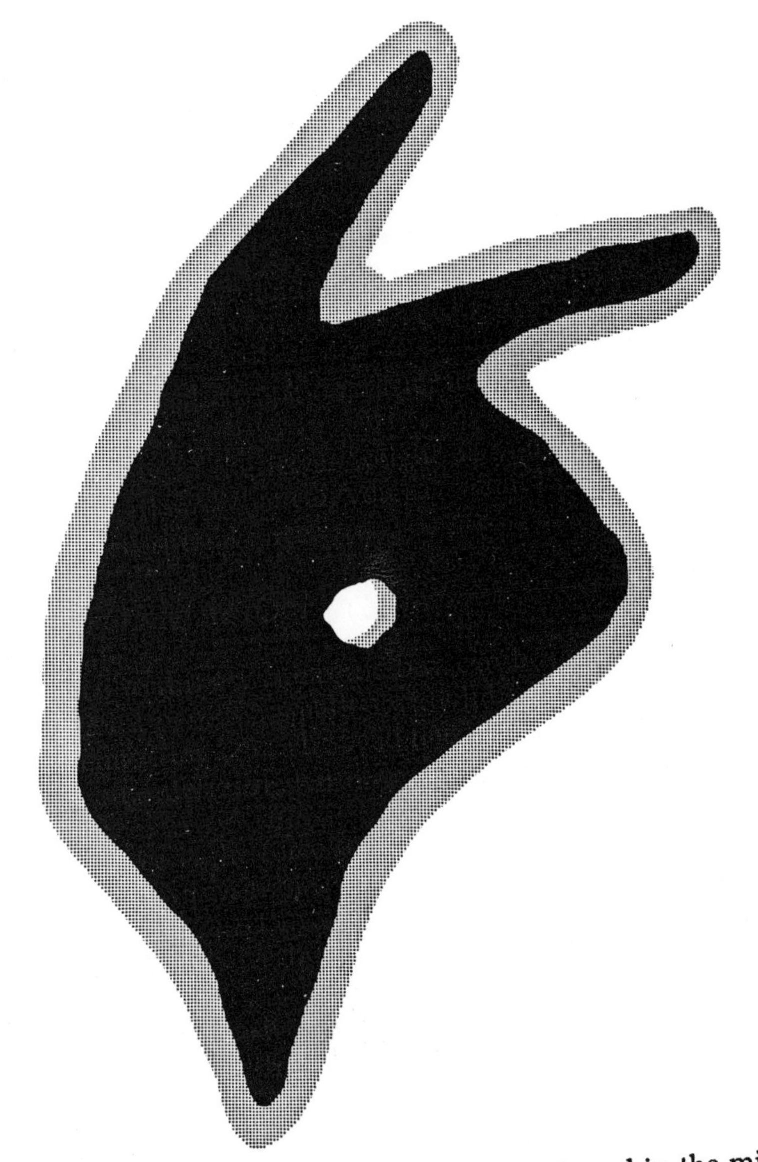

FIGURE 53-2. Light creating a shadow, darkened in the middle.

ACTIVITY 54: What Path Does Light Follow?

MATERIALS NEEDED

- Three or four 5-×-8-in. cards
- A small wooden block for each card
- Glue or thumbtacks
- Flashlight or projector
- Ruler
- Scissors

PROCEDURE

1. Cut a small hole in the center of each card.
2. Attach one of the wooden blocks to each card, using glue or thumbtacks, so the cards will stand.
3. Space the cards about 30 cm. (1 ft.) apart, with the center holes lined up.
4. Have someone hold the light so that it shines into the hole of one of the end cards while you look through the hole of the card at the other end.
5. What do you see?
6. Now move one of the cards about one inch to the side and repeat step 4.
7. What happened? What does this tell you about the path light travels?

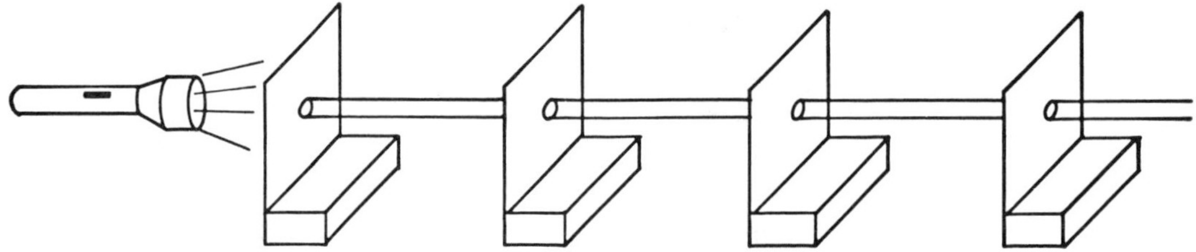

FIGURE 54-1. Flashlight shining through cards.

TEACHER INFORMATION

This activity will help children realize that light travels in a straight path. Unless the cards are positioned with the holes in a straight line, the light does not pass through the holes in the cards.

ACTIVITY 55: How Does Color Affect Energy Absorbed from Light?

MATERIALS NEEDED

- Two equally calibrated thermometers
- Heat lamp (or at least a 300-watt bulb)
- One sheet of white paper and one sheet of black paper of the same thickness
- Paper and pencil

PROCEDURE

1. Prop the thermometers in an upright position about 20 cm. (8 in.) apart, facing in the same direction.
2. Record the temperatures of both thermometers.
3. Place the sheet of white paper in front of one thermometer and the black paper in front of the other.
4. Shine the heat lamp at the sheets of paper in such a way that it faces both equally. It should be about 40–50 cm. (16–20 in.) away from the papers.
5. After the heat lamp has shone on the papers for about two minutes, check and record the temperatures of the two thermometers again.
6. Repeat for two more minutes and again record the temperatures.
7. What changes do you see in the first and last temperature readings and how do they differ with the two thermometers?
8. What can you say about the effect of color in this activity?

FIGURE 55-1. Heat lamp, sheets of paper, and thermometers.

TEACHER INFORMATION

Dark materials have a greater tendency to absorb heat than do light materials. The thermometers behind the two sheets of paper will reflect this tendency.

On a sunny day, direct sunlight could be used instead of the heat lamp. As an enrichment (or perhaps introductory) activity, invite students to go to the parking lot (on a warm day) and feel the surfaces of cars of various colors. Have them check to see if there is any difference in temperature. If so, which colors tend to be warmest?

ACTIVITY 56: What Happened to the Pencil?

MATERIALS NEEDED

- Clear tumbler or bowl
- Water
- Pencil or spoon

PROCEDURE

1. Fill the tumbler or bowl about two-thirds full of water.
2. Put the pencil or spoon into the water.
3. Look at the pencil or spoon from the top and from the side.
4. What appears to happen to the pencil or spoon at the water level? What ideas do you have about this effect?

TEACHER INFORMATION

Light travels at different speeds through different substances, creating a bending effect on any light rays that enter a substance at an angle. This is called *refraction*. Light travels faster through air than it does through water. The bending of the light rays as they pass from air to water or from water to air results in an optical illusion as the object in the water appears to bend at the surface of the water.

This effect is also seen with a boat oar or canoe paddle—it looks broken. (See also Activity 7.)

ACTIVITY 57: Can You Find the Coin?

MATERIALS NEEDED

- Pan or opaque bowl
- Water
- Coin or button

PROCEDURE

1. Place the coin in the pan.
2. Stand in such a position that the coin is just hidden from your view by the edge of the pan.
3. Without shifting your position, have your partner slowly fill the pan with water, being careful not to disturb the coin at the bottom of the pan.
4. What happened to the coin as your partner poured water into the bowl?
5. What do you think could have caused this?

TEACHER INFORMATION

As in Activity 56, refraction comes into play here. Again, an optical illusion is created as the coin appears to rest higher in the bowl if water is present. Light bends as it leaves the water and enters the air, traveling toward the eye. (See also Activity 6.)

ACTIVITY 58: How Can a Postage Stamp Hide Under Clear Glass?

MATERIALS NEEDED

- Empty short jar (such as peanut butter jar) with lid
- Water
- Postage stamp or sticker

PROCEDURE

1. Put the stamp on the table.
2. Fill the jar with water and put the lid on.
3. Place the jar on the stamp.
4. Look at the stamp.
5. Explain your observations.

TEACHER INFORMATION

As light passes from water to air the light bends (refracts) because it travels through these materials at different speeds. In this activity the refraction makes the stamp appear higher than it really is. When it is looked at from an angle, reflected light from the stamp doesn't reach the eyes, so the stamp seems to have disappeared. The lid on the jar prevents the observer from looking straight down on the stamp.

ACTIVITY 59: What Makes Light Bend?

MATERIALS NEEDED

- Aquarium three-fourths full of water
- Flashlight or projector
- Milk
- Two chalkboard erasers that are chalky
- One sheet of paper
- Tape

PROCEDURE

1. Pour milk into the aquarium, a little at a time, until the water has a cloudy appearance.
2. Wrap and tape the paper around the flashlight like a tube, to concentrate the light into a narrow beam.
3. Turn the room lights off.
4. Aim the light at the water on an angle. Have someone clap the chalkboard erasers together over the aquarium to make the beam of light easier to see in the air.
5. Observe carefully the angle of the light beam as it extends from the flashlight to the water and as it continues through the water.
6. What happens to the light beam as it enters the water? What do you think causes the change?

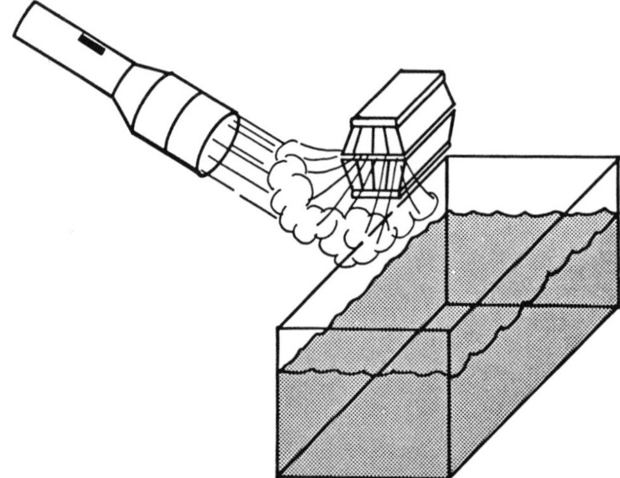

FIGURE 59-1. Aquarium, flashlight, and two chalkboard erasers.

TEACHER INFORMATION

This experiment makes the phenomenon of refraction easily visible. With the chalk dust, the light can be seen in the air and the milk makes it easily observable in the water.

ACTIVITY 60: How Does Water Affect the Way Light Travels?

MATERIALS NEEDED

- Glass jar with lid
- Paper
- Markers
- Water

PROCEDURE

1. Draw a simple diagram on the paper and color it with dark or bright colors.
2. Hang the paper on the wall or lean it against something on a table.
3. Fill the jar with water and put the lid on.
4. Hold the jar between your eyes and your diagram.
5. What do you see?
6. Keeping your eyes on the diagram, hold the jar at different distances from your eyes and from the diagram.
7. Explain your observations.

TEACHER INFORMATION

The jar filled with water acts like a convex lens and inverts the image.

ACTIVITY 61: How Can You Make a Lens from a Drop of Water?

MATERIALS NEEDED

- Small sheet of clear plastic or glass
- Eye dropper
- Water
- Book

PROCEDURE

1. Place a drop of water on the sheet of plastic.
2. Lay the plastic over the page of a book and look at a letter or punctuation mark through the drop of water.
3. What does the drop of water do to the images on the paper?
4. Examine other things through the drop of water, such as a piece of cloth or the back of your hand, by laying the plastic on them.
5. Explain what happened and why.

TEACHER INFORMATION

Any transparent substance with a convex surface will cause light rays to bend and converge. Many vision-aiding devices are based on this principle, including eyeglasses, hand lenses, binoculars, microscopes, and telescopes. The drop of water isn't the best lens, because it must be handled carefully and the degree of surface curve is difficult to control, but it is a lens.

ACTIVITY 62: How Are Convex and Concave Lenses Different?

MATERIALS NEEDED

- Convex lens
- Concave lens
- Piece of plain glass
- Flashlight or projector
- Sheet of paper
- Tape
- White surface

PROCEDURE

1. Roll the paper into a tube around the end of the flashlight and tape it in place.
2. Shine the light on a white surface.
3. Hold each lens and the glass, one at a time, in the path of the light. What happened each time?

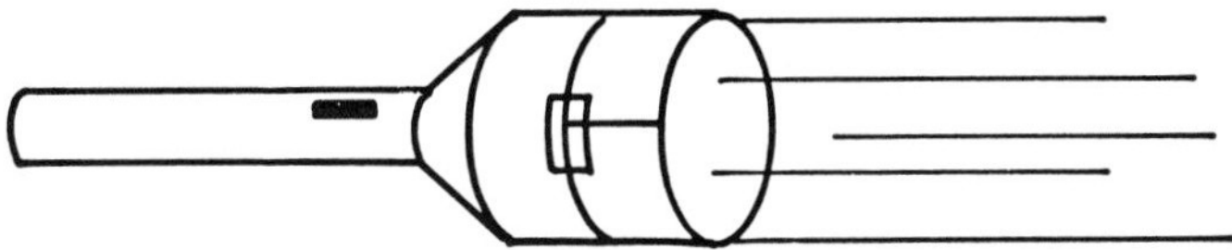

FIGURE 62-1. Flashlight with paper tube around it.

TEACHER INFORMATION

When light passes between media of differing densities (such as air and glass or air and water) the light can be refracted, or bent. Convex lenses are thicker in the middle than on the edges and cause light rays to converge, or come together. Concave lenses are thicker on the edges than in the middle and cause light rays to diverge. A convex lens in the path of the light will concentrate the light on the white surface, causing it to appear brighter, while a concave lens will spread the beam of light over a larger surface.

ACTIVITY 63: How Can You Measure the Magnifying Power of a Lens?

MATERIALS NEEDED

- Hand lens
- Lined paper

PROCEDURE

1. Lay the hand lens on the lined paper and count the number of lines from one edge of the lens to the other.
2. Pick up the lens and hold it in such a position that the lines on the paper come into focus.
3. How many lines do you see in the lens?
4. Compare the number of lines in step 1 with the number of lines in step 3.
5. From your information, what would you say is the magnifying power of your lens: Two power? Three power? Five power?

TEACHER INFORMATION

If the lens itself spans six lines but only three lines can be seen through the lens when held in focus position, the lens is about two power. If only two of the six can be seen through the lens in focus position, the lens is about three power. It makes things look about three times as large as they are. This is not an accurate measurement of lens magnification, but it will provide a close estimate. If you are using a ten-power lens, you will need to use lines, or other equally spaced objects, that are quite close together in order to get a workable count. The smaller and more powerful the lens, the closer the counted objects will need to be.

ACTIVITY 64: How Does a Lens Affect the Way Light Travels?

(Teacher-supervised activity)

MATERIALS NEEDED

- Candle
- Match
- White cardboard
- Magnifying glass
- Pan

PROCEDURE

1. Prop the cardboard on a table.
2. Stand the candle in a pan or other nonflammable container about 60–90 cm. (2–3 ft.) away from the cardboard.
3. Light the candle.
4. Hold the magnifying glass near the cardboard. Move it slowly toward the flame until a clear image of the candle appears on the cardboard.
5. Do you see anything strange about the flame? What effect do you think the magnifying glass has on what you see?

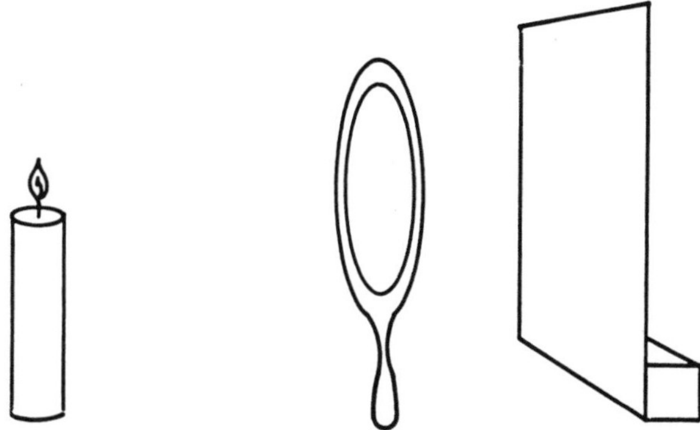

FIGURE 64-1. Candle, lens, and cardboard.

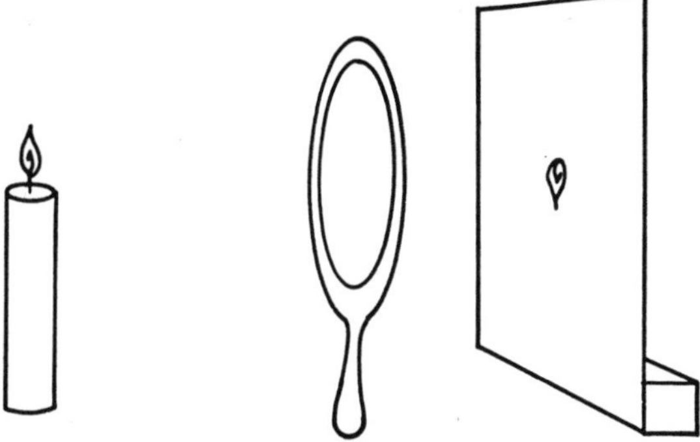

FIGURE 64-2. Candle, lens, and cardboard, with inverted image.

TEACHER INFORMATION

The bending of light through refraction (see also Activities 56 and 57) results in an inverse image of the flame as it is projected onto the cardboard. The same thing happens to the eye. Images are projected onto the back of the eye upside down, but they are reversed to their true perspective as they are interpreted by the mind.

ACTIVITY 65: What Color Is White?

(Upper grades)

MATERIALS NEEDED

- White posterboard
- Compass
- String 1 m. (1 yd.) long
- Crayons
- Scissors

PROCEDURE

1. With your compass, draw a circle 15 cm. (6 in.) in diameter on the posterboard.
2. Cut out the circle with the scissors.
3. Draw three equal pie-shaped sections on the posterboard and color them red, green, and blue.

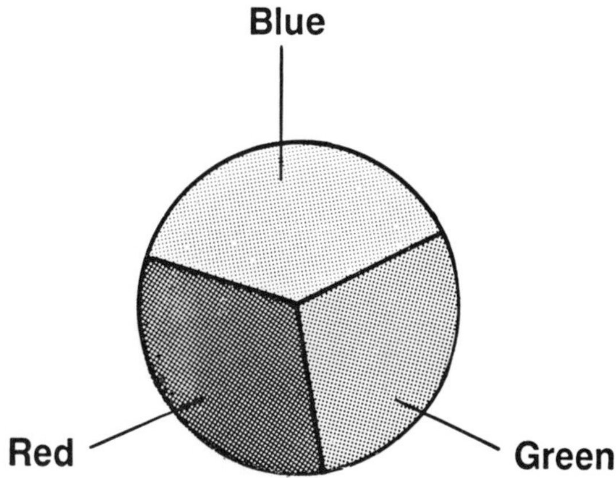

FIGURE 65-1. Divided and colored circle with two holes punched.

4. Make two small holes near the center of the circle.
5. Thread the string through the holes (in one end and out the other) and tie the ends of the string together forming a loop which passes through the two holes of the disk.
6. Center the disk on the string loop and make the disk spin by alternately stretching and relaxing the string.
7. As the disk spins, watch the colored side.
8. What happens to the colors? Why do you think this happens?
9. Try the same thing with another disk and different colors. Expand the activity with other ideas; for example, use only two sections and coloring them with complementary colors, such as yellow and blue. Each time you try a new color combination, make a prediction of what you will see as the disk spins.

TEACHER INFORMATION

As the primary colors spin, they should blend together to form a grayish white. If one of the colors seems to dominate, some of that color should be replaced with more of the other two colors. Blue might need a bit more than its share. Students will enjoy experimenting with various color combinations and testing their predictions of the resulting blends.

The disk may spin better if its weight is increased by doubling the thickness of posterboard or pasting the disk onto cardboard. Another option is to mount the disk onto a sanding pad designed for a quarter-inch drill. The drill could then be used to spin the disk. If a drill is used, the disk must be secured well, as it could fly off and cause injury. This is less likely to happen if you use a drill with a variable-speed switch and keep it at low speed.

ACTIVITY 66: What Does a Prism Do to Light?

MATERIALS NEEDED

- Prism
- Projector or flashlight
- Screen, white paper, or white wall

PROCEDURE

1. Shine the projector light on the screen or other white surface.
2. What do you think will happen if you place the prism in the path of the beam of light?
3. Place the prism in the path of the beam of light. Were your predictions accurate?
4. What is white light?
5. Which color seems to bend the most as light passes through the prism? Which the least?

TEACHER INFORMATION

White light is a combination of many colors. Each color has its own wave length and is bent to a different degree as light passes through a prism, forming a continuous spectrum. Violet has the shortest waves and is bent the most. Red has the longest waves and is bent the least. Five other "pure" colors exist in the spectrum between violet and red. In order, these are indigo, blue, green, yellow, and orange. Sometimes blue and indigo are treated as one color.

Water droplets in the air can act as a prism when conditions are right, thus creating a rainbow. Many jewelry stores sell leaded glass crystals cut in different shapes; these crystals produce beautiful rainbows.

ACTIVITY 67: How Can You Make a Prism?

MATERIALS NEEDED

- Mirror
- Tray or pan
- A sunny day
- Water
- White surface

PROCEDURE

1. Place the tray on a table or on the floor in direct sunlight. Put about 2–3 cm. (1 in.) of water in the tray.
2. Place a mirror in the tray and focus the reflected sunlight on the white surface. At least part of the mirror should be submerged in the water. If the white surface is not available, tape a sheet of white paper onto the wall.
3. What do you see in the reflection on the white surface?

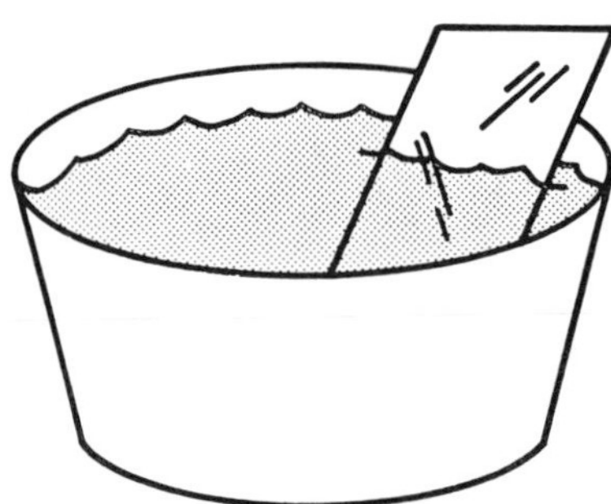

FIGURE 67-1. Mirror leaning in a tray, mostly submerged.

TEACHER INFORMATION

As light passes through a transparent substance (water) at an angle, the light rays are bent. White light contains many other colors, each of which bends to a different degree. Thus, the reflected light on the wall shows a separation of those colors. The colors separate as light passes through a glass prism, and the same effect is produced in this activity with a water prism. This same phenomenon occurs in nature as water droplets in the air separate the colors in sunlight. We see it as a rainbow. Rainbows can sometimes be seen in fine sprays of water, such as that produced by some lawn sprinklers.

ACTIVITY 68: What Affects the Quality of Reflection?

MATERIALS NEEDED

- Tin can
- Damp cloth
- Dry cloth
- Toothpaste
- Sandpaper

PROCEDURE

1. Polish the bottom of the can by rubbing it with toothpaste, using a damp cloth. Shine it with a dry cloth.
2. Look at your reflection in the polished surface.
3. Scuff the polished surface lightly with the sandpaper.
4. Look at your reflection again.
5. Explain the difference in your reflection before and after the sandpaper treatment. What made the difference? Why do you think this happened?

TEACHER INFORMATION

A polished surface reflects light rays in a consistent pattern. A rough surface diffuses light rays (reflects them in all directions), preventing a clear focus.

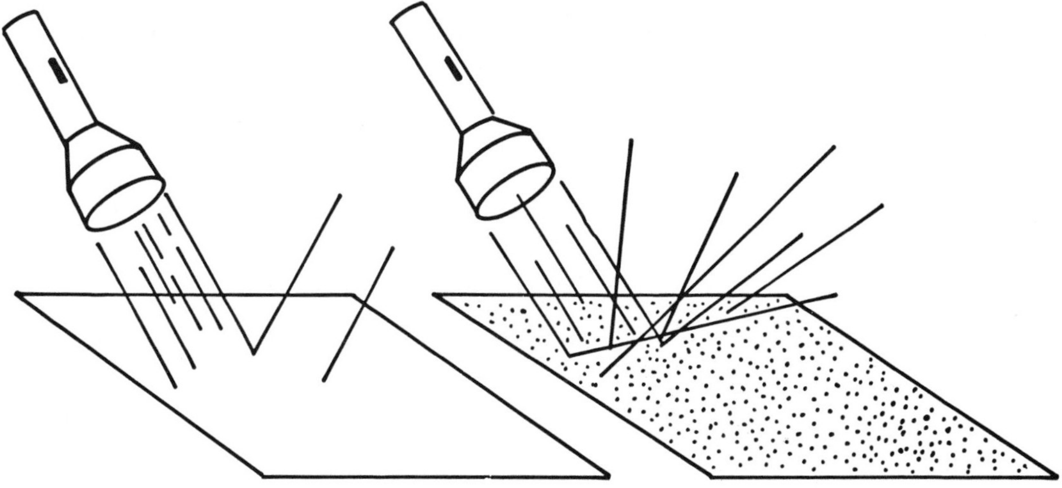

FIGURE 68-1. Two flashlights, two surfaces.

ACTIVITY 69: What Is the Difference Between Reflected Light and Source Light?

MATERIALS NEEDED

- Mirror

PROCEDURE

1. Look briefly at the light in your room.
2. Now hold the mirror so that you can see the room lights in the mirror.
3. Which of these is the "source light" and which is "reflected light?"
4. If you were to cover the source light, what would happen to the reflected light?
5. If you cover the reflected light, what happens to the source light?
6. Light reflects from your desk and enables you to see the desk. Is it source light or reflected light?
7. Does the sun give off source light or reflected light? What about the moon? Explain.

TEACHER INFORMATION

We receive light by two means—direct and reflected. There are relatively few sources of direct light (source light) but almost everything we see gives off reflected light. The exceptions to this are those that produce light, such as a light bulb, fluorescent light tubes, a burning match, and the sun. Other objects can be seen only when there is light to be reflected from one or more of these sources.

ACTIVITY 70: What Is Reflected Light?

MATERIALS NEEDED

- Projector or flashlight
- Two chalkboard erasers
- Mirror
- Darkened room

PROCEDURE

1. Arrange the projector and the mirror so that the light from the projector can be focused on the mirror.
2. With the room darkened, shine the projector light on the mirror at an angle.
3. Clap the chalkboard erasers together lightly in the beam of light and notice the angles of the light beam as it approaches and as it leaves the mirror. How do they compare?
4. Change the position of the projector so the light from the projector shines toward the mirror from different angles. Use chalk dust as needed to keep the light beam visible.
5. Each time you change the position of the projector, compare the angle of the light beam approaching the mirror to the angle of the reflected light beam.

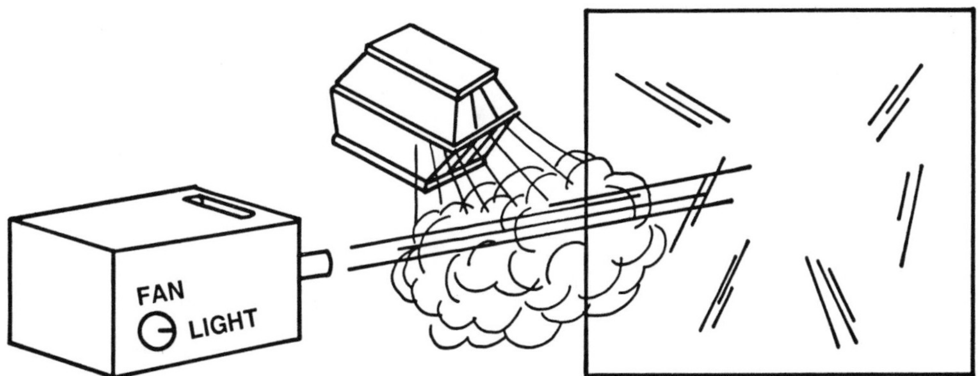

FIGURE 70-1. Projector, mirror, and two chalkboard erasers.

TEACHER INFORMATION

When light is reflected from a mirror, it is always reflected at the same angle as the angle of the light from the source to the mirror. In other words, the reflected angle is always equal to the approaching angle.

ACTIVITY 71: How Is Light Reflection Like the Bounce of a Ball?

MATERIALS NEEDED

- Rubber ball
- Darkened room
- Mirror
- Flashlight or projector

PROCEDURE

1. Bounce the ball from the floor as straight as you can.
2. Now bounce the ball to your partner.
3. Try bouncing the ball at different angles. Notice the angle of the ball's path as it approaches the floor and compare it with the angle of its path as it leaves the floor. How do they compare?
4. Now place the mirror on the floor and "bounce" the light from the flashlight off the mirror, first shining the light straight down at the mirror, then at different angles.
5. Compare the angles of light approaching and leaving the mirror. How do they compare with the angles of the bouncing ball approaching and leaving the floor?

FIGURE 71-1. Bouncing ball.

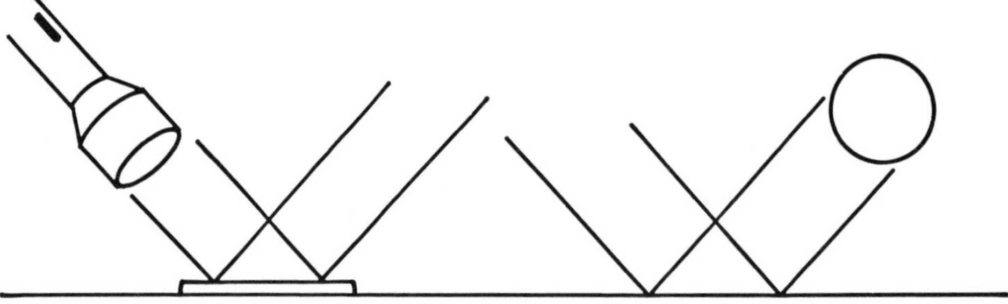

FIGURE 71-2. Bouncing ball and reflecting light.

TEACHER INFORMATION

The purpose of the activity of bouncing the ball is to provide a familiar model. The student should notice that the angle of incidence (angle of the ball's path as it approaches the floor) equals the angle of reflection (angle of the ball's path as it leaves the floor).

ACTIVITY 72: How Many Images Can You See?

(Teacher-supervised activity)

MATERIALS NEEDED

- Two mirrors
- Knife
- Small object

PROCEDURE

1. Check to be sure one of the mirrors is not important for other uses, because you will damage it in step 2 of this activity.
2. Use the knife to scrape away the silvering from the back of one mirror to form a small peep hole about a half inch in diameter right in the center of the mirror.
3. Hold the two mirrors a few inches apart with the reflecting surfaces facing each other (Figure 72-1).
4. Hold a small object between the mirrors and look at it through the peep hole (Figure 72-2).
5. What do you see?
6. Hold the object in different positions and tilt the mirrors at different angles.
7. Explain what you see and why you think it happens.

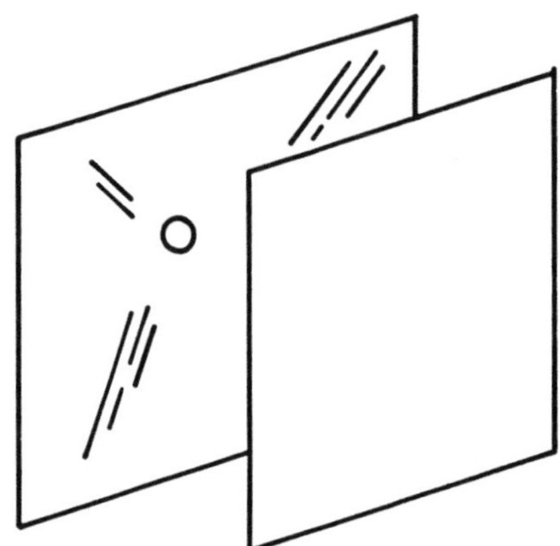

FIGURE 72-1. Two mirrors facing each other, with a peep hole in one.

FIGURE 72-2. A small object held between the mirrors.

TEACHER INFORMATION

As light is reflected from one mirror to the other, an infinite number of images can be seen if the mirrors are kept parallel to each other. As the mirrors are held at a slant with respect to each other, fewer images will be seen because the slant brings the image closer to the top of the mirror with each reflection.

ACTIVITY 73: How Well Can You Control the Reflection of Light?

(Upper grades)

MATERIALS NEEDED

- Projector or flashlight
- Several partners
- One mirror for each person
- Darkened room

PROCEDURE

1. Arrange the people with mirrors in a pattern such that light can be reflected from one to the other.
2. From what you know about the reflected angles of light, see if the group can direct the light from the projector to one mirror and have it reflected from the first mirror to a second mirror. From the second to a third?
3. Determine who will reflect the light to whom in order to reflect the projector light all around the group.
4. Pick a spot on the wall opposite the last person and light up that spot with reflected light. Be sure the light from the projector reflects from all mirrors before lighting up the spot on the wall.
5. With the light reflecting from all mirrors, compare the angle of reflection (the light leaving the mirror) with the angle of incidence (the light approaching the mirror) for each mirror. If necessary, have someone stand in the middle and clap two chalkboard erasers together lightly to make the beams more visible.
6. How does the angle of reflection compare with the angle of incidence?

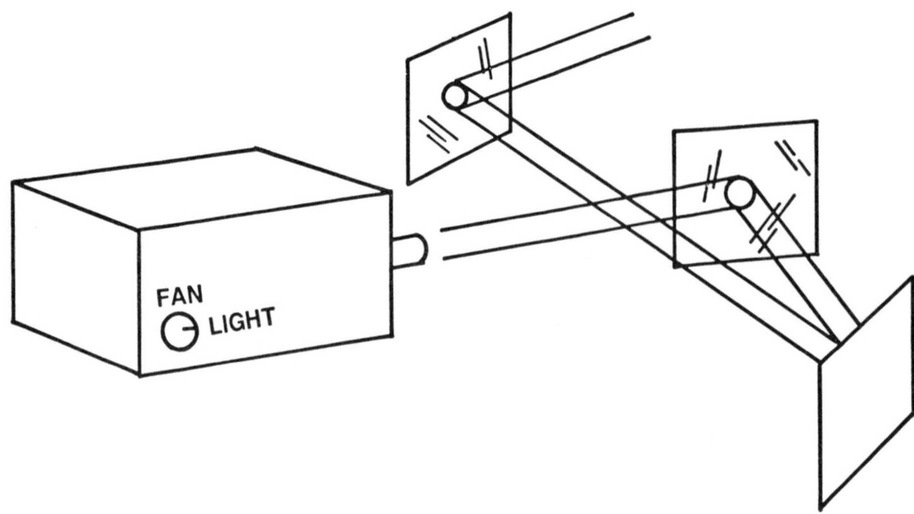

FIGURE 73-1. Projector and series of mirrors.

TEACHER INFORMATION

Students will enjoy the challenge of reflecting the light from mirror to mirror in various patterns. They should notice that the angle of reflection and the angle of incidence are equal.

ACTIVITY 74: How Does a Periscope Work?

(Teacher-supervised activity for upper grades)

MATERIALS NEEDED

- Two 1-quart milk cartons
- Two mirrors
- Knife or scissors
- Tape

PROCEDURE

1. Cut the tops off both milk cartons.
2. Cut an opening about 5 cm. (2 in.) in diameter in one side of each carton, near the bottom.
3. Tape a mirror in the bottom of each carton, facing the opening at a 45-degree angle.
4. Tape the cartons together at the open ends to make a long tube.
5. Look into the mirror at one end of your periscope. What do you see?
6. Can you put your periscope together in such a way that you can look behind you? To your right?

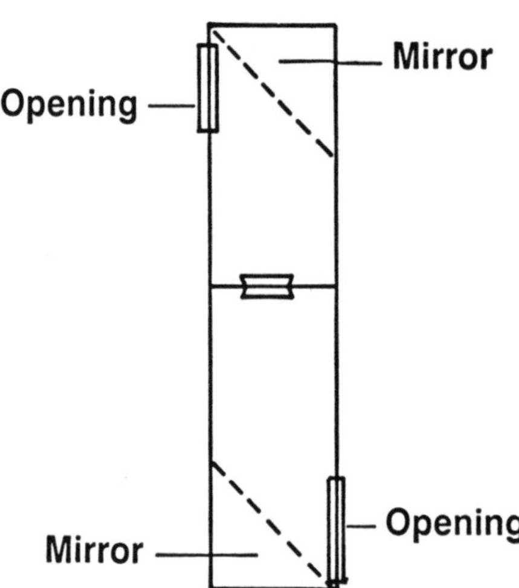

FIGURE 74-1. Milk carton periscope.

TEACHER INFORMATION

The periscope activity is likely to attract a lot of interest and could be used as an enrichment activity. It is an application of the concept of angle of reflection students learn about in other activites of this unit. Students might enjoy expanding their periscopes to include three, four, or more milk cartons to make the periscope longer or to give it creative shapes. Additional mirrors might be needed as students expand with creative ideas. Other tubes could be substituted for the milk cartons.

ACTIVITY 75: How Can You Pour Light?

(Enrichment activity)

MATERIALS NEEDED

- Tall, slim olive jar with lid
- Flashlight
- Nail
- Masking tape or plastic tape
- Newspaper or light cardboard
- Hammer
- Water

PROCEDURE

1. With the hammer and nail, make two holes in the lid of the jar. The holes should be near the edge but opposite each other. One hole should be quite small. Work the nail in the other hole to enlarge it a bit.
2. Fill the jar about two-thirds full of water and put the lid on (Figure 75-1).

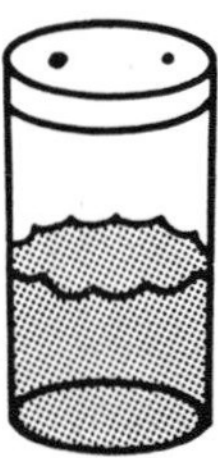

FIGURE 75-1. Jar with lid on, showing two different-sized holes.

3. Put tape over the holes in the lid until you are ready to pour.
4. Lay the jar and flashlight end to end, with the face of the flashlight at the bottom of the jar.
5. Roll the newspaper around the jar and flashlight to enclose them in a light-tight tube. Tape the tube together so it will stay (Figure 75-2).

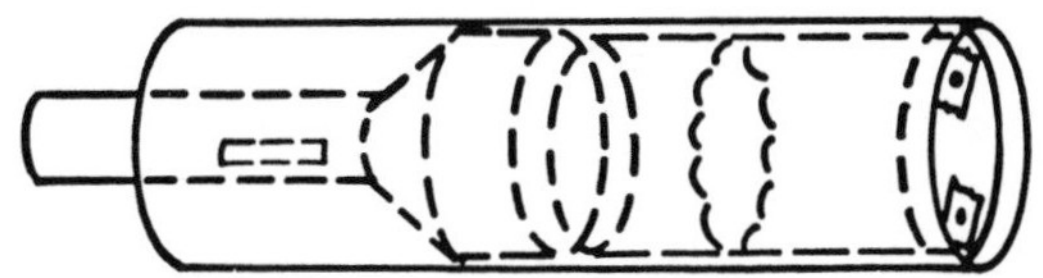

FIGURE 75-2. Flashlight and jar taped together.

6. Slide the flashlight out of the tube, turn it on, and slide it back into the tube. Darken the room.
7. Hold the apparatus upright and remove the tape from the lid. With the large nail hole down, pour the water into the pan (Figure 75-3).
8. What happened to the beam of light as the water poured into the pan?
9. Do you have any idea what caused this?

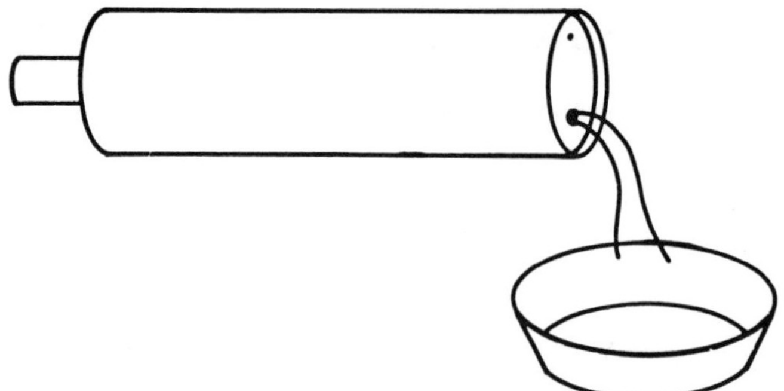

FIGURE 75-3. System with water pouring from larger hole.

TEACHER INFORMATION

Although light travels in straight lines, it is reflected internally at the water's surface and follows the path of the stream of water. Because of the phenomenon of internal reflection, fiber optics can be used to direct light anywhere a wire can go, even into the veins and arteries of the human body.

ACTIVITY 76: How Can You Make a Glass Disappear?

(Upper Grades)

MATERIALS NEEDED

- Two large glass jars
- Two small jars or drinking glasses
- Water
- Cooking oil

PROCEDURE

1. Place the two small jars inside the large jars.
2. Fill one pair of jars with water.
3. Can you see the small jar?
4. Fill the other pair of jars with cooking oil.
5. Can you see the small jar?
6. Explain your observations.

TEACHER INFORMATION

As light passes from one transparent material to another (such as air, water, and glass), the light is bent at the boundary between the two materials. This happens because of the differing speeds at which the materials transmit light. Light moves at about the same speed through petroleum products (including cooking oil) as it does through glass. Therefore, as light passes between glass and oil, it doesn't bend at the boundaries, leaving the boundaries invisible.

ACTIVITY 77: What Is Color?

MATERIALS NEEDED

- White posterboard
- Black India ink
- Newspapers
- String 1 m. (1 yd.) long
- Small pointed paintbrush
- Scissors
- Compass

PROCEDURE

1. Use the compass to draw a circle on the posterboard 15 cm. (6 in.) in diameter. Cut out the circle with the scissors (Figure 77-1).

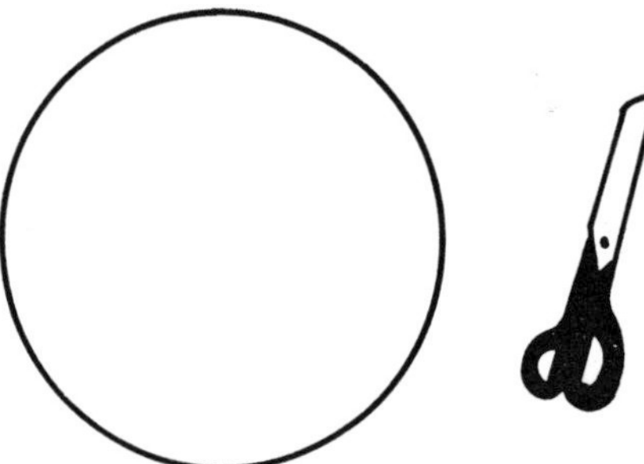

FIGURE 77-1. Circle drawn on paper, scissors.

2. Put a layer of several thicknesses of newspaper on the table and place your white disk on the newspaper.
3. With the India ink and paintbrush, paint your disk in one of the patterns shown in Figure 77-2. Let it dry.

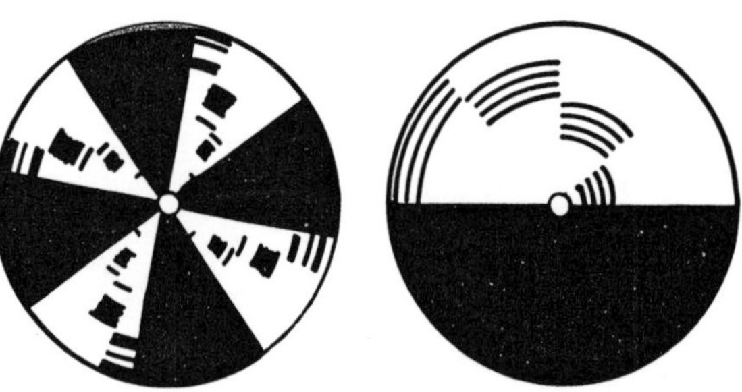

FIGURE 77-2. Disk patterns.

4. Make two small holes on opposite sides of the center point, each about 1 cm. (3/8 in.) from the center point (Figure 77-3).

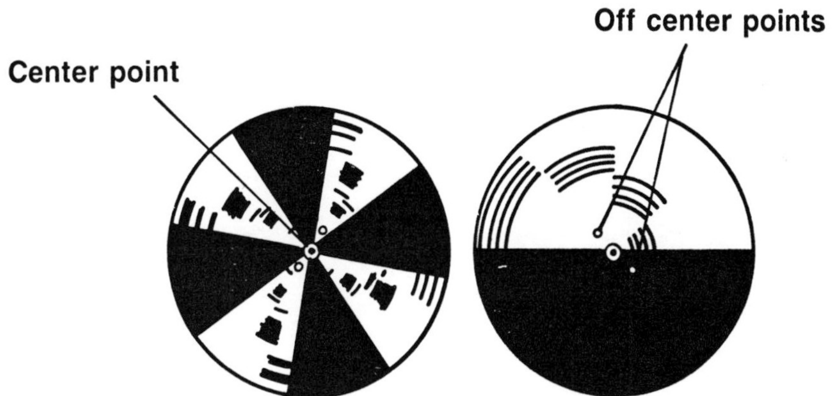

FIGURE 77-3. Center point and holes marked on patterns.

5. Thread the string through the holes of the disk and tie the ends together.
6. Put one finger of each hand through the string, wind up the disk on the string. Make the disk spin by successively pulling and relaxing the string.
7. As the disk spins, watch the painted side.
8. What do you see? Can you explain it?

TEACHER INFORMATION

When the retina receives repeated flashes of white light, they are interpreted by the brain as color. Such flashes of white light are produced by the spinning black-and-white disk. This phenomenon was discovered by Benham in the nineteenth century. If you have a phonograph turntable with adjustable speed, the effect can be studied by making a hole in the center of the disk and laying it on the turntable.

Section 5

SOUND

TO THE TEACHER

Sound is a very important part of our lives. It is one of the first stimuli to which newborn infants react, and its presence or absence shapes and affects us throughout our entire lives. This section introduces sound, its causes and uses. A study of sound lends itself very well to concrete activities, with many possibilities for discovery/inquiry. No attempt is made to introduce the physiology of the ear, although you may choose to teach it in relation to this area.

A study of sound can be greatly expanded in the Language Arts area to develop and enrich listening skills. Music can be integrated through discussion of musical terms found within the section. The final activities on inventing and playing musical instruments could lead to additional study of ancient methods and modern electronic methods of producing music.

Throughout the study, children should be encouraged to bring and demonstrate their own musical instruments. If there is a high school or university nearby, the musical director may be willing to cooperate in providing musicians and instruments. Most communities have choral groups that might be willing to perform. A note to parents asking for the names of people who play unusual musical instruments could produce interesting and entertaining results.

As the importance of sound is discussed, the value of being able to hear and speak clearly should be emphasized. Children should know that people of all ages suffer from hearing loss and that almost everyone develops some degree of impairment as he or she grows older.

Sometime near the beginning of the study, the class should discuss, and perhaps list, ways sound can help us; for example, communication, warning, entertainment, aesthetics, and protection. Sound can also be harmful. Loud noise can injure the ears. Sound can be pleasing and soothing to an individual, but it can also be disturbing and irritating. The loudness of sound is measured in decibels. For public protection, many communities have laws restricting the decibel levels that can be produced by any means. As electronic sound equipment becomes more common, children should understand reasons for attempts to control noise levels.

In discussing pitch, or the frequency of vibrations per second, children should be aware that the human ear cannot detect the frequency of very high (fast) and very low (slow) vibrations. Dog whistles are too high-pitched to be heard by people, but they can be heard by dogs and some other animals.

Resource people can be involved frequently in this study. These might include individuals of all ages who have hearing handicaps, a nurse, a doctor, an audiologist, a sound specialist (architect), a music store owner, a musician, someone who makes or plays unusual musical instruments, or any others you may find helpful.

This is an area rich in "take-home-and-talk-about-it" activities. Taking home concrete objects to show and talk about will help children develop increased language ability and be a source of strong motivation in science.

Little attention has been given to the areas of electronics in sound. The study of earth and space introduces such areas as radar, sonar, and radio telescopes. The study of static electricity and current electricity considers the role of the electron, in a simple way, through television, radio, and stereo.

ACTIVITY 78: What Is Sound?

MATERIALS NEEDED

- Paper and pencil

PROCEDURE

You have been in this room many times before. Maybe there are things about it you haven't noticed. Try this:

1. Close your eyes and be very quiet for three minutes. Listen carefully. Do you hear anything? Describe it on a piece of paper.
2. If you heard new sounds, what were they and why do you think you haven't heard them before?
3. How did the quiet make you feel?

TEACHER INFORMATION

Many people are not aware of background sounds in their environment. Students may remark that it has never been this quiet before. Others may realize that they heard new sounds because they had really never listened for them before. This is an opportunity to talk about developing listening skills through paying attention or concentrating. Specialists in sound control (acoustics) can design nearly soundproof rooms where even voices at a normal conversational level cannot be heard. Usually people become accustomed to background noise of a low decibel level and ignore it.

A discussion of "how quiet makes me feel" could lead to an art, poetry (Haiku is an excellent approach for this type of creative poetry with older children), or creative-language experience ("What are some quiet words?").

An architect or sound control specialist could be used as a resource person.

ACTIVITY 79: What Are Some Things Sounds Tell Us?

MATERIALS NEEDED

- Cassette player or phonograph
- Tape or record of common sounds
- Pencil and paper

PROCEDURE

1. Play the tape and listen to the sounds.
2. Describe or name as many sounds as you can.
3. What can you say about sounds in your life?

TEACHER INFORMATION

Many teachers enjoy preparing tapes of different sounds. You may want to prepare one on everyday sounds, such as phone ringing, water running, dog barking, bird chirping, car starting, animal noises (sound toys available for young children are good sources), automobile horns, musical instruments, jet airplane taking off. Many schools have sound records for use with kindergarten and primary grades. Check your media center or library.

Take a sound field trip. Take several tape recorders on a field trip and try to collect as many sounds as you can.

If children have tape recorders at home you may want to encourage them to record common sounds, bring them to school, and have other members of the class guess what they are.

Play soft classical music and loud rock music. Have children make a painting or color a picture showing how each makes them feel.

Classify sounds into categories; for example, warning sounds: siren, bell, honking horn, growling dog, screeching brakes. (Mothers' voices as they continue to call children often change in interesting ways.)

Have a class discussion of how sounds help us and occasionally harm us (too loud may damage ears or make us nervous).

ACTIVITY 80: How Well Can You Match Sounds?

(Early grades)

MATERIALS NEEDED

- At least 12 six-ounce unmarked metal cans
- Small objects
- Tape

PREPARATION

Prepare the cans ahead of time. Place small objects in a pair of cans and then seal the cans with tape.

PROCEDURE

1. Shake the cans and listen to the noise they make.
2. Can you hear the different sounds they make?
3. Do any of the cans make the same sound?
4. If you find cans that sound alike, put them next to each other.
5. Have a friend listen to the cans and see if he or she agrees.
6. You may want to make more cans with different sounds to see how well your friends can tell differences.

TEACHER INFORMATION

This is a preschool or early-grade activity. Older children may be interested in constructing the "shakers" for younger groups. Materials used in the cans to make noise could include dried rice, beans, or peas; marbles; BBs; gravel; sand; bits of Styrofoam; puffed rice; or any other small objects found around the home. Be sure children cannot see in the cans and that the cans are prepared in pairs with approximately the same amount of material in each set of cans.

ACTIVITY 81: How Are Sounds Made?

MATERIALS NEEDED

- Shoe box with lid
- Same-colored elastics of various lengths and thicknesses
- Different-colored elastics of various lengths and thicknesses

PROCEDURE

1. Stretch four or five elastics of different thicknesses and lengths around a shoe box with the lid removed.
2. Use your index finger to pluck the elastics. What do you see? What do you hear?
3. Try different lengths and thicknesses. Look and listen.
4. What happened? What can you say about this?
5. Find some elastics that are of different colors but the same lengths as the original ones. Match them carefully and stretch them over the box. Pluck them again. What do you see? What do you hear? Can you think of a reason for using colored elastics?
6. Put the lid on the shoe box and repeat the activity. What happened? What can you say about this?

TEACHER INFORMATION

The main purpose of this activity is to reinforce the idea that sound may be produced by vibration. In addition, this activity introduces the idea of pitch (high and low sounds) in relation to the rate of vibration (the faster the vibration, the higher the pitch).

Resonance is introduced when the lid is put on the shoe box.

Older children may have had some experience with these concepts; however, this activity is intended to create awareness of pitch and resonance only. Later experiences should help children gain understanding as they are presented in different ways.

The use of carefully matched colored elastics should help children discover that color does not affect sound.

ACTIVITY 82: What Causes Sound?

MATERIALS NEEDED

- 50 cm. (20 in.) of monofilament fish line with a wooden dowel 10 cm. (4 in.) long attached to each end
- Shoe box with lid
- Toothpick
- Pencil

PROCEDURE

1. Put the shoe box on the edge of a table or desk.
2. Remove the lid, make a hole in one end of the box with your pencil, thread the fish line through the hole, and secure it with the toothpick (Figure 82-1).

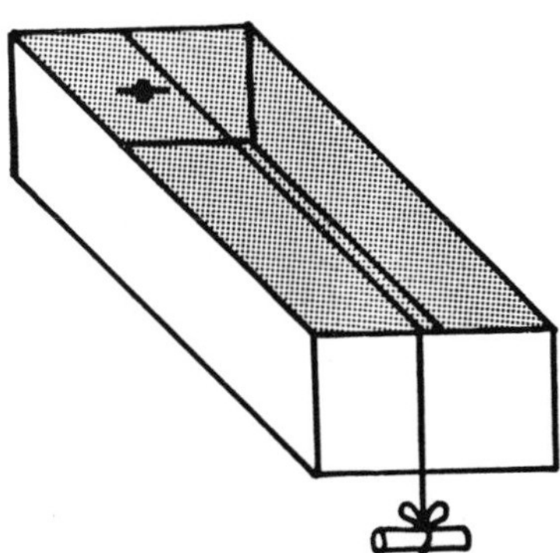

FIGURE 82-1. Open shoe box.

3. Put the lid on the box and stretch the fish line lengthwise across the top of the box. Put one dowel under the fish line near one end of the lid (Figure 82-2).

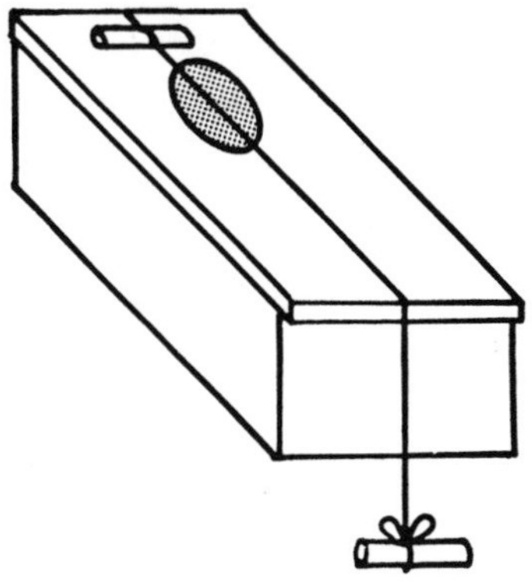

FIGURE 82-2. Box with lid.

4. Slowly pull down on the dowel and pluck the fish line. What do you hear? What do you see?
5. As you pluck the line, pull down on the dowel to stretch it tighter. Watch and listen. What do you see? What do you hear? Try to play a simple tune. What might happen if you cut a hole in the lid of the shoe box? Try it.

TEACHER INFORMATION

This activity should help children discover the relationship between the rate (speed) of vibration and the pitch (high-low) of sound. You may want to relate this activity to the previous one with elastics. The hole cut in the lid will increase the resonance. Resonance is a way of increasing the intensity of a sound by causing one object (vibrating monoline) to create a sympathetic vibration (of about the same frequency) in another object (the walls of the shoe box).

The dowel on the top of the lid serves as a bridge to keep the string elevated enough to vibrate freely; stringed instruments use the same principles. A guitar, violin, cello, or viola could be used for comparison.

ACTIVITY 83: How Do We Produce Sounds?

MATERIALS NEEDED

- Prepared shoe box from Activity 82

PROCEDURE

1. Hold your hand around the front of your throat.
2. Hum and talk. Make high sounds and low sounds. Make soft sounds and loud sounds. What happened?
3. Pluck the string stretched across the shoe box. Make it tighter as you continue to pluck. What happens?
4. Can you explain how your vocal cords work?

TEACHER INFORMATION

Our vocal cords are caused to vibrate by air passing over them. Muscles in our throat tighten and loosen the cords to produce higher and lower sounds. The amount of air we pass by the cords determines loudness and softness. This is a reason proper breathing technique is so important to singers. Activity 84 will ask children to repeat portions of this activity and further develop this idea.

ACTIVITY 84: Can Sounds Be Shaped?

MATERIALS NEEDED

- Paper and pencils

PROCEDURE

1. Take a deep breath and hum a note. Hold the note while you slowly open your mouth as wide as you can.
2. Hold your tongue and say some words.
3. Let go of your tongue and say the phrase "black bug's blood," rapidly several times.
4. List ways we change or "shape" the sounds our vocal cords make.
5. How many ways can you imitate how your parents call you to come home, or to get ready for school?

TEACHER INFORMATION

Our vocal cords produce pitch and loudness of sound but we depend on our throat, mouth, tongue, and teeth to produce the phonetic "shaping" of the sounds. This ability to produce phonetic differences is one of the reasons we are able to develop the highly complex, interrelated process we call vocal communication.

For enrichment, introduce a unit on nonverbal communication in social studies or language arts.

ACTIVITY 85: How Can Sounds Be Produced? (Part I)

MATERIALS NEEDED

- Eight glass soda bottles of the same size and shape
- Water
- Paper slips numbered 1 to 8
- Pencil

PROCEDURE

1. Pour water to different levels in the bottles.
2. Blow gently across the tops of the bottles until a sound is produced. Arrange the bottles in a row according to the *pitch* of the sound from low to high.
3. You may want to add to or remove water from the bottles to make a musical scale. Under each bottle put a slip of paper numbered from one to eight.
4. Try to play a simple tune by blowing across the tops of the bottles. Can you decide what is vibrating to make the sound?
5. Use a pencil to tap the side of each bottle near the top. What happened? Check the numbers from low to high. What is vibrating to make the sound? What can you say about this?

TEACHER INFORMATION

To do this activity, children may need to be reminded of the musical meaning of the term *pitch*.

In steps 1–4, blowing across the bottle causes the air to vibrate. This is the way pipe organs and musical wind instruments produce sound. A longer column of air will cause a slower vibration and a lower pitch. When the bottles are struck in step 5, it is the glass that vibrates to produce the sound. Water will slow the rate of vibration of the glass. Therefore, the greater the amount of water, the more slowly the glass vibrates, and the lower the pitch.

Remember, water expands and contracts according to its temperature. Water also evaporates. Both of these characteristics may make the bottles change pitch.

ACTIVITY 86: How Can Sounds Be Produced? (Part II)

MATERIALS NEEDED

- Meter stick (or yardstick)
- Plastic and wood foot rulers
- One tongue depressor per student
- Pencil (optional)

PROCEDURE

1. Place the meter stick on a table with one-half extending over the edge. Hold one end of the stick firmly against the table. Push downward and release the other end. What happened? Move the stick so that different lengths extend over the edge. What is making the sound?
2. Try the foot rulers and tongue depressor. Learn to play a simple tune. You may want to mark the stick with a pencil to remind yourself of the position of each note.
3. Find a friend and see if you can learn to play a tune together.

TEACHER INFORMATION

As the length of stick protruding from the table is increased, the speed of vibration will decrease and the pitch will go down. This is a "take-home-and-talk-about-it" activity that can provide scientific understanding and oral language experience.

ACTIVITY 87: How Can Sounds Be Produced? (Part III)

MATERIALS NEEDED

- Paper drinking straws
- Garden hose 1 m. long
- Scissors
- Mouthpiece from a bugle, a trumpet, or a trombone

PROCEDURE

1. Cut one end of a paper drinking straw as shown in the illustration. Moisten the cut end and put it between your lips. Blow gently around the straw. Cut pieces from the end of the straw as it is being played. What happened? What can you say about this?

FIGURE 87-1. Drinking straw with end cut.

2. Place a mouthpiece in a garden hose. Blow into the mouthpiece to see if you can make a sound. Change the shape of the hose. What happens to the pitch of the sound?

TEACHER INFORMATION

With practice, the students will be able to make the cut end of the straw vibrate to produce sound. This is similar to a clarinet or oboe. Paper straws work better than plastic because the plastic does not compress as easily to form a reed.

When the group uses the garden hose, a child who plays the trumpet, trombone, or bugle may be able to demonstrate and help others learn to play. Changing the shape of the hose will not vary the pitch; however, cutting a length off either the straw or the hose will shorten the vibrating column of air and raise the pitch.

ACTIVITY 88: How Can Sounds Be Produced? (Part IV)

(Early grades)

MATERIALS NEEDED

- Combs of various sizes
- Kazoos
- Tissue paper 10 cm. × 20 cm. (4 in. × 8 in.)

PROCEDURE

1. Fold the tissue paper over the comb, letting it hang down each side.
2. Hum into the paper-wrapped comb. What happened? What can you say about this?
3. Hum a tune in the kazoo. How does it make a sound?
4. Raise your head so you are looking at the ceiling of the room. Hold your hand around the front of your neck. Hum a tune. What happened? What can you say about this?

TEACHER INFORMATION

Sounds are produced by vibrations. With the tissue paper and comb, sound is produced by the vocal cords, which in turn cause the paper over the comb to vibrate and alter the sound. The same occurs when a kazoo is used.

This activity can provide a review of the way sound is produced through vibration and how sounds can be altered through the vibration of another object.

Kazoos may be purchased in novelty stores that carry party noisemakers. Some music stores also carry them.

ACTIVITY 89: How Can You See Sound?

MATERIALS NEEDED

- Cardboard oatmeal drum or medium-sized tin can
- Salt, puffed wheat, or puffed rice
- Large balloon or sheet rubber
- String

PROCEDURE

1. Remove both ends from a can or cardboard container (be careful of sharp edges).
2. Stretch one thickness of a balloon over one end of the can and tie it with a string. You now have a simple drum.
3. Sprinkle salt on the drum head. Tap it and observe what happens. Hit it harder. What happened? What can you say about this?
4. Sprinkle salt or puffed rice on the drum head. Keep the drum flat and shout into the other end. Have a friend observe the results, then trade places.
5. What happened? What can you say about this?

TEACHER INFORMATION

When the drum head is tapped, the salt will form a pattern caused by the vibration. The pattern will change as the drum is hit harder.

Shouting into the can will cause the rubber diaphragm to vibrate (be sure it is tightly stretched). Pitch and loudness will change the pattern of the salt or puffed rice.

Loud musical instruments will also cause the patterns to change. Remember, for this to work, *the balloon must be stretched tightly across the can.*

ACTIVITY 90: How Can You See Your Voice?

MATERIALS NEEDED

- Prepared drum from Activity 89
- 2-cm. × 2-cm. (1-in. × 1-in.) mirror
- Glue
- Screen or white surface
- Flashlight

PROCEDURE

1. Glue the mirror to the center of the drum head.
2. Darken the room and have a friend shine a flashlight so the light from the mirror is reflected onto a screen or white place on the wall.
3. Speak in a loud voice into the can and observe the reflected light on the wall.
4. Make different sounds to see what happens.

TEACHER INFORMATION

When the child shouts into the can, the drum head will vibrate, causing the reflected pattern on the wall to change shape. Different sounds will cause different shapes. This is a method of changing sound waves into light so they may be observed. It is a simple oscilloscope. This principle is used in many technical fields such as medicine. Musical groups often use this principle to produce light shows to accompany their music. Your encyclopedia can provide additional information if children would care to explore this topic in greater depth.

ACTIVITY 91: How Does Sound Travel? (Part I)

MATERIALS NEEDED

- Box of dominoes
- Pan of water
- Small rock
- Drawing paper
- Crayons

PROCEDURE

1. Stand the dominoes on end on a solid surface approximately 3 cm. (1 in.) apart.
2. Tip the first domino forward so it hits the one next to it. What happened?
3. Matter is made up of tiny particles called molecules that react very much as the dominoes did when the first one was disturbed. Energy in the form of vibration is transferred from one molecule to another.
4. Drop a small rock into a pan of water. Observe what happens to the water. When molecules bump against each other, they transfer energy to all the other molecules around them, causing vibrations to travel in all directions.
5. Can you draw a picture of the way you think sound travels in air?

TEACHER INFORMATION

The use of dominoes will help children see how energy is transferred from one object to another. The pan of water should show how the energy is transferred in all directions (in this case, in ripples). If a large pan is used, the children may observe that the ripples bounce off solid objects and reverse direction. Echoes are caused by sound waves traveling a great distance and bouncing back in waves.

ACTIVITY 92: How Does Sound Travel? (Part II)

MATERIALS NEEDED

- Large table or desk
- Wooden foot ruler and meter stick
- Clock that ticks loudly

PROCEDURE

1. Have a friend tap an object on the table or desk loudly enough for you to hear.
2. Put your ear on the desk top and have your partner tap again.
3. Move the ticking clock one meter away and listen to it tick. Touch one end of the meter stick to your ear and the other to the clock (hold the stick lightly balanced between two fingers).
4. What happened when you put your ear to the desk and the meter stick in steps 2 and 3? What can you say about this?
5. If anyone in the class has a ticking wristwatch, see if you can hear it through a foot ruler or the meter stick.
6. What can you say about sound traveling through solid objects? Can you think of a reason for this?
7. What does the statement "I'm keeping my ear to the ground" mean? Where do you think it began?

TEACHER INFORMATION

Sound travels better through solid objects because the molecules are more tightly packed and don't have to move a great distance to bump against each other and transmit the vibrations. Sound will travel a greater distance in solids for the same reason. The exception, of course, is specially designed acoustic materials which appear to be solid but are designed with spaces to "trap" vibrations.

The tapping on the desk and the ticking of the clock should be heard more clearly when the ear is against the solid objects. The meter stick and foot ruler should be held loosely so the hand does not muffle the vibrations.

Native Americans used this principle, literally keeping their ears to the ground, to hear sounds at great distances. Buffalo herds and horses' hoofs could be heard before they were seen. "Keep your ear to the ground" means to listen carefully.

(See Activity 11 for another activity idea.)

ACTIVITY 93: How Does Sound Travel? (Part III)

MATERIALS NEEDED

- One wire coat hanger per student
- Two pieces of string 50 cm. long

PROCEDURE

1. Tie the strings to the wide ends of the hanger.

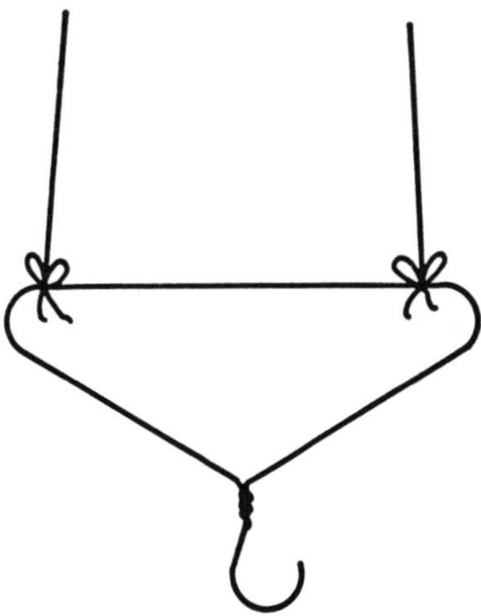

FIGURE 93-1. Upside-down coat hanger with strings attached.

2. Hold the ends of the strings and hit the hanger against a solid object. Listen to the sound it makes.
3. Wrap the ends of the string twice around each of your index fingers. Put your fingers in your ears and tap the hanger on the solid object again.
4. What happened? What can you say about this?

TEACHER INFORMATION

When struck without the fingers in the ears, the hanger will sound flat and metallic. When the fingers are placed in the ears, the sound will be a loud gong because sound travels better through the relatively solid string than through the air.

Metallic spoons or other hard solid objects may be substituted to provide an object for children to take home to demonstrate and explain. Instead of the hanger or other solid object, foam rubber may be used to demonstrate one of the principles of acoustics—sound absorption.

ACTIVITY 94: How Does Sound Travel? (Part IV)

MATERIALS NEEDED

- Ticking clock
- Foot ruler
- Meter stick
- String
- Paper cup telephone from Activity 10

PROCEDURE

1. Listen to the clock tick. Move it as far from your ear as you can and still hear the ticking. Have a friend measure the distance.
2. Put one end of the foot ruler to your ear and the clock at the other end touching the ruler. What happened?
3. Repeat step 2 using a meter stick. Substitute string for the meter stick. What happened?
4. Put the clock against one end of your paper cup telephone and listen on the other end. What can you say about this. Can you see a relationship between this activity and the one with the hanger?
5. The sticks should not be held firmly or clutched in your hand. Why?

TEACHER INFORMATION

These activities require a quiet room.

Before introducing this activity, you may want to have children tap on their desks with a solid object, listen to the sound, then put their ears to the desks and tap again.

In each instance, the sound should be louder when traveling through a solid. Thin pieces of wood such as lathing of different lengths may be substituted for the foot ruler and meter sticks. The objects should not be held firmly, as the hand will absorb the vibrations and muffle the sound. The same phenomenon occurs when the thread on the paper cup telephone is touched.

ACTIVITY 95: How Fast Does Sound Travel?

MATERIALS NEEDED

- Drum, cymbals, large metal lid or something else that will make a loud sound when visibly struck
- Stick to strike object

PROCEDURE

1. Take your drum or other object out on the school grounds. Ask other members of the class to go with you.
2. Move at least 100 meters (approximately 105 yards) away from the other students.
3. Strike the object several times so the others can see the movement of your arm and hear the sound.
4. Remember, when you see an object move at a distance you are seeing reflected light travel. When you hear the sound you are hearing sound vibrations.
5. Have the students tell you what they observed. What can you say about the speed of light and the speed of sound?
6. Discuss these questions:
   a. Would altitude affect the speed of sound?
   b. Would sound travel more easily during the day or night?
   c. Would sound travel better on a cold or a hot day?

TEACHER INFORMATION

Light travels very rapidly, over 186,000 miles a second. By comparison, sound is a slowpoke, moving at about 760 miles per hour at sea level. (Speed of sound is affected by temperature and density of the air. The speed range at sea level is about 740 to 780 as the temperature ranges from freezing to 75 degrees Fahrenheit.) Even at the short distance of 100 meters, it will be possible to see the child strike the drum before the sound is heard. Children who have been to athletic events in a large stadium may have noticed that sounds made on the playing field by athletes or bands are seen before they are heard. Airplanes, especially fast jets, are sometimes difficult to locate in the sky by their sound because the sound is traveling so much more slowly that by the time it arrives, the plane has moved to a new position.

Children should be able to answer the questions in step 6 if they remember that sound travels better in air when there are more molecules. Higher altitudes have *thinner air,* fewer molecules per cubic centimeter. Cold air contains more molecules and is *heavier.* Therefore, sound would travel better at night or on a cold day.

ACTIVITY 96: How Can Sound Be Controlled?

MATERIALS NEEDED

- Two identical shoe boxes
- Scissors
- Other materials or fabrics
- 1-in.-thick pieces of foam rubber
- Glue (optional)
- Small paper cup (optional)

PROCEDURE

1. Punch or cut a round hole approximately 2 cm. (3 in.) in both ends of each shoe box. Try to make the holes nearly the same in both boxes.
2. Cut foam rubber to line the sides, top, and bottom of one shoe box. (Be sure to cut holes in the foam rubber to match the ones in the box.)
3. Measure and cut three pieces of foam rubber so they will fit from the bottom to the top of the shoe box and about halfway across, as shown in Figure 96-1.

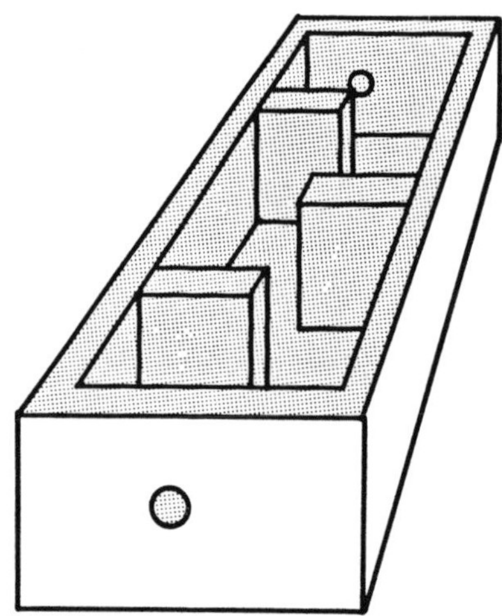

FIGURE 96-1. Foam-lined shoe box with foam dividers.

4. Put the lid on each shoe box and have a friend whisper something to you through each box. Then have your friend speak more loudly and make other kinds of sounds. Be sure your friend's mouth and your ear are against the box when the sounds are made. You may want to glue a small paper cup, with the bottom removed, over the holes in the ends. This will help collect the sound.
5. What happened? What can you say about this?
6. Try lining other shoe boxes with different materials.
7. Can you think of a way to use your oscilloscope to measure the results.

TEACHER INFORMATION

This activity will help children discover one way of deadening sound—absorption. Sound waves, traveling through the air molecules, strike the many holes in the foam rubber, are "captured," and not permitted to go on. Sound traveling through the foam-lined box will be mostly absorbed while it will travel clearly or even be amplified by the empty box.

This activity develops the concepts of resonance and acoustics in sound.

ACTIVITY 97: What Happens to Sound When There Are Fewer Molecules?

(Teacher-supervised activity)

MATERIALS NEEDED

- 4- to 8-ounce glass jar with tightly sealing lid
- Thread or string
- Hot (not boiling) water
- Small bell
- Tape

PROCEDURE

1. Use the string to suspend the bell in the jar by taping it to the inside of the lid. Be sure the bell does not touch the sides or bottom of the jar.
2. Gently shake the jar and listen to the bell.
3. Remove the lid with the bell attached and carefully pour about 2–3 cm. (1 in.) of hot water into the jar.
4. Allow the jar to stand for about 30 seconds and then replace the lid. Be sure the bell does not touch the water.
5. Gently shake the jar again and listen to the bell.
6. What happened? What can you say about this?

FIGURE 97-1. Bell in jar.

TEACHER INFORMATION

Before hot water is poured into the jar, the children should be able to hear the bell clearly. Hot water in the jar will cause the air to expand and force some of the molecules out. With fewer air molecules in the bottle, sound vibrations will not travel as easily, so the bell will not sound as loud.

Discuss the problem of communication on the moon or any other place without air.

ACTIVITY 98: What Is a Tuning Fork?

MATERIALS NEEDED

- Tuning fork
- Small dish of water
- Soft rubber mallet or rubber heel from a shoe

PROCEDURE

1. Hold the handle of the tuning fork in one hand and strike it with a rubber mallet or shoe heel. (CAUTION: Never hit the tuning fork with a hard object.)
2. Bring the double end near your ear. What happened?
3. Strike the tuning fork again. Touch the double end. What happened?
4. This time, after striking the tuning fork, lower it slowly into a dish of water. What happened?
5. Strike the tuning fork again. Gently touch the handle to a hard surface such as a table or desk.
6. Can you think of ways to make the sound of a tuning fork louder? Test your ideas.

TEACHER INFORMATION

Tuning forks may be obtained from many sources including music stores, science supply houses, and medical supply stores. Children who play stringed musical instruments may have them for use in tuning their instruments. Specially designed tuning forks are often used by doctors for general hearing screening tests. Tuning forks are keyed to a certain pitch. This depends on their thickness and length, and the material of which they are made. Most tuning forks vibrate so rapidly that it is difficult to detect movement. When the tines of a vibrating fork are lowered slowly into a dish of water, the water will splash, demonstrating that vibration is occurring. When the handle of a vibrating fork is placed on a table or desk, the sound will be amplified. If the tuning fork is touched to a large paper cup, a shoe box, or the body of a stringed instrument, the sound will be amplified.

ACTIVITY 99: Can You Make a Goblet Sing?

(Teacher demonstration)

MATERIALS NEEDED

- Four to six good-quality glass goblets
- Water
- Vinegar

PROCEDURE

1. Check the goblets carefully to be certain they have no cracked or chipped edges.
2. Add different amounts of water to each goblet (no more than half full). Put a few drops of vinegar in the water.
3. Firmly hold the goblet by the base with one hand. Moisten the fingers of your other hand with the vinegar water and rotate your fingers lightly around the rim of the goblet. What happened? Can you think why?
4. Try the other goblets. Can you describe what is happening?

TEACHER INFORMATION

Great care should be exercised in performing this activity. The goblets must be of high quality and completely free of rough edges. When this activity is properly performed, the moist fingers will cause the glass to vibrate and produce a beautiful clear tone. The combination of water and vinegar seems to produce just enough lubricant and friction to make the demonstration easier.

You may want to try sympathetic vibration with this activity. This means that the vibrations of one goblet will travel through the air and cause another glass to vibrate and produce the same tone. In order for this to occur, the condition of each glass must be almost exactly the same. Both should be dry, empty, and at the same temperature. Their physical appearance should be the same. Place them about 30 cm. (12 in.) apart. Moisten your fingers with vinegar water and cause one goblet to vibrate. While it is producing a loud tone, grasp it firmly with your hand to stop the sound. If you listen carefully, the other goblet may be making the same tone.

Sympathetic vibration may also be experienced by singing into a piano while holding the *sustain* pedal down. The vibrations of the voice will cause strings, tuned to the same pitch in the piano, to vibrate. (Sympathetic vibration was explained in relation to resonance in Activity 82.)

ACTIVITY 100: How Can Sounds Be Heard More Clearly?

MATERIALS NEEDED

- 4-ounce, 8-ounce, and 12-ounce paper cups
- Larger round tapered containers (such as popcorn drums)

PROCEDURE

1. Remove the bottoms from the paper cups and other containers.
2. Choose two friends, select different-sized containers, and go outside.
3. Have your friends walk away from you in opposite directions for about 50 paces.
4. Take a small cup, point it between your friends and say "Hello" in a loud voice into the narrower end of the cup. Next, turn to face each friend and repeat the hello at about the same volume.
5. Now fit several cups together as shown in the illustration and repeat step 4.

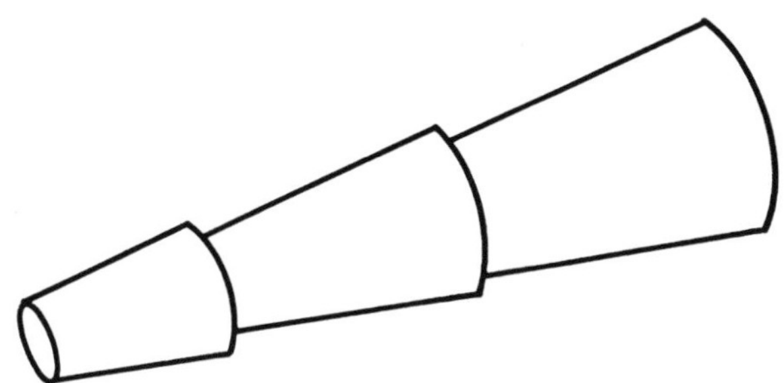

FIGURE 100-1. Paper cups nested to form a megaphone.

6. Trade places with your friends and repeat the activities. Discuss your findings. Can you explain what happened?

TEACHER INFORMATION

This activity is related to the activity with the paper cup telephone. The object the children have produced is a megaphone, which collects, concentrates, and directs sound waves. The children on the playground will discover that they can hear better when the paper cup megaphone is pointed toward them. They should also observe that as the megaphone is lengthened and widened the sound is clearer. We often cup our hands around our mouths when we shout for the same reason. Many wind instruments have bell-shaped ends.

ACTIVITY 101: What Are Some Ways to Use Sound?

(Teacher-assisted activity)

MATERIALS NEEDED

- 8-ounce paper cup
- Thin sewing needles
- Thimble
- Masking tape
- Sheet of 12-in. × 18-in. construction paper
- Old phonograph records
- Record turntable

PROCEDURE

1. Have you done the paper cup telephone activity yet? If not, perhaps you will want to try it before you begin this exploration. Ask your teacher about Activity 10.
2. Thomas Edison, a famous inventor, invented a talking machine that he called a phonograph. At first, a wax cylinder was used. It was later improved by making a round, hard disk. You can make a simple phonograph to play sound.
3. Very carefully, push a sewing needle through the lower lip of a paper cup so that the needle touches the bottom of the cup (Figure 101-1).

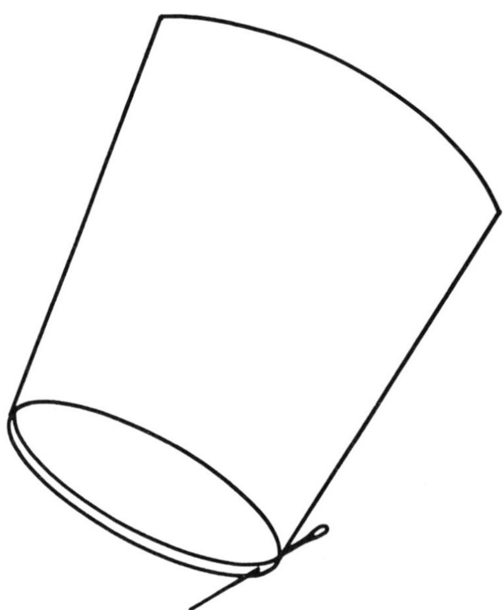

FIGURE 101-1. Paper cup with needle.

4. Put an old phonograph record (one you don't want anymore) on a revolving turntable and hold the cup by two fingers while lightly

touching the point of the needle to the grooves in the record (Figure 101-2). What happened?

FIGURE 101-2. Paper cup on phonograph record.

5. Make a sheet of construction paper into a cone held together with masking tape. Insert a sewing needle through the narrow part of the cone (Figure 101-3).

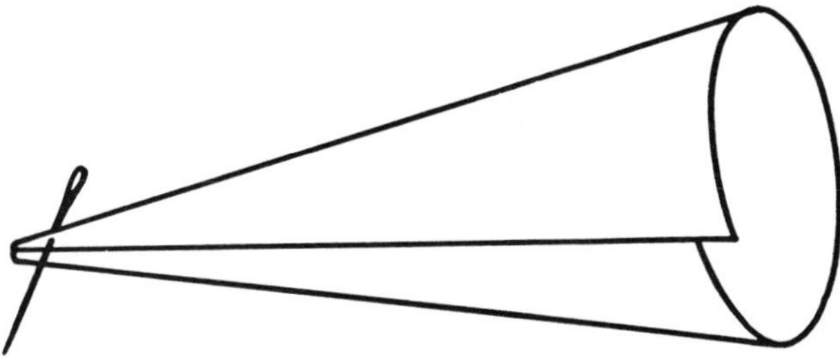

FIGURE 101-3. Needle inserted through cone.

6. Lightly touch the needle to the grooves of the record spinning on the turntable. What happened? Can you explain why?

TEACHER INFORMATION

This activity should be done individually or in small groups. It is a good "take home-talk about" activity. The paper cup telephone in Activity 10 demonstrates sound traveling better through solids and amplifying sound through concentrating the vibrations in a confined area (the paper cup). This activity is similar to the paper cup telephone in many ways. The grooves in the record cause the needle to vibrate, which transfers to the bottom of the paper cup. The shape of the cup concentrates and amplifies the sound, making it possible to hear the sound reproduced from the grooves of the record. The paper cone works in the same way, except the sound may be louder due to the size of the cone and the better vibration that is possible through thinner material.

CAUTION: Young children will need help in inserting the needles and rolling the cones.

ACTIVITY 102: Can You Think of Words That Sound Like the Object They Describe?

(Enrichment activity)

MATERIALS NEEDED

- Paper and pencils

PROCEDURE

1. Some words in our language seem to sound like the object or event they describe. Say "bark" loudly and sharply. It seems to make a sound similar to the sound a dog makes. Now try the word "wolf." Say it sharply in a deep voice. What do you hear? Words that imitate the natural sound of the object or action involved are called *onomatopoeia.*
2. Get together with several friends and, beginning with the list below, see how many words you can find that make a noise similar to the object or event:

bark	creak
wolf	knock
bear	peep
croak	puff

3. Take your list home and ask members of your family to help add to it.
4. Compare your list with those of other members of the class.
5. Write an exciting story using as many onomatopoeia words as you can.

TEACHER INFORMATION

Fairy tales, children's stories, and poetry make liberal use of onomatopoeia. The huffing and puffing of the wolf in *Three Little Pigs* is an excellent example. If children are conscious of the words and how words make them feel, their writing skills can be improved through this technique.

ACTIVITY 103: Can You Invent or Make a Musical Instrument?

(Teacher-assisted activity)

MATERIALS NEEDED

- A variety of tubes, cans, elastics, and so on, that will produce sounds (see Figures 103-1, 103-2, and 103-3)

PROCEDURE

1. Throughout history people have made and played musical instruments. The only rule seems to have been that the sound an instrument made was pleasing to the person playing it. Hollow logs were probably the first drums; reeds, the first wind instruments; and tough stems or dried animal parts such as tendons or intestines, the first stringed instruments. Today, some of our music is produced by electronics or other synthetic means. But many of the old ways of producing music are still being used, and some old ways of producing music are being revived. If you have ever seen or heard a symphony orchestra, most of the instruments being used were invented hundreds and even thousands of years ago.
2. You can invent and play your own musical instrument. Look at the illustrations here. These should give you some ideas with which to begin. Your instrument does not have to be the same. You can probably invent a better one.
3. When you have finished making your musical instrument, find some friends and see if you can learn to play a tune.

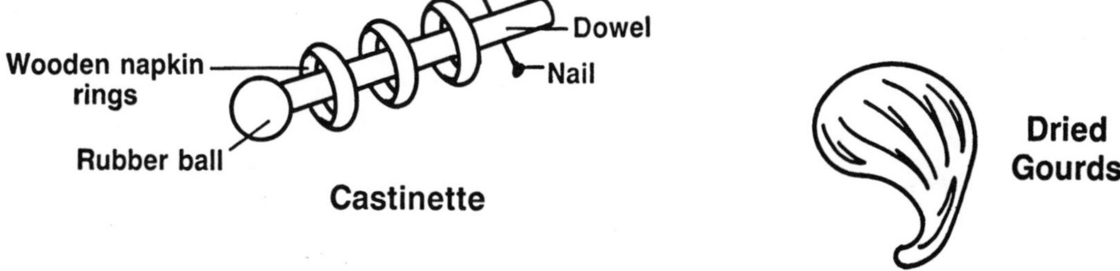

FIGURE 103-1. Homemade percussion instruments.

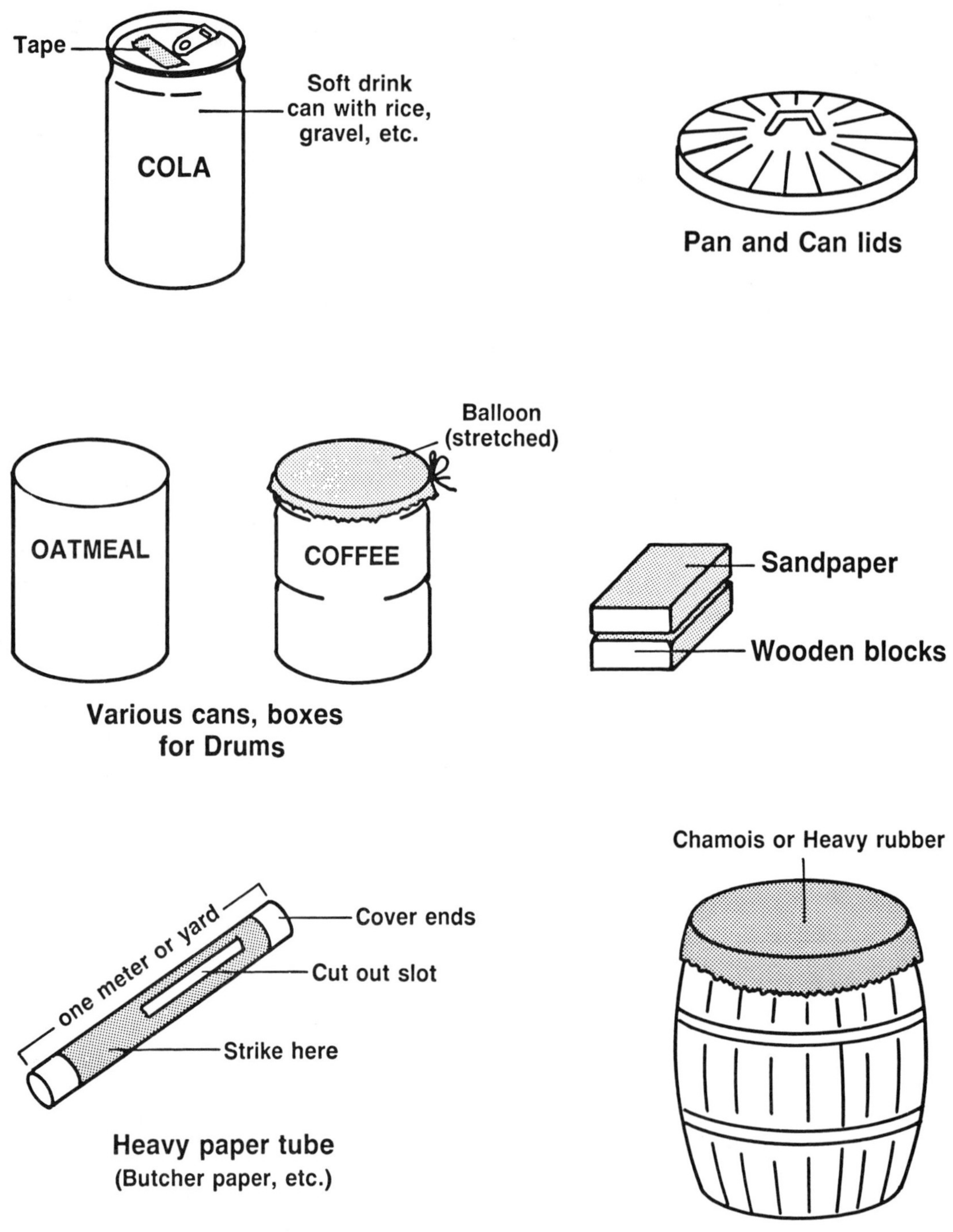

FIGURE 103-1. Homemade percussion instruments (*continued*).

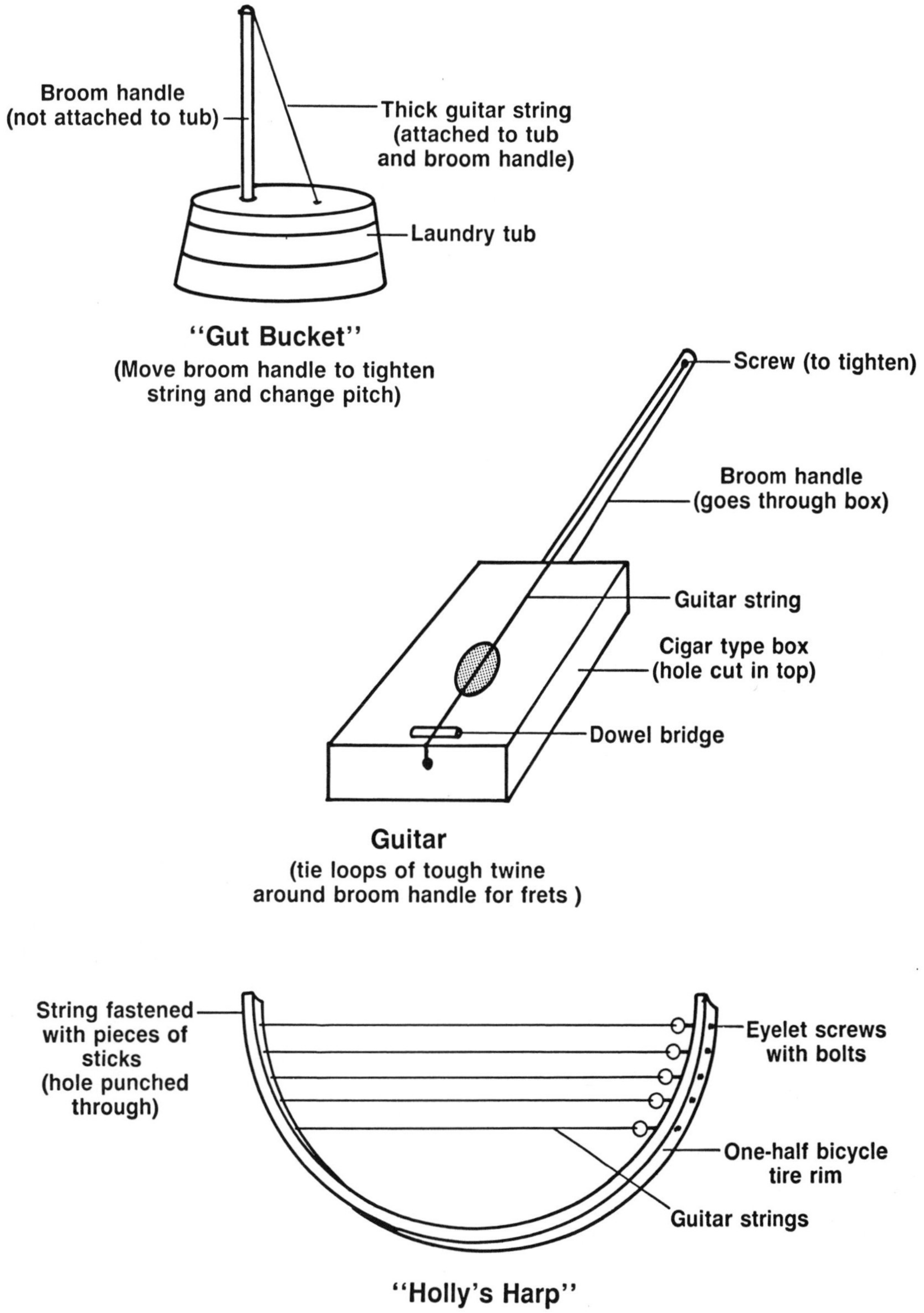

Broom handle
(not attached to tub)
Thick guitar string
(attached to tub
and broom handle)
Laundry tub
"Gut Bucket"
(Move broom handle to tighten
string and change pitch)
Screw (to tighten)
Broom handle
(goes through box)
Guitar string
Cigar type box
(hole cut in top)
Dowel bridge
Guitar
(tie loops of tough twine
around broom handle for frets)
String fastened
with pieces of
sticks
(hole punched
through)
Eyelet screws
with bolts
One-half bicycle
tire rim
Guitar strings
"Holly's Harp"

FIGURE 103-2. Homemade stringed instruments.

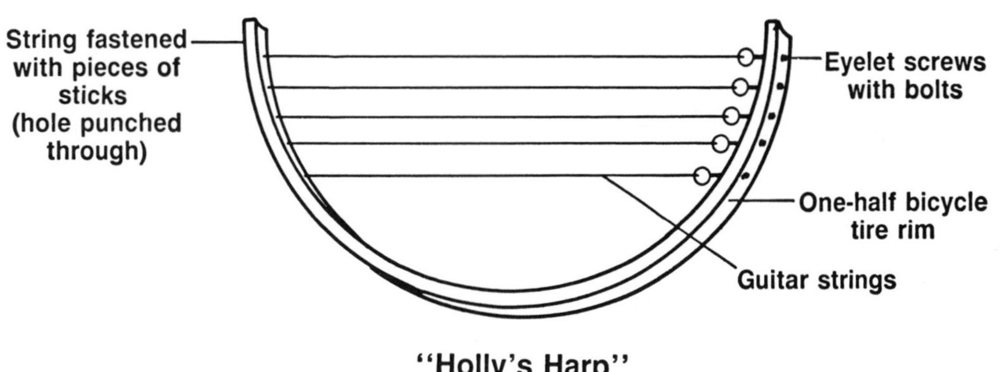

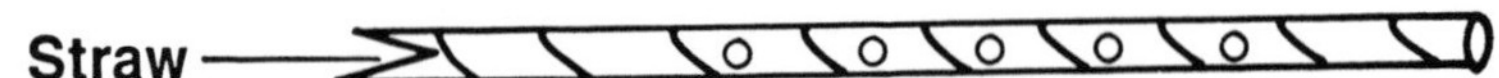

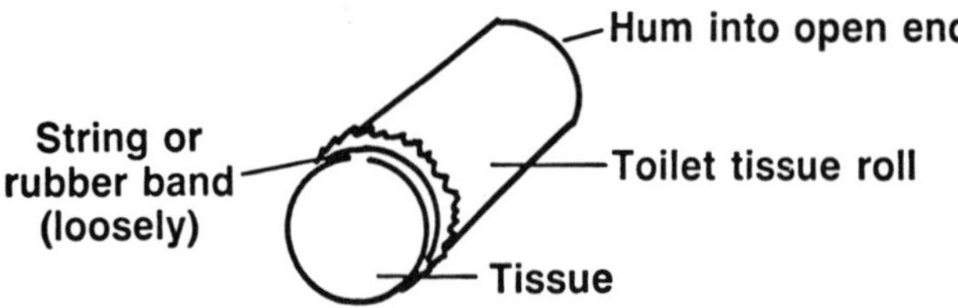

FIGURE 103-3. Homemade wind instruments.

TEACHER INFORMATION

This activity can be used in conjunction with an art class or a music class. Encourage the students to be creative as they make their instruments.

Section 6

SIMPLE MACHINES

TO THE TEACHER

Acquiring an understanding of simple machines can be a real eye-opener to the world around us. All machines, regardless of complexity, are composed of various combinations of the six simple machines. These are often applied in unique and creative ways, but they are nonetheless the same six. After some exposure to these activities, students will enjoy applying their newly acquired awareness in identifying the simple machines in common appliances and equipment—the shovel, the egg beater, the bicycle, the automobile, and so forth.

This section lends itself especially well to the discovery of scientific principles. Most of the activities suggested are safe for students to perform independently. Inquiry skills emphasized in the activities herein are: experimenting, measuring, predicting, observing, recording information, analyzing observed data, and comparing recorded information.

For most of the lever activities, a 1-in. board, which is approximately 1 m. (1 yd.) long and 10 cm. (4 in.) wide, is adequate. Others call for a lighter material, such as ½-in. plywood.

It is recommended that you prepare your levers by marking positions 1, 2, 3, 4, and 5, measured at equal intervals as indicated in Figure A.

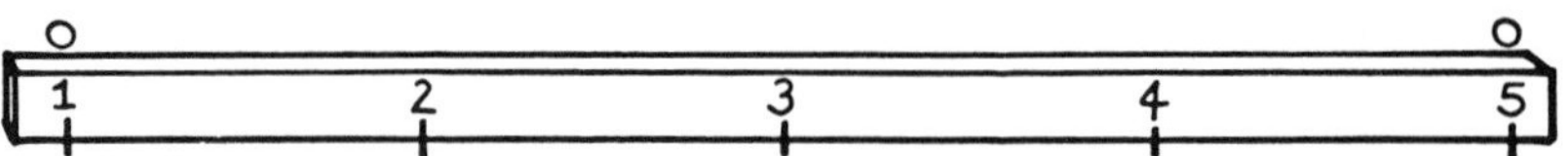

FIGURE A. Lever with points marked and eye hooks.

Eye hooks mounted at each point provide for attaching the spring balance.

Fulcrums ranging in height from 5 cm. (2 in.) to 10 cm. (4 in.) should be adequate and can be made by cutting a wedge shape from 4-in. × 4-in. post material (Figure B). Scraps that are adequate can usually be acquired at a lumber store for low or no cost.

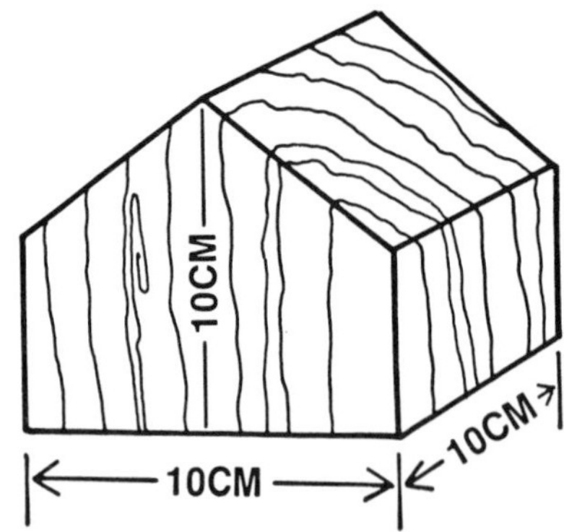

FIGURE B. 4 in. × 4 in. fulcrum.

REGARDING EARLY GRADES

Activities 104–110 can be easily adapted for younger children. Many of the later activities involve charting and mathematical comparisons that are not appropriate for the early grades. However, these activities can be used by omitting the steps involving charting and mathematics. Young children can experience the concept "Machines make work easier" by feeling it and seeing it happen. These children can be encouraged to report in terms of "easier" and "harder" instead of by mathematical comparisons. For children who have experienced the teeter-totter and the wheelbarrow, these activities will help to clarify their earlier observations.

ACTIVITY 104: What Happens When You Rub Your Hands Together?

MATERIALS NEEDED

- None

PROCEDURE

1. Rub your hands briskly together for several seconds.
2. How do your hands feel?
3. Do it again, only faster. Then quickly hold your hands on your cheeks.
4. How do your hands feel to your cheeks?

TEACHER INFORMATION

Whenever the surfaces of two objects rub together—the hands in this case—the resulting friction creates heat. In this simple activity, the heat is quickly noted and will vary according to the amount of moisture (perspiration and oil of the skin) that is present.

ACTIVITY 105: How Do Lubricants Affect Friction?

MATERIALS NEEDED

- Pan of water or sink

PROCEDURE

1. Rub your hands together briskly as you did for Activity 104.
2. How do your hands feel?
3. Next, dip your hands in the water.
4. While they're wet, rub them briskly again.
5. Do your hands feel any different? Can you explain this?

TEACHER INFORMATION

In addition to providing a cooling effect, the water also acts as a lubricant, reducing friction and thereby reducing the amount of heat produced by friction.

Reduction in friction resulting from the use of a lubricant can also be demonstrated by applying a small amount of olive oil, cooking oil, or hand lotion to the palms of the hands before rubbing.

ACTIVITY 106: How Do Starting Friction and Sliding Friction Compare?

MATERIALS NEEDED

- Two or three large books
- String 2 m. (2 yds.) long
- Spring balance

PROCEDURE

1. Tie the books into a bundle, using the string.
2. Place the books on a table or on the floor. Attach one end of the spring balance to the string wrapped around the books.

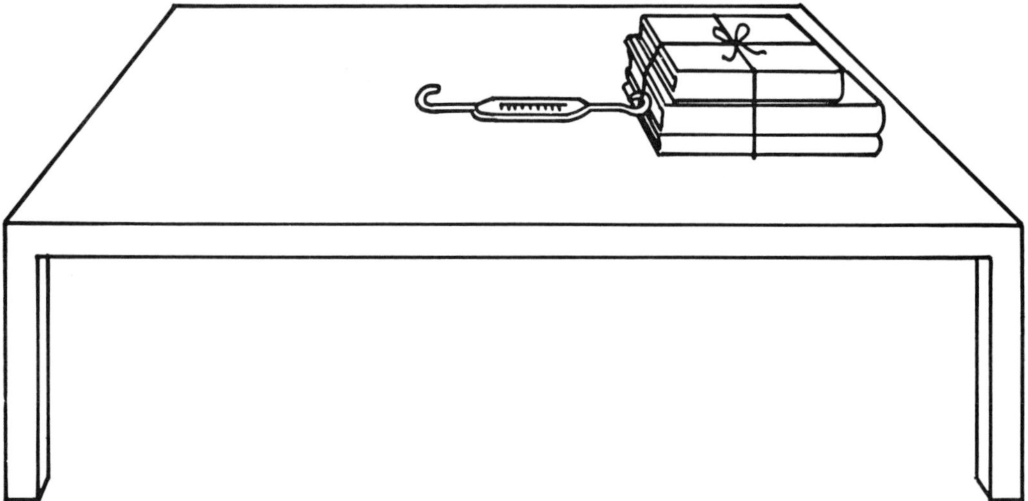

FIGURE 106-1. Bundled books with spring balance attached.

3. Holding the other end of the spring balance and watching the indicator needle carefully, pull the books 50 to 100 cm. (1½ to 3 ft.) across the table (or floor).
4. What was the reading on the spring balance when the books first began to move?
5. What was the reading on the spring balance as the books moved steadily across the table?
6. Repeat the activity, being sure to pull the books in a steady, not jerking, manner.
7. Is the amount of force required to start the books moving equal to the amount of force needed to keep them moving? If not, which is greater?
8. Repeat to verify your findings, if you wish.

TEACHER INFORMATION

Starting friction is greater than *sliding friction.* More force is required to start an object than to keep it sliding. One factor is inertia—the tendency of an object at rest to remain at rest and of an object in motion to remain in motion.

ACTIVITY 107: How Does Rolling Friction Compare with Sliding Friction?

MATERIALS NEEDED

- Two or three large books
- String 2 m. (2 yds.) long
- Spring balance
- At least six round pencils

PROCEDURE

1. Tie the books into a bundle, using the string.
2. Place the bundle of books on a table or on the floor.
3. Attach one end of the spring balance to the string wrapped around the books.
4. While holding the other end of the spring balance and watching the indicator needle carefully, slide the books steadily 25 to 50 cm. (10 to 20 in.) across the floor (or table).
5. Record the amount of force needed to slide the books.
6. Next place the pencils side by side, about 5 to 8 cm. (2 to 3 in.) apart.
7. Place the books on the pencils at one end of the row.
8. Pull the books again with the spring balance and record the amount of force required.
9. Did the pencils change the force needed to drag the books across the table? If so, how much difference did they make?

TEACHER INFORMATION

Rolling friction is less than sliding friction. This principle is used in wheels and bearings in a wide variety of applications, from wheels under a table to the workings of complex machinery. The Egyptians probably used wheels to move large stones when they built the pyramids.

ACTIVITY 108: What Is the Advantage of a First-Class Lever?

(Teacher-supervised activity)

MATERIALS NEEDED

- Board 10 cm. (4 in.) wide and 1 m. (1 yd.) long (or other suitable lever)
- Fulcrum
- Book

PROCEDURE

1. Place the fulcrum under the lever (board) at the middle (position 3 in the illustration).

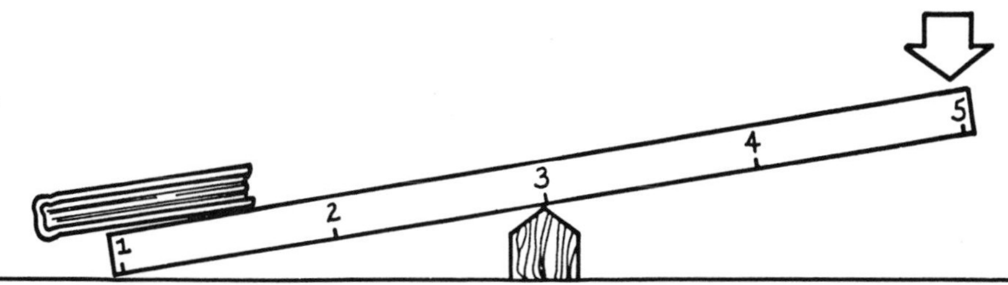

FIGURE 108-1. Lever on fulcrum—positions 1–5 noted, book, and arrow marking effort point.

2. Place the book on the lever at position 1. Push down on the lever at position 5.
3. What happened to the book as you pushed down on the other end of the lever?
4. Repeat this procedure with the fulcrum at position 2 and again at position 4.
5. Is the same amount of effort required to raise the book regardless of the fulcrum position?
6. How does the required effort change as you move the fulcrum away from the book?
7. How does the required effort change as you move the fulcrum closer to the book?
8. Try to lift some other objects with your lever, such as a box of ditto paper. Do not try to lift a piano or other objects that are heavy and tall, as they might tip over.
9. To lift a heavy object, would you place the fulcrum near the object, away from the object, or does it matter?

TEACHER INFORMATION

The fulcrum divides a first-class lever into two parts, called the effort arm and the load arm. The load arm is the end upon which the load rests. The effort arm is the end we apply a force to in order to move the load.

With the fulcrum between the load arm and the effort arm, the first-class lever changes the direction of the load; that is, we move the load up by pressing down on the opposite end of the lever.

With a first-class lever, moving the fulcrum toward the load decreases the amount of force necessary to lift the load. When the fulcrum is closer to the load, we gain in force but lose speed and distance. When the fulcrum is closer to the effort, we gain in speed and distance but lose force.

Examples of first-class levers include scissors, pliers, and teeter-totters.

Note: If a piano is used to verify responses to step 9, it should be closely supervised. Be sure to lift at the end of the piano rather than at the side. Use a heavy, thick board and a strong fulcrum.

ACTIVITY 109: What Type of Simple Machine Is the Teeter-Totter?

MATERIALS NEEDED

- Teeter-totter

PROCEDURE

1. Place the teeter-totter in such a position that it will balance with you on one end and a classmate on the other end.
2. Change the position of the teeter-totter on the fulcrum (bar in the middle) and try to balance with the same person.
3. What happened?
4. Now adjust the teeter-totter so you can balance with a different classmate.
5. What did you have to do? Why?

TEACHER INFORMATION

You might prefer to have students do this activity independently during their free time, but you, or a student who understands the principle of the first-class lever, should follow up to help assure correct learning.

The teeter-totter is a first-class lever. Either end could be called the effort arm or the load arm, but if you arbitrarily assign each end of the teeter-totter a name, the principles learned in Activity 108 will apply.

ACTIVITY 110: How Can a Lever Be Used to Lift Heavy Things?

(Teacher demonstration)

MATERIALS NEEDED

- Lever (2-in. plank)
- Fulcrum
- Automobile

PROCEDURE

1. Place the plank on the ground and drive an automobile into such a position that one tire is on one end of the plank.
2. Set the parking brake.
3. Lift the end of the plank opposite the wheel and place the fulcrum under the plank near the wheel.
4. Push down on the effort arm of the lever.
5. What can you do with the lever that you couldn't do without it?

TEACHER INFORMATION

This activity is suggested as a teacher demonstration because of the obvious risks involved. It demonstrates that levers can be used to lift very heavy loads with relatively little effort. Perhaps student assistants could be used safely for some tasks, but care should be taken to avoid unnecessary risks.

Consider having students try to lift one side of the automobile before using the lever. Be very careful because of possible back injuries. One student can lift a corner of the car using a lever, while several students could not do it without the lever.

ACTIVITY 111: How Can You Predict the Effort Required to Lift a Load with a First-Class Lever?

MATERIALS NEEDED

- Lever 1 m. (1 yd.) long (preferably lightweight, such as ½-in. plywood)
- String
- Fulcrum 3–10 cm. high (1–4 in.)
- Spring balance
- Two or three books
- "Record of Measurement I" chart
- Pencil

PROCEDURE

1. Tie the books into a bundle. Place the fulcrum under position 3 as indicated in Figure 111-1.

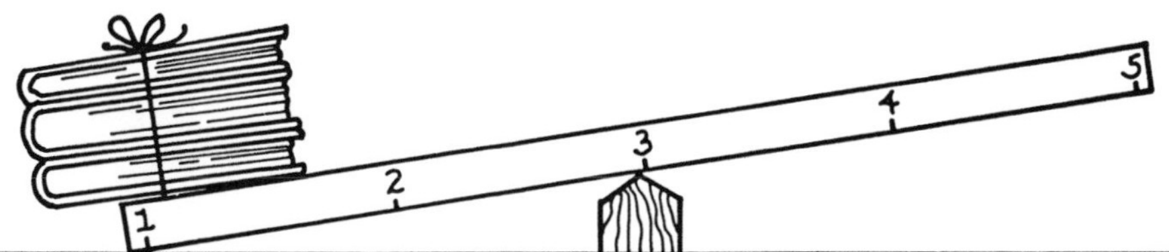

FIGURE 111-1. Lever with fulcrum and positions 1–5 noted.

2. Place the books on the lever at position 1.
3. Use the "Record of Measurement I" chart for recording your measurements in the remainder of this activity.
4. Attach the spring balance at position 5. Pull down and record the force required to lift the books.
5. Weigh the books and compare with the force required above.
6. With the books on the lever at position 1 and the spring balance attached at position 5, move the fulcrum to position 4.
7. Pull down on the spring balance and record the force required to lift the books.
8. Repeat the above procedure with the fulcrum at position 2.
9. Compare your findings.
10. Estimate the force required to lift the books with the fulcrum halfway between positions 2 and 3. Record your estimate.
11. Try it. Record the actual force required. How close was your estimate?
12. Estimate the force necessary to lift the books with the fulcrum halfway between positions 3 and 4. Record your estimate.
13. Try it. Record your results. Did you do any better?

TEACHER INFORMATION

The effort required to lift an object with the first-class lever is proportionate to the comparative lengths of the load arm and the effort arm. For example, with the fulcrum at position 3, the two arms are equal in length. If the load weighs 1 kg. (or 1 lb.), the effort required to lift it should be 1 kg. (or 1 lb.).

With the fulcrum in position 4, the load arm is three times as long as the effort arm and the effort required to lift 1 kg. (or 1 lb.) will be about 3 kg. (or 3 lbs.).

With the fulcrum in position 2, the effort arm is three times as long as the load arm and the effort required to lift 1 kg. (or 1 lb.) will be about .33 kg. (or ⅓ lb.).

The degree of accuracy of the figures is affected by the degree of precision in positioning the load, fulcrum, and effort, and by the weight of the board itself. The results are therefore only approximate.

Name______________________ Date______________________

RECORD OF MEASUREMENT I

Actual weight of the load = ______________________ kg.

Load Position	Effort Position	Fulcrum Position	Force
1	5	3	______________
1	5	4	______________
1	5	2	______________
1	5	between 2 and 3	Estimate: __________ Actual: __________
1	5	between 3 and 4	Estimate: __________ Actual: __________

ACTIVITY 112: What Do We Lose As We Gain Force with a Lever?

MATERIALS NEEDED

- Lever 1 m. (1 yd.) long (preferably lightweight, such as ½-in. plywood)
- Pencil
- Spring balance
- Fulcrum at least 10 cm. (4 in.) high
- Two or three books
- String
- "Record of Measurement II" chart
- Ruler

PROCEDURE

1. Use the "Record of Measurement II" chart for recording your measurements in the remainder of this activity.
2. Tie the books into a bundle. Place the fulcrum under position 3 as indicated in Figure 112-1.

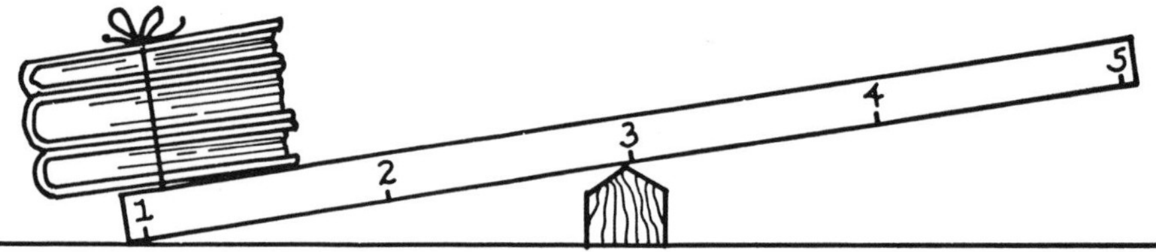

FIGURE 112-1. Lever with fulcrum and positions 1–5 noted.

3. Review Activity 111 by doing the following (Figure 112-2):
   a. Place the books at position 1.
   b. Attach the spring balance at position 5, pull down, and record the force required to lift the books.
   c. Weigh the books and compare with the force required above.
   d. With the books on the lever at position 1 and the spring balance attached at position 5, move the fulcrum to position 4.
   e. Pull down on the spring balance and record the force required to lift the books.
   f. Repeat the above procedure with the fulcrum at position 2.
   g. Compare your findings.
4. In addition to measuring the force required to lift the load for the various fulcrum positions, use the ruler to measure the distances traveled by the effort arm while the load arm travels the distances indicated on the chart.
5. With the last two fulcrum positions, estimate travel distances of the effort arm. Record your estimates.

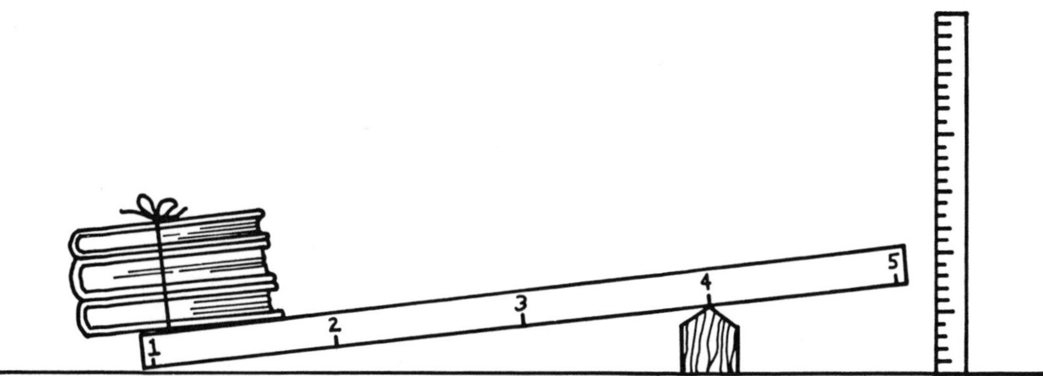

FIGURE 112-2. Lever with fulcrum, books, and ruler.

6. Try these and record the actual results.
7. As the force required at the effort arm decreases, does the distance the effort arm travels increase or decrease?
8. Write a statement about the force required to lift a load, the distance the load travels, and the distance the effort arm travels as the fulcrum is moved closer and closer to the load.
9. The lever you used here is called a first-class lever. Notice how it compares to the second-class lever and the third-class lever in other activities.

TEACHER INFORMATION

The total amount of work required to lift a load is not decreased by the use of a lever. In using a first-class lever (as in this activity), we can decrease the amount of force required to lift a load by moving the fulcrum closer to the load.

As the fulcrum moves closer to the load and the effort required to lift the load is decreased, the effort arm travels a greater distance and the load travels a lesser distance. We gain in terms of force required but we sacrifice speed and distance.

The amount of force required to lift a given load using a first-class lever can be computed using the following formula:

$$\text{load} \times \text{length of load arm} = \text{effort} \times \text{length of effort arm}$$

For example, if we have a 200-kg. load and we can apply only 50 kg. of force to lift the load, the effort arm must be four times as long as the load arm. As the effort required to lift the load is divided by four, the speed and distance traveled by the load will also be divided by four.

Name________________________ Date________________________

RECORD OF MEASUREMENT II

Weight of the load = ______________________________ kg.

Load Position	Effort Position	Fulcrum Position	Force	Travel Distance Load Arm	 Effort Art
1	5	3	_____	10 cm.	_____
1	5	4	_____	5 cm.	_____
1	5	2	_____	5 cm.	_____
1	5	Between 2 & 3	Estimate: _____ Actual: _____	5 cm.	Estimate: _____ Actual: _____
1	5	Between 3 & 4	Estimate: _____ Actual: _____	10 cm.	Estimate: _____ Actual: _____

ACTIVITY 113: How Is a Second-Class Lever Different from a First-Class Lever?

MATERIALS NEEDED

- Lever
- Fulcrum
- Two or three books
- String

PROCEDURE

1. Tie the books into a bundle.
2. Place the fulcrum at position 5 and hang the books, by their string, from position 4, as illustrated in Figure 113-1.

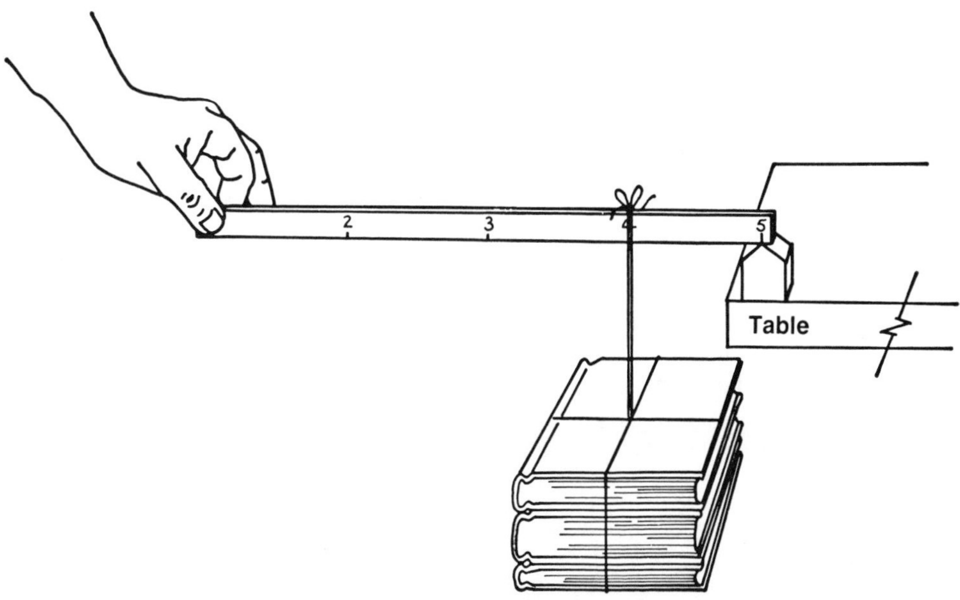

FIGURE 113-1. Lever, books, and fulcrum.

3. Holding the lever at position 1, lift the books.
4. Move the books to position 3, then 2, then 1, each time lifting from position 1.
5. Is it easier to lift when the load is closer to the fulcrum or farther from the fulcrum?
6. With the books at position 4, the fulcrum still at position 5, and the effort still applied at position 1, what is the length of the load arm? The effort arm?

7. This is a second-class lever. Notice the relative positions of the fulcrum, the load, and the effort for this second-class lever. How do these compare with the first-class lever you used in the previous activities?

TEACHER INFORMATION

With the load placed between the fulcrum and the effort, we now have a second-class lever. The length of both arms is measured from the fulcrum, so with the load at position 3, the effort arm is twice the length of the load arm.

As with the first-class lever, the shorter the load arm and the longer the effort arm, the less effort required to lift the load. The effort arm travels farther and faster, however, than the load.

A major difference between the first-class lever and the second-class lever is that the second-class lever does not reverse the direction of the load; both effort and load travel in the same direction.

Examples of second-class levers include the paper cutter, the nutcracker, and the wheelbarrow.

ACTIVITY 114: What Do You Gain and What Do You Lose by Using a Second-Class Lever?

MATERIALS NEEDED

- Lever
- Fulcrum
- Two or three books
- Pencil
- String
- Spring balance
- Meter stick
- "Record of Measurement III" chart

PROCEDURE

1. Use the "Record of Measurement III" chart for recording your measurements in the remainder of this activity.
2. Tie the books into a bundle.
3. Weigh the books and record the results.
4. Place the fulcrum at position 5 and suspend the books, by the string, from position 1.

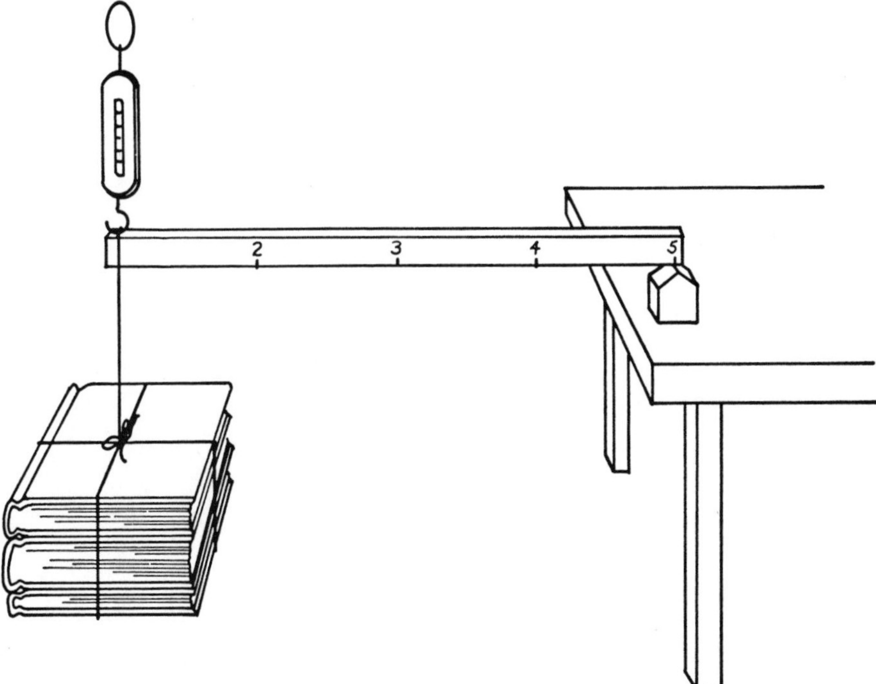

FIGURE 114-1. Lever with books, fulcrum, and positions noted.

5. Record the amount of force required to lift the books, with the spring balance also at position 1, and compare this force to the weight of the books.
6. Measure the distance traveled by the spring balance (effort) as the books (load) travel 20 cm. (8 in.).
7. Next, move the load to position 3 and record the force indicated on the spring balance. With the load between effort and fulcrum, you now have a second-class lever.
8. How does the amount of force required compare with the actual weight of the books.
9. Lift the load, measuring the distance traveled by the effort as the load is raised 10 cm. (4 in.). Record the results.
10. How does the distance traveled by the load arm compare with the distance traveled by the effort arm?
11. If you were to move the load to position 4, how much force do you think would be required to lift the books? Record your estimate.
12. Try it and record the results. How did you do?
13. With the load at position 4, how far do you think the load will travel as you lift the effort 20 cm (8 in.)? Record your estimate.

TEACHER INFORMATION

The formula for computing effort and travel distance is the same for the second-class lever as for the first-class lever (see Activity 111). Remember to measure the length of each arm from the fulcrum.

Name______________________________ Date________________

RECORD OF MEASUREMENT III

Weight of the load = _______________ kg.

Load Position	Effort Position	Fulcrum Position	Force	Travel Distance Load Arm	Effort Arm
1	1	5	_____	20 cm.	_____
3	1	5	_____	10 cm.	_____
4	1	5	Estimate: _____ Actual: _____	Estimate: _____ Actual: _____	20 cm.
2	1	5	Estimate: _____ Actual: _____	Estimate: _____ Actual: _____	20 cm.

ACTIVITY 115: What Is a Third-Class Lever?

MATERIALS NEEDED

- Lever
- Table
- Two or three books
- Strings

PROCEDURE

1. Tie the books into a bundle and weigh them.
2. Use the edge of the table as a fulcrum. (You might need to have someone sit on the table to hold it down.)
3. Place the end of the lever under the edge of the table so your fulcrum (table's edge) is at position 5.
4. Suspend the books, by their string, at position 1.
5. Holding the lever at position 3, lift the books.
6. Is the effort required to lift the books greater or less than the actual weight of the books?
7. Move your hand to position 2 and lift the load.

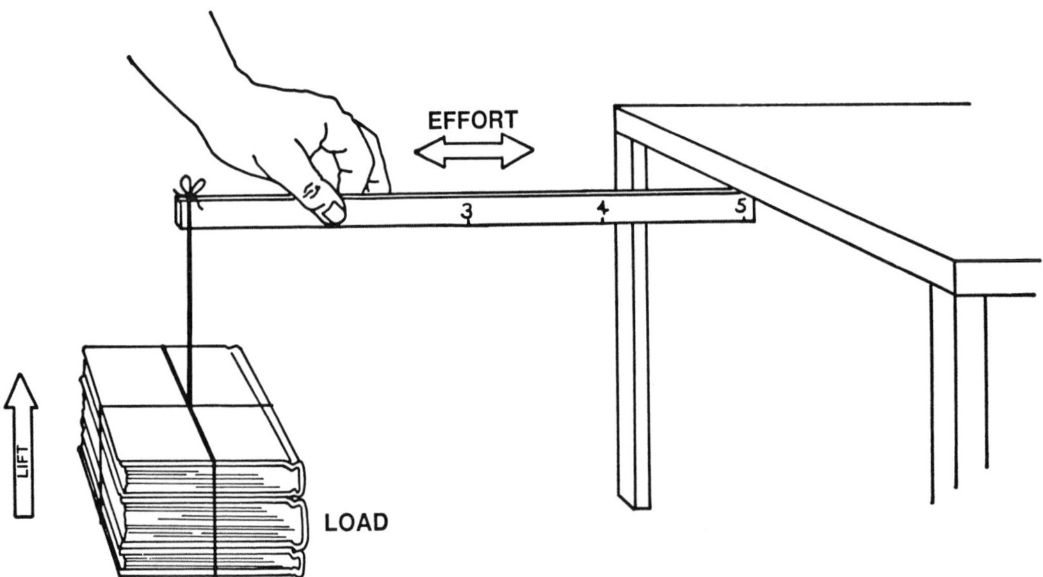

FIGURE 115-1. Table, lever, and books showing effort arm and load arm.

8. Lift the load from position 4.
9. Is it easier to lift the load as the effort (your hand) moves closer to the fulcrum (the table's edge)?
10. How is the third-class lever different from the first-class and second-class levers you have been using?

TEACHER INFORMATION

As explained in earlier activities, second-class levers decrease the amount of effort required to lift a load, but in so doing they increase the distance the effort must travel to lift the load a given distance. The third-class lever reverses the advantage. With the effort now between the fulcrum and the load, the effort required to lift the load is greater than the actual weight of the load. The load, however, travels faster and farther than does the effort.

As with the other types of levers, the lengths of both the effort arm and the load arm are measured from the fulcrum.

The speed and distance advantage of the third-class lever is helpful in the use of such items as the fishing pole, axe, and broom. Our arms and legs are also third-class levers, with the joint as the fulcrum, the distance from joint to hand or foot as the load arm. These third-class levers offer advantages in speed and distance as a person swings a bat or a golf club, throws a baseball, or kicks a soccer ball.

ACTIVITY 116: What Is Gained and What Is Lost by Using a Third-Class Lever?

MATERIALS NEEDED

- Lever
- Table
- Two or three books
- Pencil
- String
- Spring balance
- Meter stick
- "Record of Measurement IV" chart

PROCEDURE

1. Use the "Record of Measurement IV" chart for recording your measurements in the remainder of this activity.
2. Tie the books into a bundle.
3. Weigh the books and record the weight.
4. Use the edge of the table as a fulcrum. (You might need to have someone sit on the table to hold it down.)
5. Place the end of the lever under the edge of the table so your fulcrum (table's edge) is at position 5.
6. Suspend the books, by their string, at position 1.
7. Attach one end of the spring balance to the lever at position 3.

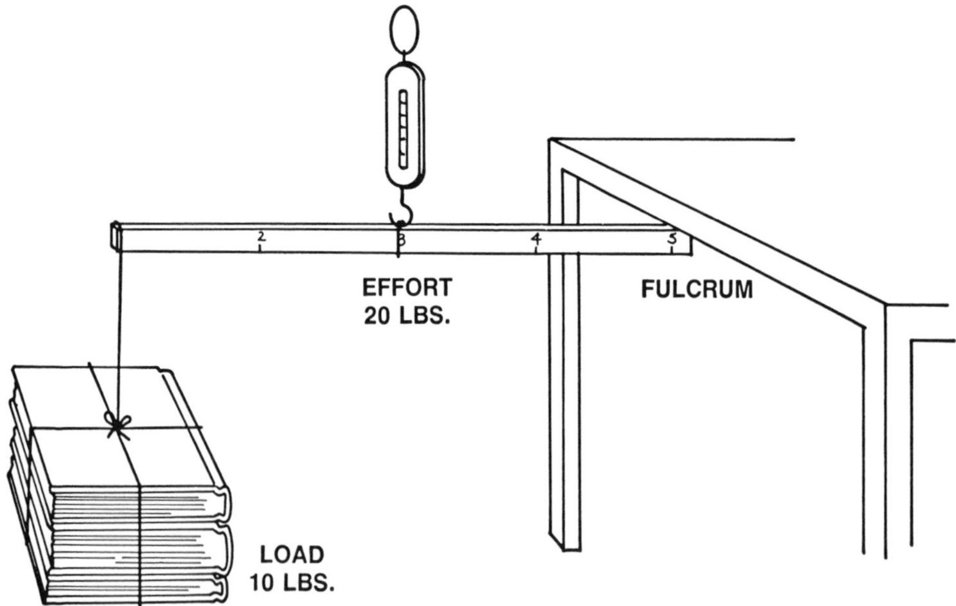

FIGURE 116-1. Third-class lever system with 10-lb. load and 20-lb. effort.

8. Holding the other end of the spring balance, lift with enough force to support the books. You are using a third-class lever.
9. Record the reading at the indicator and compare with the actual weight of the books.
10. Lift the load from position 3 and measure the travel distance of the load as the effort travels 10 cm.
11. Using your skills for predicting, which you have learned in earlier activities, estimate the force required to lift the load with the effort being shifted to position 2.
12. Try it, record the results, and compare with your estimate.
13. Leaving the effort at position 2, predict the travel distance of the load as the effort travels 10 cm.
14. Next, predict the outcomes with the effort being applied at position 4 and the effort traveling 5 cm. and record the results.
15. Try it. Were your predictions close?
16. Select another point on the lever—somewhere between the numbers. Predict effort and distances and test your predictions.

TEACHER INFORMATION

The formula for computing effort and travel distances for a third-class lever is the same as for first- and second-class levers. Remember to measure the lengths of the effort and load arms from the fulcrum.

With the system set up as indicated above, the effort required to lift a 10-lb. load would be 20 lbs., since the load arm is twice the length of the effort arm.

Name________________________ Date____________

RECORD OF MEASUREMENT IV

Weight of the load = ____________ kg.

Load Position	Effort Position	Fulcrum Position	Force	Travel Distance Load Arm	Effort Arm
1	3	5	_____	_____	10 cm.
1	2	5	Estimate: _____ Actual: _____	Estimate: _____ Actual: _____	10 cm.
1	4	5	Estimate: _____ Actual: _____	Estimate: _____ Actual: _____	5 cm.
1	?	1	Estimate: _____ Actual: _____	Estimate: _____ Actual: _____	5 cm.

ACTIVITY 117: What Is the Wheel-and-Axle?

MATERIALS NEEDED

- Compass
- Stiff paper at least 10 cm. square
- Pencil
- Scissors
- Tape measure

PROCEDURE

1. Use the compass to make a circle on the paper.
2. Cut out the circle.
3. Insert the pencil through the center of the circle. You have made a wheel and axle.

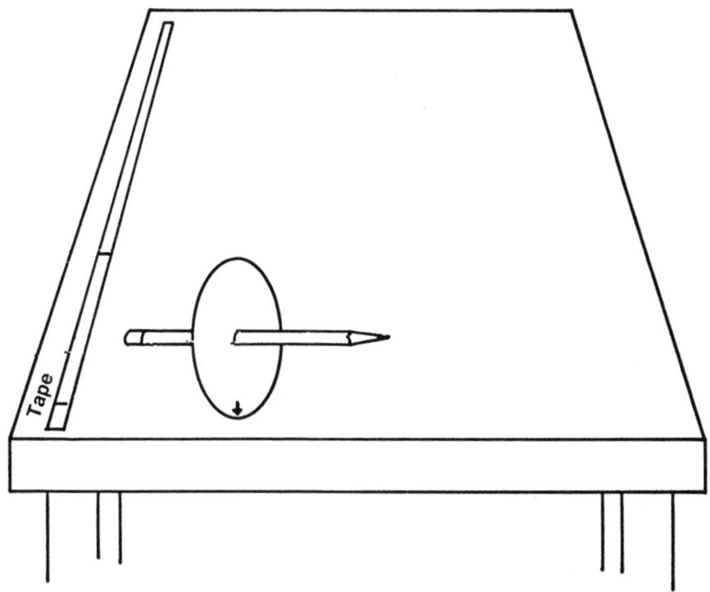

FIGURE 117-1. Pencil and paper wheel on table.

4. Roll your wheel and axle along the tabletop. How many times does the pencil rotate as the wheel rotates once?
5. Measure the distance the wheel traveled in one complete rotation.
6. Remove the pencil from the wheel, place the pencil on the table, and measure the distance it travels in one complete rotation.
7. How far would the pencil travel if rotated ten times?
8. Insert the pencil (axle) back into the wheel. How far does it travel now in ten rotations?
9. Name one advantage of the wheel and axle.

TEACHER INFORMATION

The wheel and axle is a form of the lever. When the wheel or the axle turns, the other turns also. If the wheel turns around the axle, as on bearings, it is not a wheel and axle.

If the wheel is turning the axle, it is a form of second-class lever (Figure 117-2). The fulcrum is at the center of the axle. The radius of the wheel is the effort arm of the lever and the radius of the axle is the load arm. There is increased force but less speed and distance.

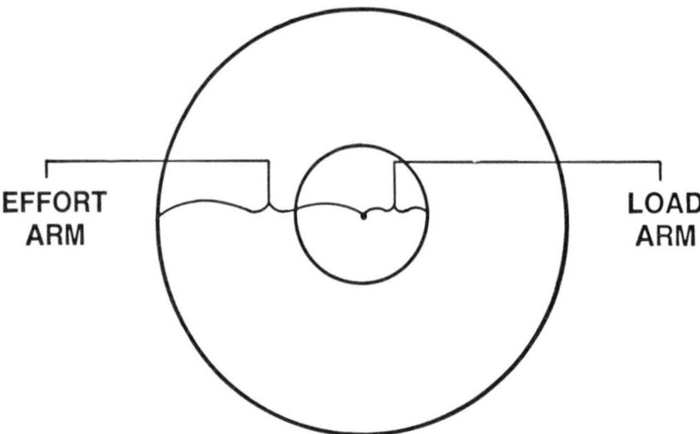

FIGURE 117-2. Wheel and axle showing load and effort as second-class lever.

If the axle is turning the wheel, it becomes a form of the third-class lever, with a gain in speed and distance but a decrease in force (Figure 117-3). The fulcrum is at the center of the axle. The radius of the wheel is the load arm and the radius of the axle is the effort arm.

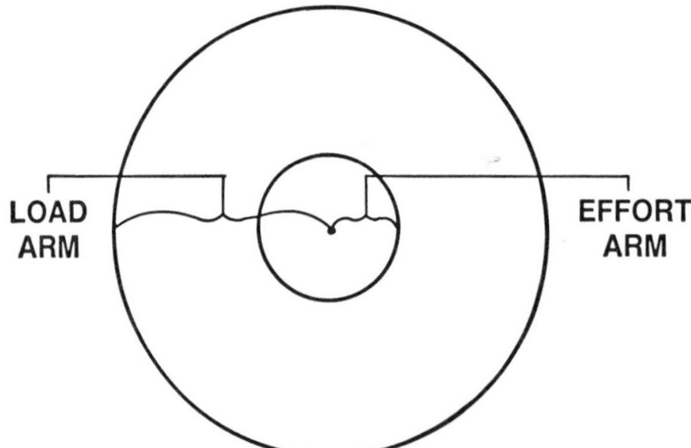

FIGURE 117-3. Wheel and axle showing load and effort as third-class lever.

Examples of the wheel and axle acting as a second-class lever include the door-knob, the screwdriver, and the steering wheel of an automobile.

ACTIVITY 118: What Type of Simple Machine Is the Pencil Sharpener?

MATERIALS NEEDED

- Pencil sharpener with suction mount
- String about 2 m. long
- Book

PROCEDURE

1. Clamp the pencil sharpener to the side of a file cabinet or other vertical surface and remove the cover.
2. Turn the handle of the pencil sharpener around, noting that it goes all the way around, just like a wheel.
3. Tie the book in such a way that a long string is left, from which the book can be suspended.
4. Notice the amount of effort required to lift the book. Tie the end of the string firmly around the end of the pencil sharpener shaft. Use tape if necessary to keep it from slippping.
5. Allow the book to hang freely, and support the pencil sharpener with your hands to keep it from pulling loose.

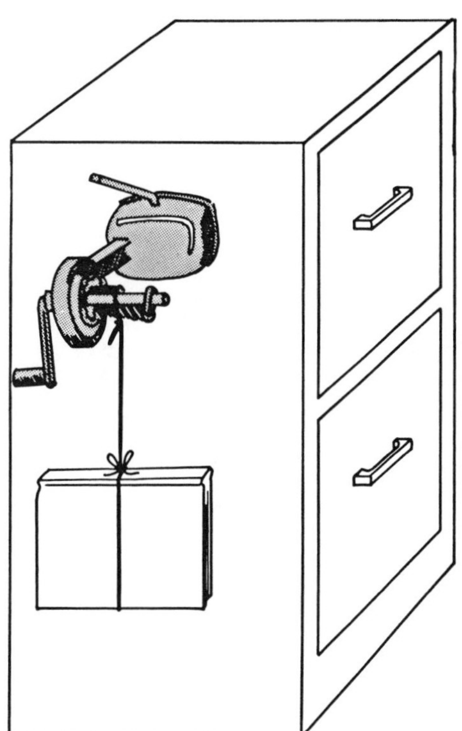

FIGURE 118-1. Pencil sharpener on vertical surface, with book tied.

6. Turn the pencil sharpener handle around several times, making sure the string is winding around the shaft.
7. Is more or less force required to lift the book with this wheel and axle than to lift the books directly?
8. See if you can locate a picture of an old well with a windlass for raising a bucket full of water. What similarities do you see between the windlass and your pencil sharpener?
9. What type of machine is the pencil sharpener? The windlass?

TEACHER INFORMATION

A wheel does not have to be a complete wheel in order to be considered a wheel and axle. It can be just a crank, as with the pencil sharpener used above or the water-well windlass referred to. The crank makes a complete circle when used, just as though it were a complete wheel. A type of windlass called a winch is often found on boat trailers and four-wheel-drive vehicles.

ACTIVITY 119: What Is a Fixed Pulley?

MATERIALS NEEDED

- Single-wheel pulley
- Crossbar
- Spring balance
- Meter stick
- Cord or heavy string
- Pencil
- "Measuring with a Fixed Pulley" chart
- Bundle of books (or other heavy object)

PROCEDURE

1. Use the "Measuring with a Fixed Pulley" chart for recording your measurements in the remainder of this activity.
2. Weigh the books with the spring balance and record the results.
3. Arrange your pulley, crossbar, spring balance, cord, and bundle of books as shown in Figure 119-1, with the pulley attached to the crossbar.

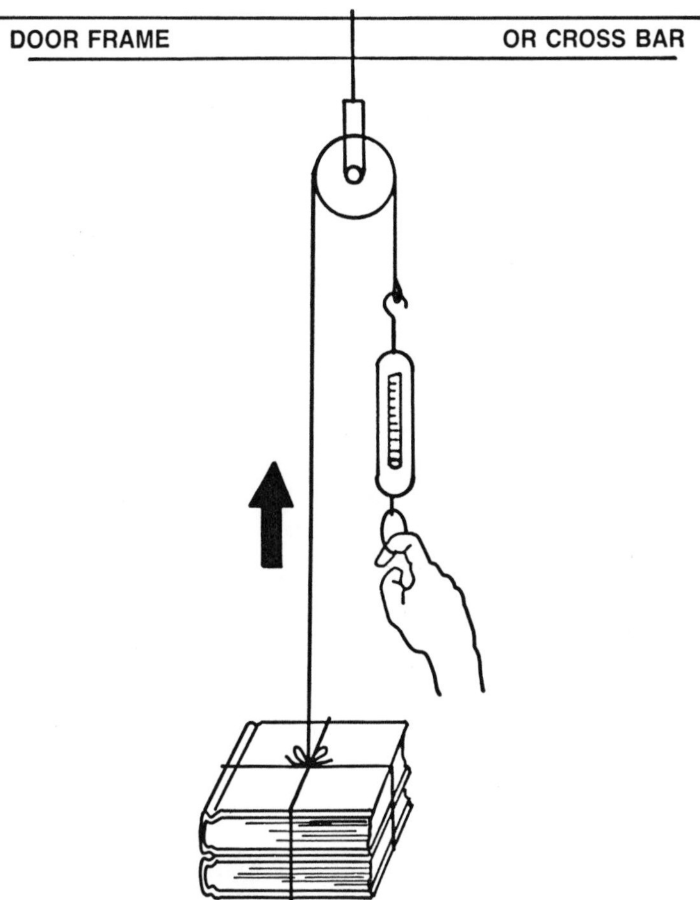

FIGURE 119-1. Pulley system with books.

4. Pull down on the spring balance to lift the books. Be sure to pull straight down and not to the side.
5. Pull down steadily on the spring far enough to lift the load 20 cm. Record the following information on your chart:
   a. Direction the load (books) moved as the effort (spring balance) moved downward.
   b. Distance moved by the effort as the load moved 20 cm.
   c. Amount of force required to lift the books.
6. Examine the information in your chart. Was lifting the books using the pulley different in any way from lifting the books without the pulley? Consider these questions:
   a. Did the pulley decrease the amount of force needed to lift the books?
   b. Did the pulley cause the books to move a greater or lesser distance than the effort moved?
   c. Did the pulley cause the books to move in the opposite direction from that of the effort?
7. With the pulley fastened to the crossbar, as it has been for this activity, it is called a fixed pulley. This simply means that the pulley does not move up or down, but remains in a fixed position.
8. What is accomplished by using a fixed pulley?

TEACHER INFORMATION

When you use a fixed pulley, the load moves up or down but the pulley itself is fastened to a stationary object and therefore remains in a fixed position.

A fixed pulley does not alter the amount of force required to lift an object, but it reverses the direction of the force; that is, as the force is applied in a downward direction the load is lifted in an upward direction.

The fixed pulley is a form of turning first-class lever (see Figure 119-2). Think of the fulcrum as being at the center of the axle, the effort at one edge of the pulley wheel, and the load at the other edge. As with other first-class levers, the fulcrum is between the effort and the load. Curtains, drapes, and louvered blinds use fixed pulleys.

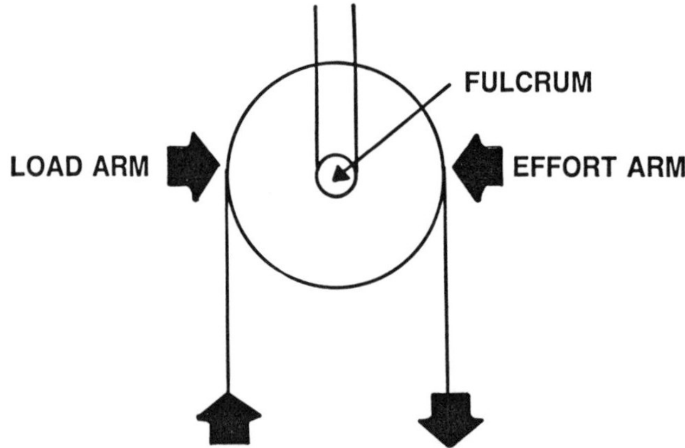

FIGURE 119-2. Fixed pulley system showing it as a first-class lever.

Name______________________________ Date______________________________

MEASURING WITH A FIXED PULLEY

Weight = ___________________________ kg.
Force = ______________________________

TRAVEL DIRECTION

What is the direction the load (books) moves as the effort (spring balance) moves downward?

____

TRAVEL DISTANCE

What is the distance moved by the effort as the load moves 20 cm.?

____

ACTIVITY 120: What Is a Movable Pulley?

MATERIALS NEEDED

- Pulley
- Crossbar
- Spring balance
- Meter stick
- Cord or string
- Pencil
- "Measuring with a Movable Pulley" chart
- Bundle of books (or other heavy object)

PROCEDURE

1. Use the "Measuring with a Movable Pulley" chart for recording your measurements in the remainder of this activity.
2. Weigh the books with the spring balance and record the results.
3. Arrange your pulley, crossbar, spring balance, cord, and bundle of books as shown in Figure 120-1, with one end of the cord attached to the crossbar.

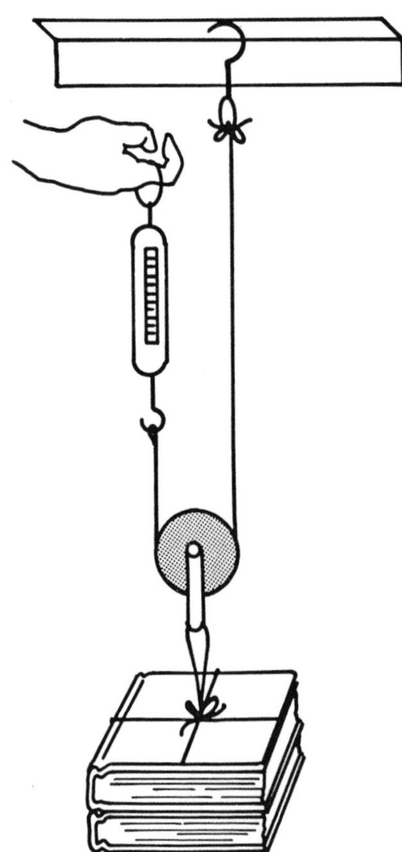

FIGURE 120-1. Movable pulley system.

4. Lift the books by pulling up on the spring balance. Note the force indicated on the spring balance as you lift in a steady motion. Record this amount as the force required to lift the books.
5. Compare the weight of the books with the amount of force required to lift the books using the movable pulley.
6. Measure and record the distance traveled by the effort (spring balance) as the load (books) travels 20 cm.
7. Notice and record the direction traveled by load and effort as you lift the load.
8. Estimate the distance the load will travel as the effort travels 30 cm.
9. Try it. Record the results and compare with your estimate.
10. Examine the information in your chart and consider these questions:
    a. Did the pulley decrease the amount of force needed to lift the books?
    b. Did the pulley cause the load to move a greater or lesser distance than the effort moved?
    c. Did the pulley cause the load to move in the opposite direction from that of the effort?
11. With the pulley fastened to the load, as it has been for this activity, and one end of the cord fastened to the crossbar, the pulley is called a movable pulley. The pulley itself moves up or down with the load.
12. What effect does a movable pulley have on the the force required to lift a load?
13. What effect does a movable pulley have on the distance a load travels compared with the distance traveled by the effort?
14. What effect does a movable pulley have on the direction of the load compared with the direction of the effort?

TEACHER INFORMATION

A movable pulley is attached to the load and therefore moves up and down with the load.

When you use a movable pulley, the direction of travel does not change. The load travels in the same direction as the effort. However, the amount of force required to lift a load is less than the actual weight of the object. The travel distance of the load is less than that of the effort. Thus, the movable pulley offers an advantage as to force required, but it does so at the expense of travel distance and speed.

In computing the gain or loss from using a movable pulley, use the following as a guide:

a. The load will travel half the distance of the effort.

b. The force required to lift the load is half the actual weight of the object.

Note: The force required will be increased by whatever friction is involved as the pulley turns on the axle, the string rubs against the sides of the groove in the pulley, and so forth.

ENRICHMENT

After students have completed this activity, challenge them to use their pulley to lift objects of various weights. After weighing each object they should use their previous knowledge to predict the amount of force that will be required to lift the object using the pulley. This will reinforce their knowledge of the movable pulley and strengthen their predicting skills.

Name________________________________ Date________________________________

MEASURING WITH A MOVABLE PULLEY

Weight =____________________________kg.
Force =____________________________

TRAVEL DISTANCE

What is the distance traveled by the effort (spring balance) as the load (books) moves 20 cm.?

____

What is your estimated distance the load would travel as the effort moves 30 cm.?

____

What is the actual distance?

____

TRAVEL DIRECTION

What is the direction traveled by the load and effort as you lift the load?

____

ACTIVITY 121: What Can Be Gained by Combining Fixed and Movable Pulleys?

MATERIALS NEEDED

- Two pulleys
- Crossbar
- Spring balance
- Meter stick
- Cord or heavy string
- Pencil
- "Measuring with a Combined Fixed and Movable Pulley" chart
- Bundle of books (or other heavy object)

PROCEDURE

1. Use the "Measuring with a Combined Fixed and Movable Pulley" chart for recording your measurements in the remainder of this activity.
2. Weigh the books and record the weight.
3. Arrange the pulleys, crossbar, spring balance, cord, and bundle of books as illustrated in Figure 121-1. Notice that one pulley and one end of the cord are attached to the crossbar.

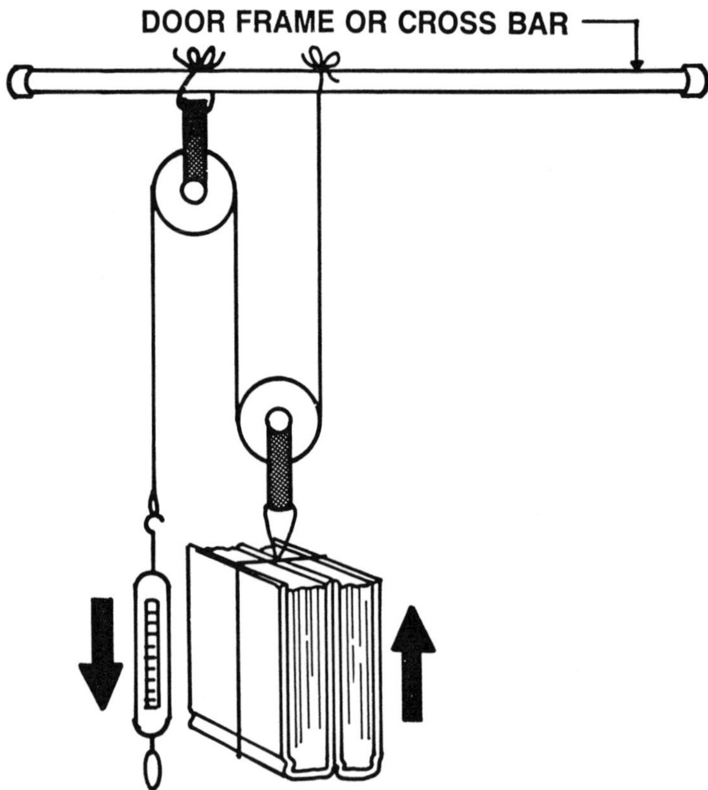

FIGURE 121-1. Pulley system with one fixed pulley and one movable pulley.

4. You now have a pulley system that includes a fixed pulley and a movable pulley.
5. From your previous experience, see if you can predict the answers to the following questions. Record your predictions.
   a. Which direction will the load (books) move as you pull down at the effort position (spring balance)?
   b. Considering the actual weight of the books, how much force will be required to lift the load?
   c. How far will the load travel as the effort travels 40 cm.?
6. After recording your predictions, test them by actual measurement. Record your actual measurements and compare them with your predictions.
7. Now record the following predictions on the second part of the chart.
8. Predict the travel distance of the effort necessary to lift the load 5 cm.
9. Change the number of books in your bundle, record the weight of your new load, and predict the amount of force necessary to lift it.
10. After recording your predictions, test them and record your actual measurements.
11. Were your predictions closer this time?
12. Can you think of any situation where it would be helpful to combine a fixed pulley with a movable pulley?

TEACHER INFORMATION

A combination of a fixed pulley and a movable pulley offers the advantages of both. A load can be lifted with half as much force as would be expected by considering the actual weight of the objects (because of the movable pulley) and the load can be moved upward by pulling downward (because of the stationary pulley).

This system, including a fixed pulley combined with a movable pulley, is called a *block and tackle.* It is used for lifting automobile motors, for raising and lowering scaffolds for painters, and for many other purposes.

ENRICHMENT

Allow students to experiment with various combinations of pulleys and test the mechanical advantage of their creations.

Combinations of more than one fixed pulley and an equal number of movable pulleys multiply the mechanical advantage of the movable pulley and decrease efficiency in terms of travel distance. For instance, in a system involving a double fixed pulley and a double movable pulley, a load of 4 lbs. would be lifted with approximately 1 lb. of force at the effort position, but the effort must travel 4 cm. (or inches) for each cm. (or inch) the load is to be lifted.

If a strong overhead beam (such as a tree branch) is available, students would enjoy experimenting with their pulleys in lifting heavier objects, such as each other, the teacher, or several students at a time. Such an activity should be closely supervised to assure safety. Beware of possible broken ropes and falls. Vertical distance lifted should be limited to minimize risk of injury.

Name____________________ Date____________________

MEASURING WITH A COMBINED FIXED AND MOVABLE PULLEY

Part One

Weight________________kg.

	Predicted Results	*Measured Results*
Load direction	________	________
Force required	________	________
Load distance	________	________

Part Two

Weight________________kg.

	Predicted Results	*Measured Results*
Load distance	________	________
Force required	________	________

ACTIVITY 122: What Is an Inclined Plane?

MATERIALS NEEDED

- Board at least 1½ m. (4½ ft.) long
- Roller skate (or toy truck or small wagon)
- Cord or heavy string
- Pencil
- "Measuring an Inclined Plane" chart
- Spring balance
- Box of rocks (or books or other item)

PROCEDURE

1. Use the "Measuring an Inclined Plane" chart for recording your measurements in the remainder of this activity.
2. Using the string, attach the load to the roller skate.
3. Weigh the load, including the roller skate, and record its weight.
4. Place the board on a stairway, with one end at the bottom of the stairs and the other end resting on the fourth step.
5. Attach the spring balance to the skate and pull the load up the inclined plane (board). As you pull in a steady manner, notice the force indicated by the needle and record the results.

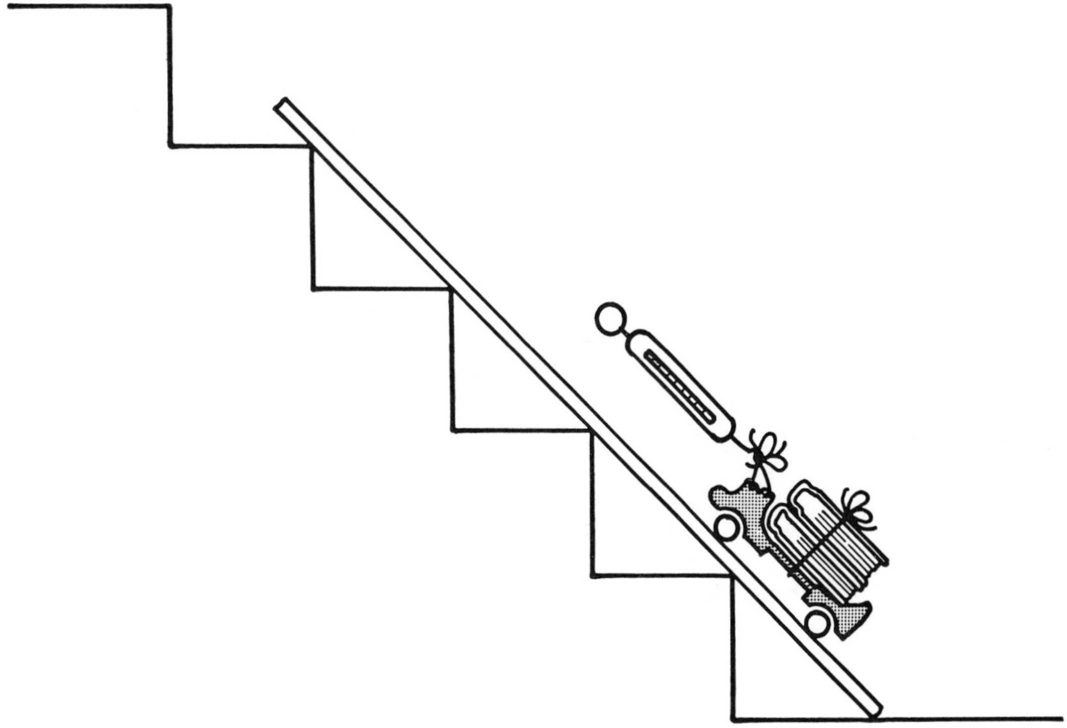

FIGURE 122-1. Roller skate with load on inclined plane.

6. Compare the weight of the load with the force needed to pull the load up the inclined plane.
7. As you pulled the load up the inclined plane, was more force or less force required than the actual weight of the load?
8. Move the top of the board down to the first step (Figure 122-2).

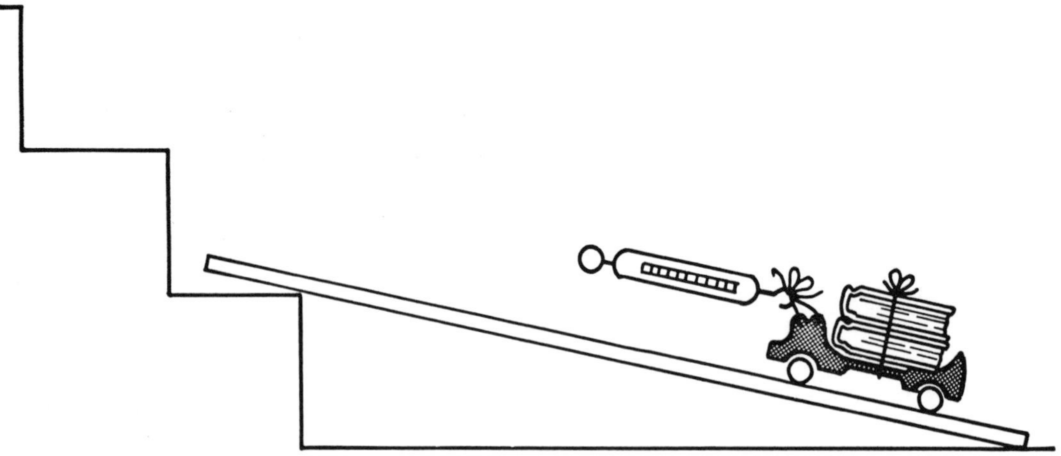

FIGURE 122-2. System in new position.

9. Judging from your first experience, how much force do you think will be required to pull the load up the slope? Record your prediction.
10. After recording your prediction, attach the spring balance to the load and try it.
11. Record the results. How close was your estimate?
12. Now predict the force required with the board on the second step. Try it after recording your prediction.
13. Was your estimate closer this time?
14. If your load weighed 100 lbs., how much force would you need to apply to push it up the inclined plane with the top of the inclined plane resting on the first step?
15. Think of some ways inclined planes would be useful. Write down two of them and show them to your teacher.

TEACHER INFORMATION

An *inclined plane* is a slanting surface. It provides a mechanical advantage of force. We can move a load up an inclined plane with less force than would be indicated by the actual weight of the object (provided the friction isn't too great).

As with the use of any other machine, the total work required is not reduced but only redistributed. The advantage gained in force is sacrificed in distance and speed.

Mechanical advantage is computed by dividing the length of the inclined plane by the height, as in Figure 122-3.

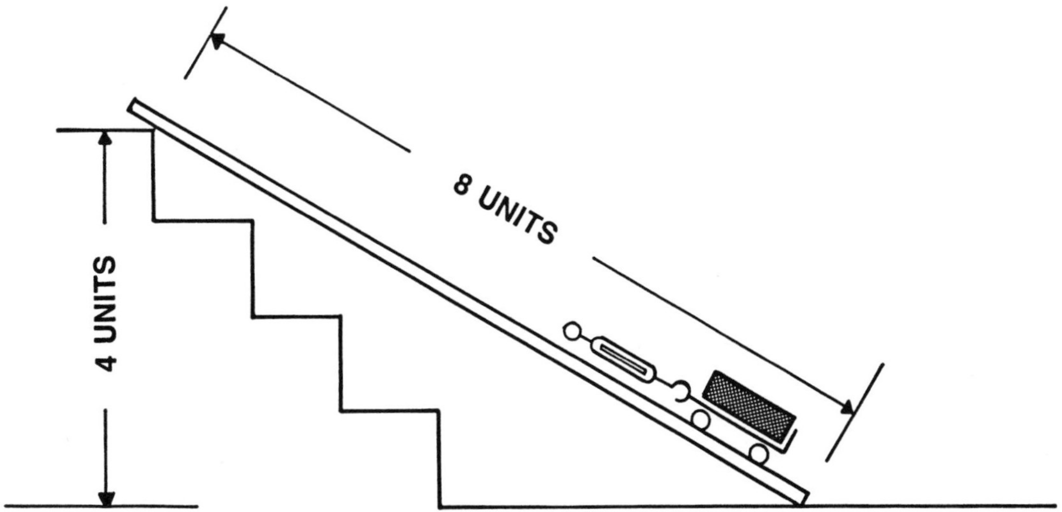

FIGURE 122-3. Inclined plane system.

The weight of the object is twice the force required to move the object up the ramp (if friction were eliminated), but we must move the object twice as far as if we lifted it straight up (eight units instead of two units).

Application of the inclined plane is illustrated as barrels of oil are rolled up a ramp, as a car drives up a mountain on a winding road, and as a person walks up a stairway or up the sloping floor of a theater.

Note: If it is inconvenient for students to use a stairway for their work with the inclined plane, have them support the end of their board on a stack of books or some other sturdy, adjustable support.

Name________________________________ Date________________________________

MEASURING AN INCLINED PLANE

Weight = ____kg.

Position of Upper End	Position of Lower End	Force
4th step	bottom	more/less
1st step	bottom	Estimate________________________ Actual________________________
2nd step	bottom	Estimate________________________ Actual________________________

ACTIVITY 123: What Is a Wedge?

MATERIALS NEEDED

- Wedge
- Stack of books
- Board

PROCEDURE

1. Stack the books up on one end of the board.
2. Place your fingers under the end of the board near the books and lift it up about 3 to 8 cm. Notice the force required to lift the books.
3. Now place the tip of the wedge under the same end of the board (Figure 123-1).

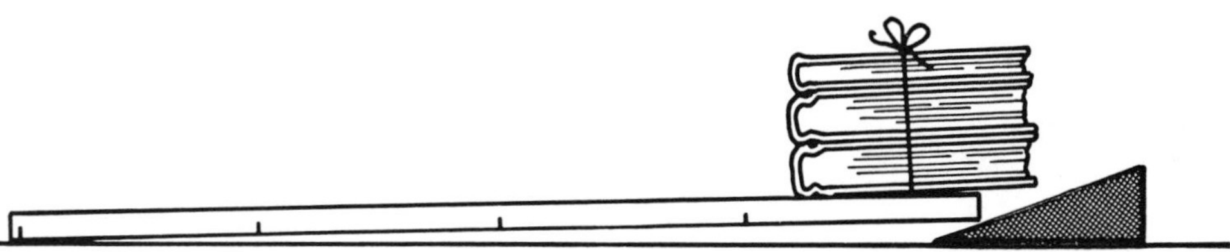

FIGURE 123-1. Board, books, and wedge.

4. Tap the wedge with your foot, forcing it under the end of the board.
5. What is happening to the load of books?
6. Can you tell whether the force required to drive the wedge under the board is greater or less than the force required to lift the load directly?
7. Why does the wedge so strongly resist being forced under the board?

TEACHER INFORMATION

Two wedges can be made by sawing a block of wood in half diagonally (Figure 123-2). Note that each wedge looks like an inclined plane. It differs from the inclined plane only in its application. When it is used as an inclined plane, an object (load) moves up the incline. When it is used as a wedge, the inclined plane moves into, or under, the object.

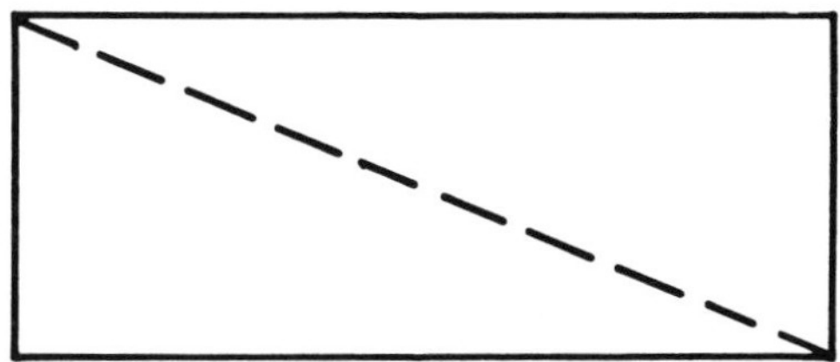

FIGURE 123-2. Rectangle showing diagonal cut.

We gain in force and also change the direction of the force by using the wedge.

The longer or thinner the wedge, the greater the gain in force and the greater the loss in distance; that is, the farther the wedge must go under an object to lift it a given amount.

The maximum distance a load can be moved by a wedge is the thickness of the big end of the wedge.

The ideal mechanical advantage of the wedge can be computed by dividing the length of the wedge by the thickness of the big end. However, because of the great amount of friction involved, the actual mechanical advantage is usually significantly less than the ideal. Friction, however, is helpful because it keeps the wedge from slipping out.

Applications of the wedge are the axe, chisel, pin, nail, knife blade, woodsplitter's wedge, and so forth.

ENRICHMENT

If a short log, a sledge hammer, and a woodsplitting wedge could be acquired, a demonstration of the use of the wedge in actually splitting the log would provide an excellent experience in seeing the usefulness of the wedge. **CAUTION: Splitting wood may splinter, so use care and be sure children stand back a safe distance.**

ACTIVITY 124: What Is a Screw?

MATERIALS NEEDED

- Pencil
- Sheet of white paper
- Scissors
- Black marker
- Large wood screw

PROCEDURE

1. Cut a triangle from a sheet of white paper by cutting diagonally, from corner to corner (Figure 124-1).

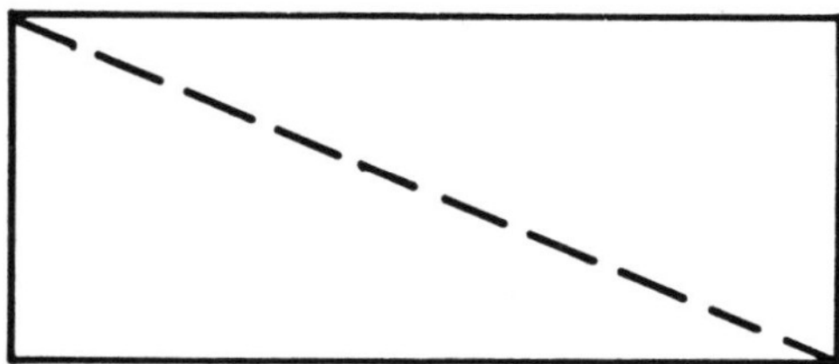

FIGURE 124-1. Rectangle showing diagonal cut.

2. Using the marker, make a heavy black line along the hypotenuse (the longest side), as in Figure 124-2.

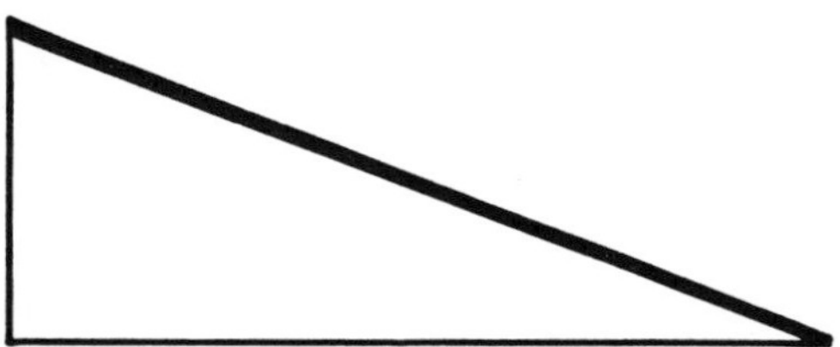

FIGURE 124-2. Triangle with darkened hypotenuse.

3. Hold the triangle upright on top of your table or desk. Which of the simple machines we have already studied does the triangle now look like?
4. Beginning with the short side, wrap the paper triangle around a pencil (Figure 124-3).
5. Hold the wrapped pencil side by side with the large wood screw.
6. Does the heavy line of the triangle resemble the threads of the screw?
7. How would you say the threads of a screw compare to an inclined plane? Think about how the triangle with its black edge looked before you wrapped it around the pencil.

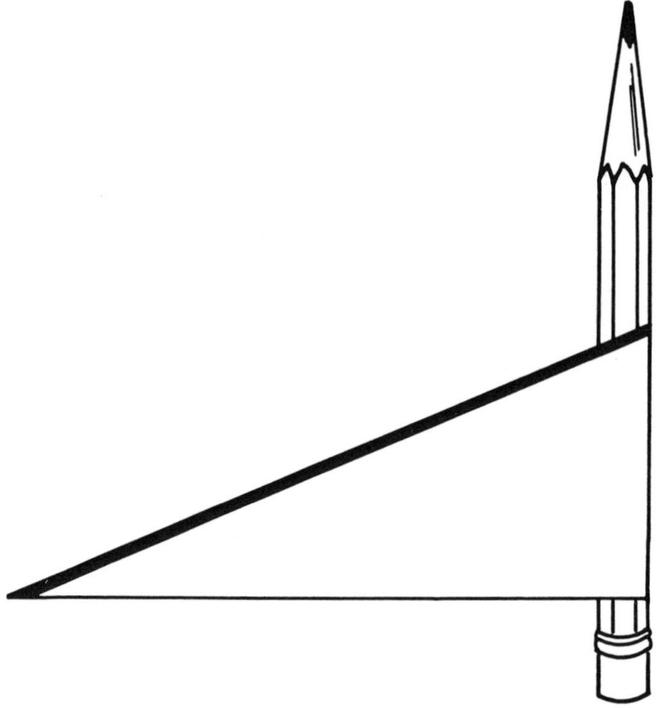

FIGURE 124-3. Triangle being wrapped around pencil.

TEACHER INFORMATION

The screw is a form of inclined plane that winds around in a spiral. The spiral-shaped ridge around the screw is called the *thread*.

ACTIVITY 125: What Kind of Simple Machine Is the Screwdriver?

MATERIALS NEEDED

- Wood screw
- Board (pine or other soft wood)
- Screwdriver

PROCEDURE

1. Try to push the screw into the board with your fingers.
2. Place the tip of the screwdriver on the head of the screw and try to push the screw into the board without turning the screwdriver.
3. Did the screw go any farther than when you pushed with your hand?
4. Now turn the screwdriver as you press down hard with it on the head of the screw.
5. Can you get the screw into the board this time?
6. Notice how far the screwdriver handle travels as the screw turns around once.
7. How far does the screw move into the board as the screwdriver handle turns around the screw into the board?
8. What can you say about the gain or loss in force and in distance as you turn the screw into the board?
9. Make a list of ways people make use of the screw.
10. What kind of machine is the screwdriver?

TEACHER INFORMATION

The screw offers a gain in force but at the expense of distance and speed. The head of the screw travels much faster and farther in a circular direction than the distance the screw moves into the board.

The screw also changes the direction of the effort from a turning motion to a pulling motion.

The ideal mechanical advantage of the screw is computed by dividing the circumference of the screw (distance it travels in one complete turn) by the pitch (distance between two threads). However, the actual mechanical advantage of the screw is greatly reduced by friction.

Friction helps by keeping the screw from turning backward or pulling out. The loss of force due to friction is made up by using another machine, the screwdriver. The screwdriver is a form of the wheel and axle.

The principle of the screw is applied in the use of the base of a light bulb, a bolt, a crescent wrench, caps on jars and bottles, and the piano stool.

Section 7

MAGNETISM

TO THE TEACHER

A study of magnetism is often a very helpful beginning point for introducing structured inquiry/discovery activities. Be certain to warn the children that magnets will break or lose their magnetism if dropped or hit together. In the case of U-shaped magnets a piece of soft iron called a *keeper* should be placed across the ends.

Section 7 is nongraded; however, some activities may seem more appropriate to certain age levels. Each teacher should feel free to reorganize and eliminate materials according to the particular group, keeping in mind the level of psychological development that may influence the understanding of certain concepts. Inquiry and the use of concrete materials is a major purpose of this unit.

Many of the activities in this section seem to be most effective when presented to individuals, small groups, or teams. If your classroom organization permits, the materials should be put in a science learning center, with time provided for children to move through the sequence at their own rate. Classroom discussions to reinforce the concepts should follow. If classroom demonstrations are used initially, children should perform the activities and then the materials should be left on the science table for children to explore individually.

Many children are fascinated by magnets. They seem almost like magic. There is a natural desire on the part of some children to explore and share their discoveries with friends and others outside the classroom. Most magnets are fairly expensive, but many school supply outlets sell strips of small magnets (for notices on bulletin boards, refrigerator doors, and so on) at a reasonable cost. If possible, try to get a number of these small magnets for out-of-school activities. Ideally, each child should have a pair of these small *alnico* (aluminum, nickel, cobalt) magnets.

A word of caution: Audio tapes are magnetic. If they come near a strong magnet, they may be erased. Spring-operated watch mechanisms may also become magnetized in a strong magnetic field.

ACTIVITY 126: Which Rock Is Different?

MATERIALS NEEDED

- Several similar rocks
- One lodestone
- Paper clip

PROCEDURE

1. One of these rocks can do something the others cannot.
2. Can you find it?
3. What can you say about it?

TEACHER INFORMATION

The children may choose a rock other than the magnetic lodestone. If this occurs and their reasons for the choice are logical, their answers should be accepted, as the process of inquiry is our objective. However, since it is assumed that most children have had some experience with magnets (kindergarten), a paper clip or other magnetic material on the table may assist in the discovery.

Lodestone or magnetite is a particular type of iron ore that occurs naturally and has magnetic properties. Lodestones may be purchased from a science supply house at a nominal cost.

ACTIVITY 127: Where Did the First Metal Magnet Come From?

MATERIALS NEEDED

- Nonmagnetized needle
- Lodestone
- Paper clip

PROCEDURE

1. Is the needle a magnet?
2. How might you test it?
3. Rub it 20 times in the same direction with the magnetic rock.
4. Test your needle again. Is it a magnet?
5. What can you say about this?

TEACHER INFORMATION

Magnetism has been known for centuries. References to this "magical" property occur in Chinese and Greek mythology. This activity might provide opportunities for creative writing about the discovery of magnetism. Your encyclopedia can provide information about the history of lodestones.

ACTIVITY 128: What Materials Will a Magnet Pick Up?

MATERIALS NEEDED

- A tray of magnetic and nonmagnetic materials, such as a Canadian nickel, a United States nickel, and brass and steel safety pins (be sure to include gold-colored, silver-colored, and other colored items)
- Magnet
- Audio tape, filmstrip, or book on magnetism

PROCEDURE

1. What are some things magnets can pick up or attract?
2. If you would care to learn more about magnetism, ask your teacher for an audio tape, a filmstrip, or a book on this topic.

TEACHER INFORMATION

Occasionally, teachers will have the children make piles of magnetic and nonmagnetic materials. It is not recommended that small children be asked to write lists of their findings.

As students experiment with the materials, it is hoped that they will become motivated to seek the answer to the title question through the use of reference materials. An audio tape, library book, encyclopedia, filmstrip, or even classroom textbook can provide an explanation.

The answer should be made easy to locate. Note the words "care to learn" in step 2. If the child is not sufficiently motivated to find the answer at this time, he or she will be introduced to it later. (By the way, the materials magnets will pick up are those made of iron, nickel, steel, and cobalt.)

ACTIVITY 129: What Do Magnets Look Like?

MATERIALS NEEDED

- A large collection of magnets of different sizes, shapes, materials, and colors
- Magnetic materials, such as paper clips, for testing

PROCEDURE

Use these materials to answer the question: What do magnets look like?

TEACHER INFORMATION

The answer to the question is simple. Magnets can look like almost anything. You cannot tell if something is a magnet by its appearance. If possible obtain "cow magnets" from feed and grain stores. These magnets are put in the stomach of cattle to collect bits of metal that have been eaten.

Children often have the idea that magnetism has something to do with the shape of the magnets, as magnets are most often shown in horseshoe or bar shapes. Activity 130 is included to help children see that shape is not directly related to the property of magnetism.

Students might have unusual magnets of their own that they could bring to add variety to the shapes of magnets used.

ACTIVITY 130: How Do Magnets Get Their Names?

MATERIALS NEEDED

- The magnets used in Activity 129

PROCEDURE

1. Magnets often get their names from their shapes or what they do. See if you can find magnets that might have the following names:
   bar magnet
   cylindrical magnet
   disk (or disc) magnet
   U-shaped magnet
   horseshoe magnet
   cow magnet
2. Can you name any others?

TEACHER INFORMATION

The purpose of this activity is to reinforce the preceding one. It may have some value in helping children learn new names for geometric shapes and provide a basic vocabulary for further study of magnets.

Since magnets are so much a part of our everyday life, your children may bring in many new and unusual magnets to add to the collection.

ACTIVITY 131: Which Magnet Is Strongest?

MATERIALS NEEDED

- The magnets used in Activities 129 and 130
- Paper clip
- Ruler
- Spring scale

PROCEDURE

Use these materials to answer the question: Which magnet is the strongest?

TEACHER INFORMATION

This is the first activity in this section in which children are asked to develop their own investigation. Often children will begin by putting two magnets together to see which one seems to "pull" harder. You may need to point out that this will not show which one is pulling harder. To help in the investigation, a spring scale, ruler, and paper clip are provided, but the children should not be given direction on how to use them. The purpose of the activity is to encourage creative inquiry. Success should be evaluated on the amount of creative exploration children undertake.

Younger children will often choose the largest magnet as the strongest. Teachers of young children should keep in mind the work of Piaget with preoperational thinking in utilizing this activity.

ACTIVITY 132: Through Which Substances Can Magnetism Pass?

MATERIALS NEEDED

- Paper clip suspended from a string toward a large mounted magnet
- Variety of magnetic and nonmagnetic materials, such as a piece of plastic, wood, aluminum foil, paper, iron lid
- String

PROCEDURE

1. What keeps the clip up?
2. Place different materials between the clip and the magnet.
3. What happened?
4. What can you say about this?

TEACHER INFORMATION

For the apparatus identified in "Materials Needed," use a string to suspend a strong magnet from a mount or ruler (Figure 132-1). Place a paper clip held by a thread below the magnet, leaving a space between the magnet and the clip.

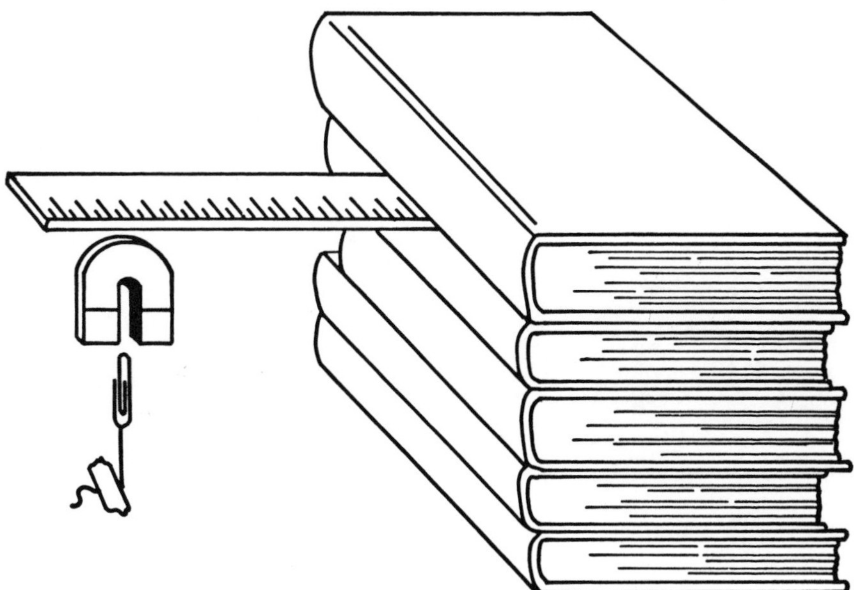

FIGURE 132-1. Large magnet mounted, with paper clip suspended.

Nonmagnetic materials will pass between the clip and magnet without disturbing the magnetic field. When the iron lid comes near the gap, the magnet will be attracted to it and the clip will probably fall. In a later class discussion, it should be demonstrated that magnetic materials will disturb or cut a magnetic field. However, substances made of a magnetic material (iron, nickel, steel, or cobalt) may be made into temporary magnets and behave like a magnet while in the magnetic field. Thus the iron lid alone may not pick up paper clips, but when it comes near or touches a strong magnet, it will temporarily become a magnet through a process called *induction.* The extent of time the magnetic material retains its magnetic properties is often related to its hardness (how tightly the molecules are packed together). The steel needle used in Activity 127 will retain its magnetism for a long period. A soft iron lid or paper clip will lose its magnetism rapidly when removed from the magnetic field. Activity 140 develops this theory in depth with a somewhat different approach.

A graphic demonstration of how a magnetic material disturbs or cuts a magnetic field is to "cut" it with scissors. Carefully bring a pair of open scissors between the magnet and the clip. Cut through the magnetic field with the scissors. Usually the clip will fall.

ACTIVITY 133: What Part of a Magnet Has the Strongest Pull?

MATERIALS NEEDED

- Bar magnet
- Paper clips

PROCEDURE

1. See how many paper clips you can make stick to different parts of the magnet.
2. What happened?
3. What can you say about this?

TEACHER INFORMATION

Many more paper clips will stick to the ends of the magnet. Few will cling to the center. Magnets are strongest at the poles.

This activity will further illustrate the theory of induction introduced in Activity 132. While the paper clips are touching the magnet, they temporarily become magnetized and several will "stick" to each other near the ends. When the clips are removed from the magnet, they rapidly lose their magnetic properties.

ACTIVITY 134: What Is a Special Property of Magnetism?

MATERIALS NEEDED

- Two bar magnets
- Stack of books
- Ruler
- Thread

PROCEDURE

1. Tie the thread to the center of one bar magnet.
2. Hold the bar magnet in the air by the thread so it can turn freely.
3. Bring each end of another bar magnet near the one that is suspended from the thread.
4. What happened?
5. What can you say about this?

FIGURE 134-1. Bar magnet suspended from thread.

TEACHER INFORMATION

Be sure the bars are correctly magnetized and that each has an "N" and an "S" marked on opposite ends. Like poles will push away. Unlike poles will attract each other. The poles of the bar magnet can be reversed by drawing the bar magnet several times across one of the poles of a powerful magnet. The direction in which the bar magnet is drawn across the pole of the larger magnet will determine the polarity of the bar magnet.

The ability to attract *and* repel each other is a special characteristic by which magnets can be identified. They have unlike poles. Activity 139 will suggest a way to illustrate that most materials made of steel develop poles and therefore are weak magnets.

ACTIVITY 135: How Can You See a Magnetic Field?

MATERIALS NEEDED

- Two thin pieces of wood at least 10 cm. (2½ in.) long
- Shaker of iron filings
- Bar magnet
- 3-in. × 5-in. card

PROCEDURE

1. Place the bar magnet between the two pieces of wood.
2. Cover the magnet with the card.
3. Sprinkle iron filings on the card.
4. Tap the card gently several times.
5. What happened?
6. What can you say about this?

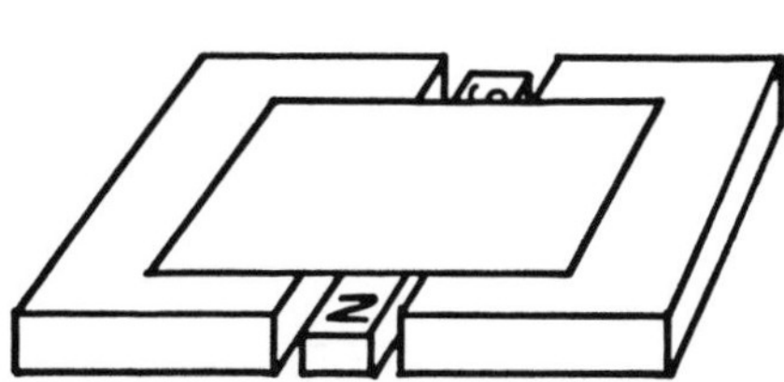

FIGURE 135-1. Blocks, card, magnet, and iron filings.

TEACHER INFORMATION

The iron filings will be aligned with the magnetic field of the bar magnet, making it visible. Note that the filings in the middle will point to the poles, while the greater number of filings will cluster at the poles. Iron filings may be purchased from science supply houses. They also occur naturally in many types of sand and may be collected by running a strong magnet through a sand pile.

As enrichment, children may want to experiment with magnets of different shapes or use light-sensitive paper in place of the card to make a permanent record.

ACTIVITY 136: What Happens When a Magnet Can Turn Freely?

MATERIALS NEEDED

- Bar magnet
- Thread

PROCEDURE

1. Hold the bar magnet by the thread.
2. Spin the magnet slightly, then give it time to slow down and completely stop.
3. Observe the position in which it stops.
4. Do this several times.
5. What happened?
6. What can you say about this?

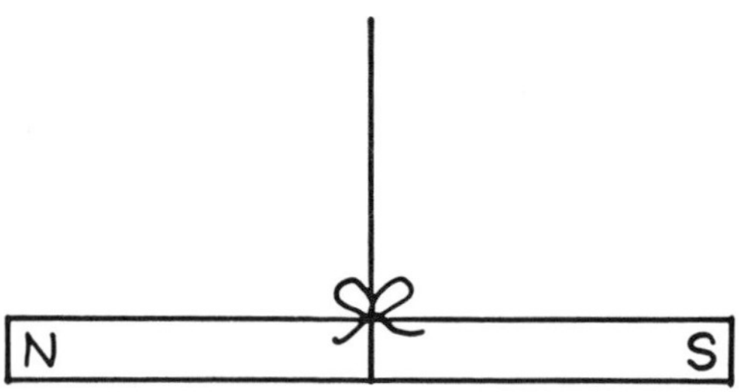

FIGURE 136-1. Bar magnet suspended from a thread.

TEACHER INFORMATION

If the bar magnet is correctly magnetized, it should stop each time with the *N* end pointing toward magnetic north. An audio tape or other reference can be used to explain that calling the *N* end of the magnet *north* has come about through common usage, as people knew about magnets and their behavior long before they understood them scientifically. Actually, since opposite poles attract, to be correct it should be called the *north-seeking* end.

Activity 139 will help students understand why scientists think magnets align this way.

ACTIVITY 137: What Is a Compass?

MATERIALS NEEDED

- Sensitive compass
- Paper clip

PROCEDURE

1. Bring the clip near the compass.
2. What happens to the compass needle?
3. What can you say about this?

TEACHER INFORMATION

A compass is a freely suspended bar magnet. If a bar magnet is brought near, it will behave just as the suspended bar magnet did in Activity 134, showing it has poles.

The children may also bring other known magnetic materials near the compass to further reinforce this idea. Understanding that a compass is a magnet is important for further investigations in this unit.

CAUTION: Very strong magnets may damage a compass by pulling the needle off its delicate support.

ACTIVITY 138: How Can You Make a Compass?

MATERIALS NEEDED

- Plastic, aluminum, or glass bowl
- Nonmagnetized needle
- Small piece of Styrofoam
- Compass
- Water
- Bar magnet
- Paper clip

PROCEDURE

1. Is the needle a magnet? Don't guess. Devise a way to find out.
2. Rub the needle 30 times in the same direction with the bar magnet. Is the needle a magnet now?
3. Fill the bowl partly full of water.
4. Stick the needle through the Styrofoam and float it in the pan of water.
5. Point the needle in different directions, then allow it to settle.

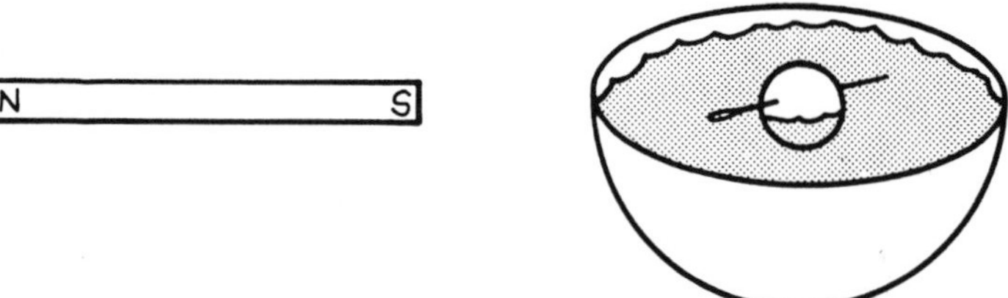

FIGURE 138-1. Needle in floating styrofoam.

6. What happened?
7. Can you see a relationship to the compass?
8. What can you say about this?

TEACHER INFORMATION

The floating needle will behave like a compass, with one end always pointing to magnetic north. A story is told that this is the same type of compass used by Christopher Columbus. Since the metal needles of the time were poor, Columbus had a lodestone to remagnetize his floating needle. A bar magnet will affect the floating needle in the same way it did the compass. By moving the bar magnet under the dish, the children can discover that magnetism goes through water.

ACTIVITY 139: What Are the Earth's Magnetic Poles?

(Classroom demonstration and total group discussion)

MATERIALS NEEDED

- 13-cm. (6-in.) Styrofoam ball cut in half
- Bar magnet
- Compasses
- Toothpicks
- Index card
- Iron filings

TEACHER INFORMATION

The concept of the earth's behaving as a large magnet with magnetic north and south poles is difficult to teach with simple inquiry/discovery activities alone. You might want to begin with a classroom discussion using one-half of a Styrofoam ball (or a grapefruit or large orange) with a bar magnet running through it and a tip sticking out of each end to represent the magnetic north and south poles. Toothpicks nearby could represent *true north* and *true south,* the axis, (an imaginary line from true north to true south) on which the earth turns.

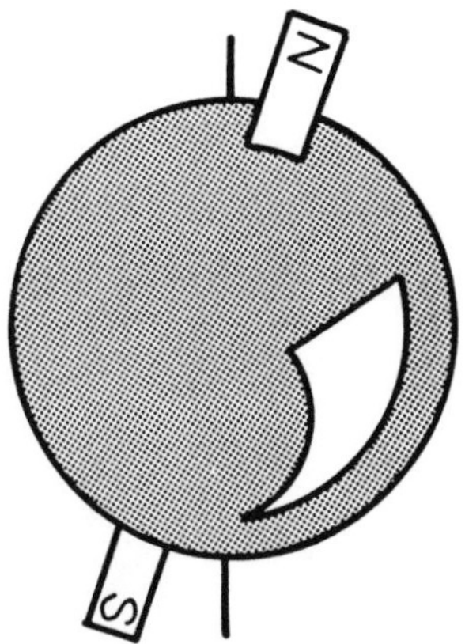

FIGURE 139-1. Ball, bar magnet, and toothpick.

To further reinforce the idea, place an index card over the bar magnet with iron filings sprinkled on it. Scientists believe this pattern represents approximately the lines of force of the earth's magnetic field, with the strongest pull at the ends or poles.

With this basic idea in mind, a compass can be brought near the ball to show that it will point to the north and the south ends or poles. This is the basic information necessary to understand this concept. In addition, you may want to discuss or try some of the following:

1. Activities 127 and 132 showed that steel and other magnetic materials will become magnetized in the presence of a magnetic field. Most materials made of steel that we use in our daily lives are weak magnets (they have poles). You can test this by holding a compass near a steel leg of a chair or table and moving it up and down the leg. Usually, one end of the compass needle will point to the leg, but, as the compass is moved up and down the leg, the needle will reverse.
2. See your encyclopedia for a discussion of northern and southern lights (aurora borealis and aurora australis). Scientists believe the stronger pull at the earth's poles attracts electrons given off from the sun. As the enter the earth's asmosphere they produce these unusual lights.
3. You may want to research the questions of why true north and south and magnetic north and south are not the same. Why do the magnetic poles migrate or change their location somewhat each year? The difference between true north and magnetic north is called the *angle of declination* and varies according to your geographic location on earth.
4. Do other planets and moons and the sun have magnetic fields?

ACTIVITY 140: How Do Materials Become Magnetized?

MATERIALS NEEDED

- Plastic tube (toothbrush container or test tube) two-thirds full of iron filings
- Strong magnet
- Compass

PROCEDURE

1. Place the tube with the iron filings flat on a table.
2. Move the compass along the side of the tube. Observe the needle.
3. Rub the tube with the iron filings 30 times in the same direction with the strong magnet. Now move the compass along the side of the tube again. Observe the needle.
4. What happened?
5. Shake the tube several times. Move the compass along the side of the tube.
6. What do you think is happening?

TEACHER INFORMATION

This activity illustrates in concrete form one of the theories scientists use to explain what happens when an object becomes magnetized. Inside materials that can be magnetized are groups or *domains* of atoms that have north and south poles but are arranged randomly (Figure 140-1).

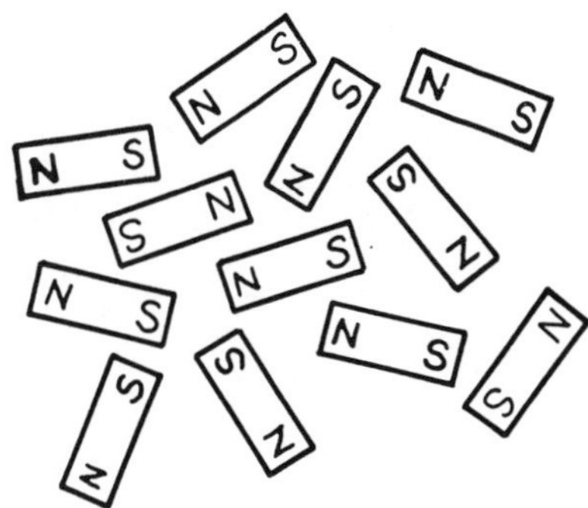

FIGURE 140-1. Domains shown in random order.

The iron filings in the plastic tube represent these domains. The compass will show that the tube does not have poles. When the *domains of atoms* come into the presence of a strong magnetic field, they line up, following the lines of force of the magnetic field (Figure 140-2).

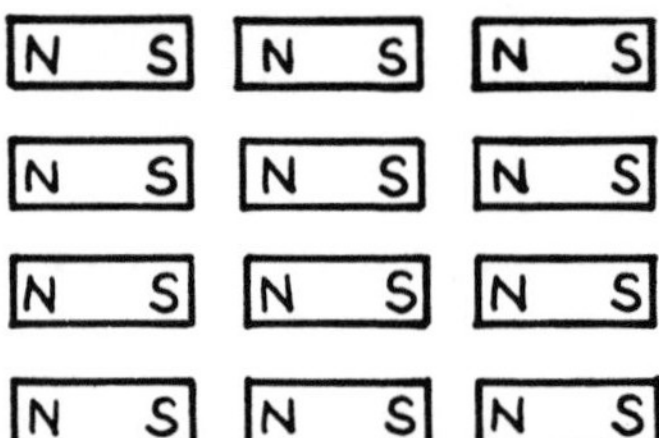

FIGURE 140-2. Domains shown in same order.

When the plastic tube is rubbed with a strong magnet, the iron filings line up inside and the compass test will show the tube has poles. Shaking the tube several times mixes the filings up and the compass test will show the tube no longer has poles.

The mixing up of the domains is one way of explaining how magnets may lose their magnetism. When an object is heated, the molecules move more rapidly and bounce against each other. Dropping or striking a magnet may jar the domains out of alignment. Magnets stored with *like* poles together seem to gradually push the domains out of position.

The domain theory may also help children understand how steel objects, such as chair and table legs, become magnetized by having their domains aligned by the powerful magnetic field of the earth.

As the domain theory is presented to children with the plastic tube model, it is important to remember that it is a simplified version, used as an introduction for concrete thinkers. Subatomic concepts consistent with this model are studied in later years.

ACTIVITY 141: How Can You Find the Poles of a Lodestone?

MATERIALS NEEDED

- Lodestone
- Compass

PROCEDURE

1. Bring the compass near different parts of the lodestone.
2. Observe the needle.
3. What happened?
4. What can you say about this?

TEACHER INFORMATION

The compass will indicate that lodestones do have poles. Some lodestones may have several poles, but they should have equal numbers of north and south poles. Some scientists believe that lodestones are magnetized and aligned to the earth's magnetic poles as the iron ore from which they are formed cools.

Since ancient deposits of lodestone have poles pointing in directions different from the present north and south it is suggested that our present north and south poles may have switched several times over the years.

The different directions in which the poles of ancient deposits point are also studied as indicators of earth movement and the theory of *continental drift.*

Section 8

STATIC ELECTRICITY

TO THE TEACHER

The topic *static electricity* has at least two things in common with *magnetism:* (1) the attraction and repulsion of one object for another, and (2) the attraction of all age groups to the topic. There is something, perhaps the element of mystery, that intrigues both young and old. Although our information about static electricity is still based largely on theory (another common thread with magnetism), much is known about its behavior. Through observation and experimentation, logical explanations of the phenomenon have developed.

Static electricity is the object of curiosity, annoyance, and humor. During a severe electrical storm the emotion associated with it is often fear, in recognition of the all-too-real danger to life and property. The lightning bolt itself is current electricity because it is moving, but it results from the build-up of an electrostatic charge. (See the Big Idea in the "Static Electricity" section of the concepts/skills index.)

This section is suitable for virtually every grade level and most activities can be easily adapted for use where needed. Activity 142 is intended as a teacher demonstration and works well as an introduction to the unit. If used this way it will raise questions, not provide answers. A better time to discuss concepts is after students have experimented, discovered, and formed general ideas about the way electrically charged objects seem to behave. Static electricity works best on a cool, clear day (moisture in the air tends to drain off the charge), but success with these activities is very high almost any time except, perhaps, on a hot, muggy day.

As you select materials to use with static electricity activities, avoid those that have been treated with antistatic chemicals. Such chemicals are often used in dishwashers (for example, antispot substances), in clothes dryers (anticling products), or on carpets (fabric protector). Often these treatments can be washed out, and the materials can then be used for static electricity activities.

ACTIVITY 142: What Is the Kissing Balloon?

(Teacher demonstration)

MATERIALS NEEDED

- Balloon
- Wool cloth
- String
- Permanent marker
- Words to the story (given below)
- Tape

PROCEDURE

1. Inflate the balloon.
2. Draw a face on the balloon, using the marker.
3. With the string, suspend the balloon from the ceiling. Adjust the height so the balloon is at the level of your head when you're standing on the floor. Do this while students are out of the room.
4. With students still out of the room, rub the "nose" of the balloon with the wool cloth. If properly charged, the balloon will now face you any time you are reasonably near. If you walk around the balloon, it will follow.
5. You are now ready for your students to return to the classroom. They should take their seats without going near the balloon.
6. Without revealing scientific principles involved, tell the following story as an introduction to your study of static electricity. Following the study, the Kissing Balloon could be used again as an evaluation. A suggestion for such an evaluation follows the story.

STORY

"Students, I'd like you to meet a friend of mine. His name is George. George, meet the smartest fourth grade in the state." (*At this point you are standing at least 2 meters (2 yards.) from "George."*)

"There are a couple of things I think you should know about George, class. First, he's nearsighted, and second, he has an awful crush on me. He likes me so much that he just can't keep his eyes off me—when he can see me that is." (*Walk over closer to "George" and he will turn to face you.*)

"You see? He just stares at me, and he keeps staring at me as long as I'm close enough for him to see me." (*Walk away.*) "When I walk away, he just looks all over, trying to find me again." (*Move closer again.*) "You'll be able to tell when I'm within his range of vision because he'll look right at me." (*Walk around "George."*) "See, I told you he likes me. Now, if you'll promise not to tell anyone, I'll let George kiss me—just once, on the cheek." (*Lean over, where your cheek is very near "George."*) "There."

"Now, for the next few days, we're going to do some things that should give you some clues about George. We'll visit with him again on another day."

Your students should be more highly motivated for their study of static electricity as a result of meeting "George."

EVALUATION

One idea for an evaluation following learning activities on static electricity is to repeat the "George" activity, put the following terms on the chalkboard, and ask students to explain why "George" behaved the way he did. Instruct them to use some of the terms from the chalkboard in their explanation:

- Static electricity
- Attraction
- Repulsion
- Transfer of electrons

Note: One of the properties of static electricity is that a charge can be held in a given location. When you rub George's nose with the wool cloth, the charge does not spread throughout the balloon, but remains localized. Otherwise, this activity would not be possible.

ACTIVITY 143: How Does Rubbing with Wool Affect Plastic Strips?

MATERIALS NEEDED

- Two plastic strips
- Wool cloth
- Sheet of paper

PROCEDURE

1. Hold the two plastic strips at one end and let them hang down.
2. Place the two plastic strips on a sheet of paper and rub with wool.
3. Carefully remove the strips, touching them only at one end.
4. Place them together and let them hang down again. What happene Why?

TEACHER INFORMATION

At step 1 the plastic strips are both neutral and therefore neither attract nor repel each other. When rubbed with wool, which gives up electrons readily, they take on a negative electrostatic charge; they gain an excess of electrons. Since they are now charged alike, they will repel each other when they are held up.

ACTIVITY 144: What Changes the Way Balloons React to Each Other?

MATERIALS NEEDED

- Two balloons of the same size
- Two pieces of string 60 cm. (2 ft.) long
- Wool cloth

PROCEDURE

1. Inflate the two balloons and tie the ends with string.
2. Hold up the two balloons by their strings so they hang about an inch or two apart.
3. Rub one balloon with the wool cloth and repeat step 2. What happened?
4. Rub the other balloon with the wool cloth and repeat step 2 again. What happened?
5. Explain.

TEACHER INFORMATION

At step 2, the balloons are neutral and do not react to each other. At step 3, the rubbed balloon has a negative charge and, in turn, induces a positive charge in the other balloon. Thus, the balloons attract each other. When the two balloons touch, electrons are transferred from the negatively charged balloon, giving the other one a negative charge, and the balloons repel each other. When both balloons have been rubbed with wool, at step 4, they have like charges (negative) and will repel each other.

ACTIVITY 145: What Will Puffed Rice Do to a Comb?

MATERIALS NEEDED

- Comb
- Wool cloth
- Puffed rice (several kernels)

PROCEDURE

1. Rub the comb with the wool cloth.
2. Bring the comb near the puffed rice. Hold the comb steady and observe until you see something different happen. It might take as long as 3 to 5 minutes. Be patient.
3. Explain what happened and why.

TEACHER INFORMATION

The comb, being rubbed with wool, takes on a negative charge. When it is held near the puffed rice, the rice becomes charged positively by induction and will leap and cling to the comb. Patience is needed at this point.

As the puffed rice remains in contact with the comb, some of the negative charge (electrons) will drain off the comb and onto the puffed rice. The puffed rice now has a negative charge—the same as the comb—and will leap from the comb. Notice that the puffed rice does not simply fall, but rather appears to be thrown from the comb by some force. The force is the electrostatic charge.

As the puffed rice sits on the table, its excess electrons will probably drain off to the table and the cycle is sometimes repeated.

ACTIVITY 146: How Can You Make Paper Dance?

MATERIALS NEEDED

- Sheet of glass (or inverted bowl)
- Plastic bag
- Two books
- Small bits of paper

PROCEDURE

1. Support the glass by placing a book under each end.
2. Place some small bits of paper under the glass.
3. Rub the top of the glass vigorously with the plastic.
4. Observe for 3 to 5 minutes.
5. What happened?
6. Why do you suppose it behaves this way?

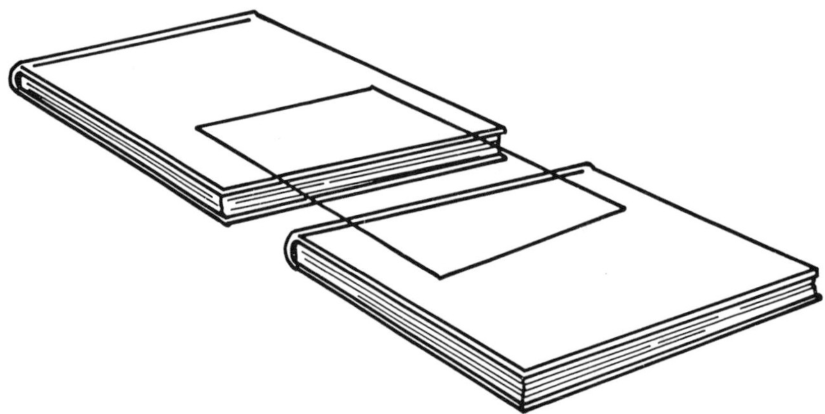

FIGURE 146-1. Glass supported by books.

TEACHER INFORMATION

Avoid paper that has been treated in any way (for example, to make erasing easy). Tissue paper works well and Styrofoam is an excellent substitute. This activity is very similar to Activity 145. See "Teacher Information" in Activity 145. In this activity, the behavior appears the same but the charges have been reversed. The glass will give up electrons readily and become positively charged. In turn, it will induce a negative charge in the bits of paper. The paper will jump up to the glass, gradually give up some electrons and fall back to the table where the process of induction is repeated.

ACTIVITY 147: Why Does Paper Leap for a Balloon?

MATERIALS NEEDED

- Balloon
- Wool cloth
- Bits of paper
- String

PROCEDURE

1. Blow up the balloon and tie the end with string.
2. Rub the balloon with the wool cloth.
3. Hold the balloon about an inch from the bits of paper and observe for 3 to 4 minutes.
4. What happened? Can you say why?

TEACHER INFORMATION

See "Teacher Information" section of Activity 145. Tissue paper works very well for the bits of paper, and Styrofoam is an excellent substitute.

ACTIVITY 148: What Does Puffed Rice Run Away From?

MATERIALS NEEDED

- Clear plastic box
- Puffed rice or vermiculite
- Wool cloth

PROCEDURE

1. Put a few pieces of vermiculite or puffed rice inside the plastic box.
2. Rub the top of the box with wool.
3. What happened?
4. Bring your finger near the top of the box.
5. What happened?
6. Can you explain your findings? Do you think the puffed rice is afraid of you?

TEACHER INFORMATION

This activity involves an element of experience with induced magnetism beyond that of earlier activities. When your finger approaches the negatively charged plastic box, your finger becomes positively charged by induction, just as the puffed rice inside the box has been. Therefore, your finger and the puffed rice have like charges. Evidence of the resultant repelling effect is seen as the puffed rice is "chased" around the box by the finger.

ACTIVITY 149: How Can You Make Salt and Pepper Dance Together?

MATERIALS NEEDED

- Balloon
- Wool cloth
- Plate with salt and pepper
- String

PROCEDURE

1. Inflate the balloon and tie the end with string.
2. Rub the balloon with wool.
3. Bring the balloon within about an inch or two of the plate.
4. Observe for 3 to 5 minutes.
5. Explain what is happening and why.

TEACHER INFORMATION

In this activity you will see the salt and pepper do a "dance" because of the principles explained in "Teacher Information" for Activity 145. You will need to caution your students to watch very carefully. Otherwise they will probably not notice that the same grains of salt and pepper are attracted to the balloon, repelled, then attracted again over and over. Notice that they don't just fall from the balloon but are *thrown* by the electrostatic force.

ACTIVITY 150: How Can You Make a String Dance?

MATERIALS NEEDED

- Balloon
- String 30–50 cm. (1 to 1½ ft.) long
- Wool cloth

PROCEDURE

1. Inflate the balloon and tie the end.
2. Charge the balloon by rubbing it with the wool cloth.
3. Bring the balloon near one end of the string, but don't let it touch.
4. What happened?
5. Can you explain why?
6. With practice you might learn to be a snake charmer!

TEACHER INFORMATION

The end of the string in this activity is charged by induction and attracted to the balloon. Students enjoy making the end of the string dance.

ACTIVITY 151: How Can You Make a Spark with Your Finger?

MATERIALS NEEDED

- Darkened room with carpeted floor

PROCEDURE

1. Turn the lights off and make the room as dark as possible.
2. Shuffle your feet across the carpet for a few steps.
3. Touch a doorknob or some other metal object. Watch carefully at your fingertip as you touch the doorknob.
4. What did you see? If you didn't see anything, try it again.

TEACHER INFORMATION

This activity is not dangerous, but it does tend to invite horseplay, so if a group of students is involved, close supervision might be needed. The objective of the activity is to see the spark that jumps between the finger and the doorknob after an electrostatic charge is built up from shuffling the feet across the room on the carpet. Students usually discover that a spark can also jump between their fingers and another person's ear or nose. The spark will sometimes be felt and heard. If the room can be darkened, it can also be seen. If some students are frightened of the spark, they should not be required to participate.

ACTIVITY 152: How Can You Make an Electroscope?

(Upper grades)

MATERIALS NEEDED

- Bottle with cork stopper
- Copper wire about 20 cm. (8 in.) long
- Lightweight aluminum foil
- Nail
- Rubber comb
- Wool cloth
- Scissors
- Ruler

PROCEDURE

1. Force the nail through the rubber stopper to make a hole for the wire.
2. Remove all insulation from both ends of the wire.
3. Insert the copper wire through the cork stopper.
4. Bend the lower end of the wire (the end that will go inside the bottle) as illustrated in Figure 152-1.

FIGURE 152-1. Assembled electroscope.

5. Cut a strip of aluminum foil approximately ½ cm. (¼ in.) wide and 3 cm. (1¼ in.) long.
6. Fold the aluminum foil in half and let it hang over the end of the wire, as illustrated. *Be sure all insulation is removed from the wire where the foil rests.*
7. Put the stopper on the bottle, being careful not to jar the strip of aluminum foil off the end of the wire.
8. Rub the comb with the wool cloth and bring the comb near the top end of the wire. As you do this, observe the foil strip carefully.

9. What happened? Can you explain why?
10. Try the same thing with other charged objects.

TEACHER INFORMATION

The electroscope is an easy-to-make device and should not be difficult to assemble for students who are motivated. They can use it to demonstrate the presence of an electrostatic charge in a comb, a balloon, or other charged object. As the charged object is brought near the upper end of the copper wire, the wire, being a conductor, carries the charge to the foil. The entire foil strip receives the same charge and the two ends repel each other.

The very thin foil stripped from a gum wrapper works better for this activity than does heavier aluminum foil used in wrapping food.

Section 9

CURRENT ELECTRICITY

TO THE TEACHER

The study of this area should follow the studies of magnetism and static electricity, as it requires background information from both.

The activities are nongraded; however, teachers of young children will need to adapt language and instruction.

The amount of electric current used in these activities (1½ to 3 volts) is perfectly safe if you follow directions to avoid overheating of circuits. Remember, if your flashlight has two batteries it uses 3 volts of electricity. *Never use household current directly.* In many activities, a high-quality transformer could substitute for batteries. Before using a transformer, have it checked by an electrician so you know exactly how much voltage it produces. Variable-voltage model train transformers are not recommended. Flashlight cells may be wrapped together securely with electrician's tape just as they fit in a flashlight.

Materials such as light sockets, bulbs, and insulated copper wire can be purchased at a hardware or electronics store. An inexpensive wire cutter and stripper (to remove insulation) is a necessary item.

Most activities are designed for individuals or small groups. Costs can be reduced by setting up a learning center and rotating groups through it. Many projects are designed to "take home and tell about" and can strengthen children's language skills.

Before you begin this section, please read all activities. Some of the same materials are used in different ways several times.

Many schools have magnets that have become weak. You can rejuvenate magnets by wrapping a coil of wire around them and sending an electric current through the wire (see activities on electromagnets). If you recharge bar magnets, be sure the current flows through the wire in the proper direction to produce the correct poles as marked (use a compass to check). A simple device for making bar magnets stronger can be made from a toilet tissue tube with a coil of wire wrapped in one direction around it. Simply insert a bar magnet in the tube and turn on the current for a few seconds. If the poles are reversed, repeat the process but turn the bar magnet around *or* switch the wires on the battery terminals.

Enrichment activities for this unit could focus on new ways to produce electric current.

Evaluation should use concrete materials, not pencil and paper.

ACTIVITY 153: What Is a Circuit?

MATERIALS NEEDED

- One 1½-volt flashlight battery
- Two 25-cm. (10 in.) lengths of single-strand insulated copper wire of 20 or 22 gauge
- Small light socket with flashlight bulb
- Small screwdriver

PROCEDURE

1. In front of you are all the materials needed to make the light turn on. Can you hook them together so the bulb lights up? If you have trouble, read the following hints:
   a. Electricity will flow from the battery (power source) only if it has a path from one terminal (end) to the other.
   b. Electric current will go through the copper wire but not through the plastic or rubber insulation (covering).
   c. The bulb must be screwed tightly in the socket.
   d. The wires must be tightly connected.
2. What happens if the path to the battery is broken? Why?

TEACHER INFORMATION

One and one-half volts of electric current from a flashlight battery is perfectly safe for classroom use. This activity may be varied according to the age of the children. You may want to give the circuit with the wires attached to younger children and let them discover how to make it work by screwing the bulb in and touching the bare ends to the battery. Older children should be able to hook up the circuit by following the hints. You may need to help them clean off (strip) about 2 cm. (1 in.) from both ends of the wire. An inexpensive wire cutter and stripper obtainable from any hardware store is most helpful.

When completed, the circuit should look like Figure 153-1.

Numbers indicating the gauge (thickness) of wire are in the reverse order of their thickness. For example, 20-gauge wire is heavier than 22-gauge. An ideal gauge for most of these activities is often called *bell wire*.

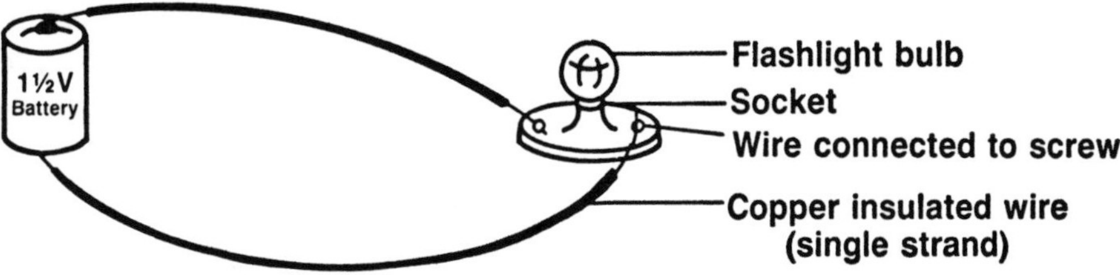

FIGURE 153-1. Battery and bulb connected to light the bulb.

ACTIVITY 154: What Is a Short Circuit?

MATERIALS NEEDED

- Complete circuit constructed in Activity 153
- One 25-cm. (10-in.) length of copper wire, similar to that used in Activity 153, stripped on both ends

PROCEDURE

1. Connect your circuit so there is a complete path and the light turns on.
2. Strip (clean off) the insulation from 1 cm. (½ in.) in the center of each wire. Does the light still go on?
3. Put the bare ends of the extra piece of wire across the bare sections of your circuit wires. Does the light go on?
4. What do you think has happened? Why?
5. Feel the ends where the bare ends are touching. Do you notice anything?
6. You have made a short circuit in your path. Discuss with your teacher and the other class members what that means.

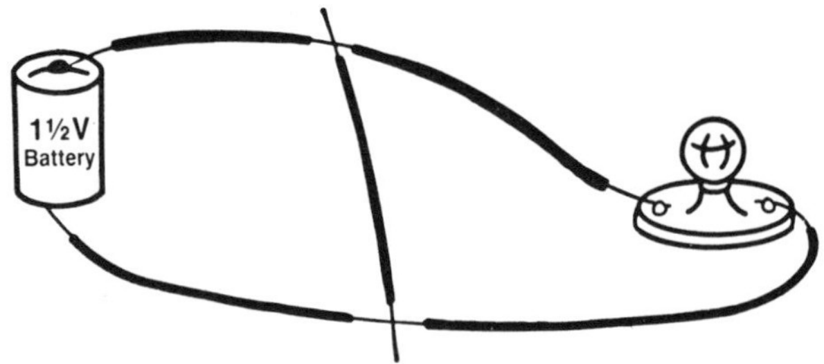

FIGURE 154-1. Battery and bulb, short-circuited.

TEACHER INFORMATION

When the additional wire is placed across the circuit, the light goes out. A general rule in electric circuits is that electricity will follow the path of least resistance. This means it will follow the shortest, easiest path or the one of least resistance back to its source (battery). In this example you have made the path shorter and avoided a resistor (the light bulb). If you permit current to flow through the short circuit for more than a few seconds, the wire will begin to heat up. This is caused by providing an easy path for electricity to flow. The amount of electricity going through the wire increases beyond its normal capacity.

ACTIVITY 155: Can You Make a Switch?

MATERIALS NEEDED

- Complete circuit used in Activities 153 and 154
- Copper or iron strip 10 cm. (4 in.) long by 2 cm. (1 in.) wide
- Strip of wood (lath) 15 cm. (6 in.) long
- Two small wood screws
- Hammer and nail
- Screwdriver

PROCEDURE

1. Use the hammer and nail to punch a hole near one end of your long copper strip.
2. Use a screw to attach the metal strip near one end of the piece of wood (if you punch a little hole in the wood, the screw will go in more easily).
3. Install the other screw in the wood so that the loose end of the metal strip touches but is not attached to it. Bend the metal strip up about 2 cm. (1 in.).
4. Cut one of your circuit wires in the middle of the bare place you made when you were constructing a short circuit.
5. Attach one end of the bare wire to each screw.
6. When you finish, your circuit should look like Figure 155-1.
7. Can you use it to make the light turn on and off? Why?

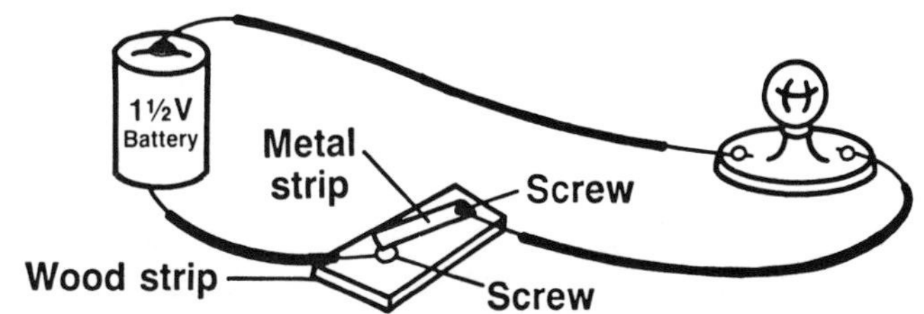

FIGURE 155-1. Battery and bulb with switch in circuit.

TEACHER INFORMATION

If possible, sheet copper should be used because it is easier to cut and there is less chance of sharp edges and corners. For best results, the wires should be under the screws when they are tightened down. The copper strip can be somewhat shorter but it should go up and down easily, since it will be used later as the key in a telegraph.

This circuit is sometimes called a *complete circuit* because it has the following:

a. A power source (battery)
b A path through which the current can flow (wire)
c. A resistor to use current (light)
d. A switch to turn it on and off

ACTIVITY 156: How Can You Make a Series Circuit?

MATERIALS NEEDED

- 1½-volt dry-cell battery
- Circuit and switch from previous activity
- Two additional small light sockets with flashlight bulbs
- Two pieces of insulated single-strand copper wire 10 cm. (4 in.) long
- Small screwdriver

PROCEDURE

1. For this and some of the following activities, we will use a 1½-volt dry-cell battery instead of a flashlight battery. It will produce the same amount of electric current, but it is easier to use and will last longer.
2. In this activity, we will add two lights to our circuit.
3. Replace the flashlight cell with the dry cell and test to be certain your circuit and switch work.
4. Disconnect one wire from your light socket and connect it to one terminal of another socket with one 10-cm. length of wire. Use another 10-cm. length of wire to connect the other terminal of your second socket to the third socket. Connect the long wire from the battery to the third socket. When you finish your circuit should look like Figure 156-1.
5. Now close the switch. Do the lights come on? Unscrew one bulb. What happened? Can you explain why?

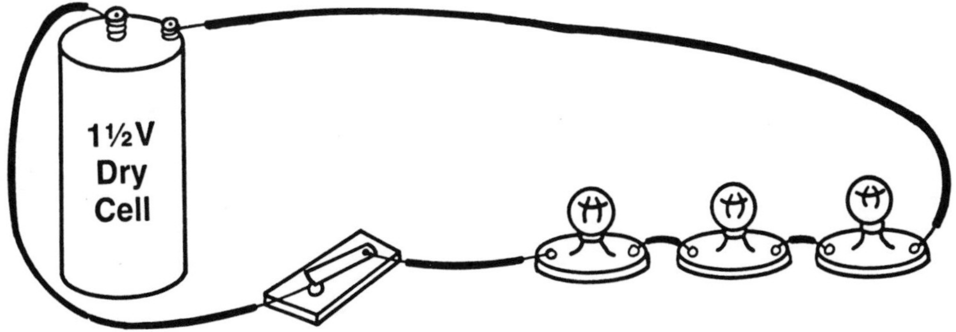

FIGURE 156-1. Battery, switch, and three bulbs wired in series.

TEACHER INFORMATION

Before letting the children use the large dry cell batteries, you may want to remove the screw caps on the terminals to remind the children not to leave the wires connected when they are not in use. Dry cells have the advantage of being easier to handle and simpler to hook up in series. They produce the same amount of voltage as a flashlight cell but they do not wear down as quickly and may produce more heat in a short-circuit situation.

Be certain the two 10-cm. lengths of wire are stripped on both ends. The circuit the students have constructed is called *series* because the electric current travels through the wire in one path and the resistors (lights) and switch are all part of that single path. If one portion of a series circuit is missing, the current will not flow, because it must have a complete path *from* the power source *to* the power source. If a light bulb is removed, the path is broken and all the lights go out.

ENRICHMENT

Compare the brightness of the lights in this circuit to that of the light in Activity 155.

ACTIVITY 157: How Can You Make a Parallel Circuit?

MATERIALS NEEDED

- Series circuit from Activity 156
- Screwdriver
- Wire stripper
- Two additional pieces of insulated single-strand copper wire 10 cm. (4 in.) long

PROCEDURE

1. Use the additional pieces of wire to change your circuit so it looks like the one in Figure 157-1.

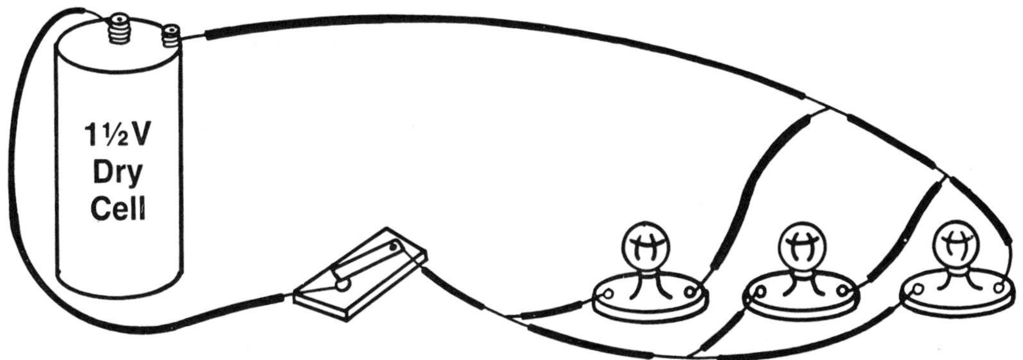

FIGURE 157-1. Battery, switch, and three bulbs in parallel.

2. Close the switch so all bulbs are lit. Unscrew one bulb. What happened? Unscrew two bulbs.
3. Can you explain how this circuit is different from the one in Activity 156?

TEACHER INFORMATION

A parallel circuit provides an independent path for the electric current to travel to each light and back to the power source. The lights will burn brighter because the current does not have to travel through a series of resistors (the other lights).

ACTIVITY 158: What Materials Will Conduct Electricity?

MATERIALS NEEDED

- Circuit used in Activity 155, with switch removed to expose bare wires
- Dry-cell battery in place of flash-light cell
- Small objects made of different materials, such as paper clips, nails, wire, wood, rubber bands, glass, plastic, coins, rocks

PROCEDURE

1. Test your circuit by touching the bare wires together. The light should go on.
2. Choose objects from the pile on the table. Touch both bare wires to each object about 2 cm. (1 in.) apart and observe the light.

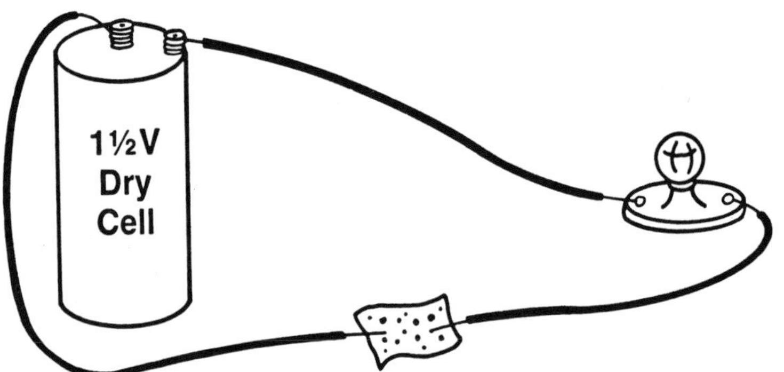

FIGURE 158-1. Battery, bulb, and conductor.

3. Use the information you have learned about circuits to explain what is happening.

TEACHER INFORMATION

This activity introduces the idea of conductors and nonconductors. Nonconductors are sometimes called insulators. Most metals are conductors to some degree since electricity will move through them. Some materials, such as glass, rubber, and plastic, are insulators and prevent the movement of electrons.

ACTIVITY 159: What Is Resistance?

MATERIALS NEEDED

- Circuit with battery and bare wires used in Activity 158
- Large writing pencil with 8 cm. (3 in.) of wood removed on one half to expose the lead (carbon core)

PROCEDURE

1. Touch the ends of the bare wire to the lead core of the pencil, as far apart as possible.
2. Slowly move the bare wires closer together and observe the light.
3. Can you use the information you have learned about conductors to explain this?
4. Have you seen anything like this principle used in a home or an automobile?

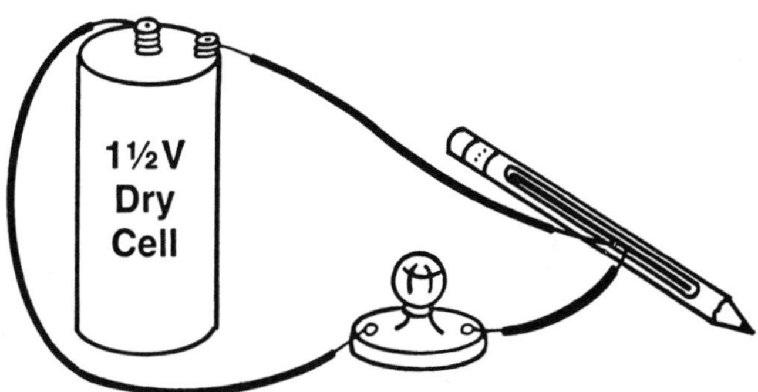

FIGURE 159-1. Battery, bulb, and lead pencil.

TEACHER INFORMATION

This is a demonstration of variable resistance. Carbon will conduct electric current but not nearly as well as copper. Because it resists the flow of current, it is an example of one kind of resistor. As the bare copper wires are moved closer together, the resistance is gradually overcome and the light gradually becomes brighter. This is the principle of the rheostat used to dim automobile dash lights, and some lights in homes, theaters, and in public buildings.

ENRICHMENT

As a teacher demonstration, connect a length of very thin iron wire to the bare ends of the copper wire. The wire will glow brightly and break rapidly. This type of resistance, when controlled, is used in light globes and many appliances that produce heat energy.

ACTIVITY 160: How Does Electric Current Affect a Compass?

MATERIALS NEEDED

- Insulated 22-gauge copper wire, 50 cm. (20 in.) long, stripped on each end
- 1½-volt dry-cell battery
- Compass

PROCEDURE

1. From your study of magnetism, do you remember that a compass is a magnet suspended so it can turn freely? The magnetic field of the earth causes it to point north unless another magnet comes near it.
2. Put your compass flat on the table and note in which direction it is pointing.
3. Connect one end of the wire to a terminal of the battery and place the wire across the top of the compass.
4. Touch the other end of the wire to the second terminal of the battery (don't connect it).
5. Move the wire to different positions on top of the compass and observe the needle as you send current through the wire.
6. What is happening? Discuss this with the class.

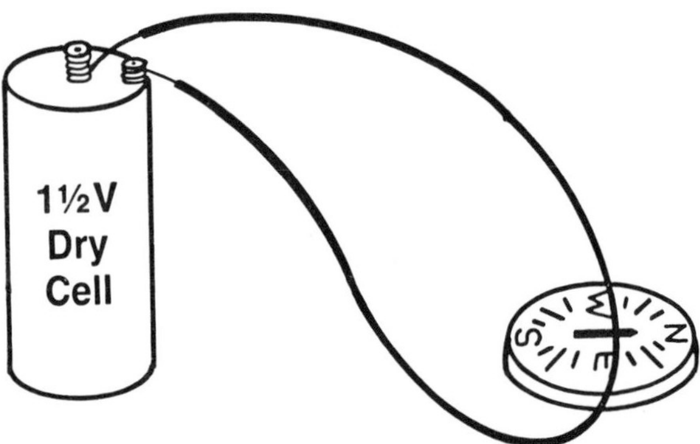

FIGURE 160-1. Battery, wire, and compass.

TEACHER INFORMATION

When an electric current flows through a wire, a magnetic field is formed around the wire. Through this activity, students may decide that electricity is in some way related to magnetism. The next activity will help them visualize what is really happening.

CAUTION: A copper wire without a resistor (such as a light bulb) is a short circuit. The wire should be connected only momentarily; otherwise, it will get very hot and the electricity will drain rapidly.

ACTIVITY 161: What Happens When Electric Current Flows Through a Wire?

MATERIALS NEEDED

- Circuit used in Activity 160
- Iron filings
- 5-in. × 7-in. card

PROCEDURE

1. Connect one end of the wire to a terminal of the battery.
2. Place the card flat and level over the middle part of the wire.
3. Connect the other end of the wire to the battery and quickly sprinkle iron filings on the card.
4. Disconnect the wire and observe the card.
5. Have you seen something like this before? Look carefully at the filings.
6. What conclusions can you make? Discuss this with the class.

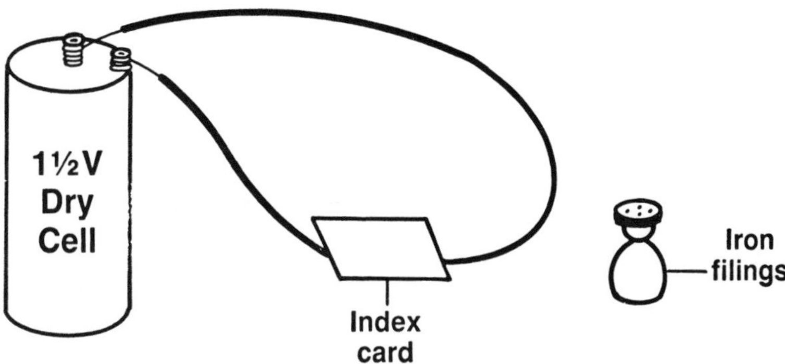

FIGURE 161-1. Battery, wire, card, and iror 'ilıngs.

TEACHER INFORMATION

When current flows through the wire, the iron filings will line up along the path of the wire because of the magnetic field created around it. Note that iron filings do not line up with the wire, but perpendicular to it instead. This indicates that the *lines of force* of the magnetic field are perpendicular to the direction of the flow of current.

ACTIVITY 162: What Is an Electromagnet?

MATERIALS NEEDED

- 1 m. (39 in.) of 22-gauge insulated copper wire stripped on both ends
- 1½-volt dry-cell battery
- Large iron nail no longer than 10 cm. (4 in.)
- Paper clips

PROCEDURE

1. In Activities 160 and 161, we learned that when an electric current flows through a wire, a magnetic field is formed around the wire.
2. Coil the wire ten times around the nail. Bring it near some paper clips. What happened?
3. Attach one end of the wire to a terminal of the battery. Bring the nail near some clips. Touch the other end of the wire to the other terminal of the battery. What happened?
4. Disconnect the wire from one terminal of the battery. Hold the nail above the table and observe what happens.
5. What can you say about this?

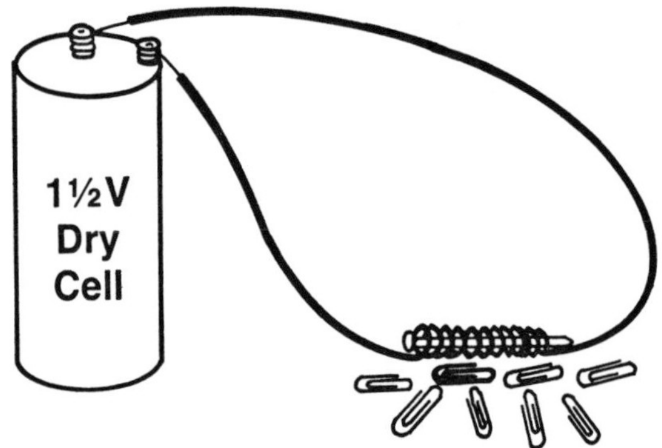

FIGURE 162-1. Electromagnet with paper clips.

TEACHER INFORMATION

The nail will not pick up paper clips until current flows through the coil of wire. The coil of wire creates a magnetic field that causes the soft iron nail to become a temporary magnet and attract the clips. When the electric current is cut off, the nail will gradually lose its magnetism and the clips will fall off. This is another form of induction, similar to that discussed in Section 7, "Magnetism."

The nail you use should be no longer than 10 cm. (4 in.). Very large, thick nails will retain their magnetic properties for a longer period of time and will not release the paper clips readily when the current is turned off.

ACTIVITY 163: What Is a Way to Change the Strength of an Electromagnet?

MATERIALS NEEDED

- Same as those for Activity 162

PROCEDURE

1. As you perform the activities with electromagnets, remember not to leave them connected to the battery any longer than necessary.
2. Use your electromagnet with 10 coils to pick up as many paper clips as you can at one time. Record the number of clips it picked up.
3. Wrap 10 more coils of wire around the nail, connect it to the battery and see how many clips you can pick up at one time Record the number.
4. What do you think would happen if you wrapped 10 more coils around your electromagnet? Try it.
5. What can you say about this?

TEACHER INFORMATION

Increasing the number of coils of wire will increase the strength of the magnetic field. This is one way to make an electromagnet stronger. Using a stronger electric current will also increase the force of an electromagnet.

ACTIVITY 164: What Is Another Way to Change the Strength of an Electromagnet?

MATERIALS NEEDED

- Two 1½-volt dry-cell batteries
- 1 m. of insulated copper wire
- One 10-cm. (4-in.) length of insulated copper wire stripped at both ends
- One large nail
- Box of paper clips
- Paper and pencil

PROCEDURE

1. Make an electromagnet with ten coils of wire.
2. Use one battery with your electromagnet and see how many clips you can pick up at one time. Record the results.
3. Observe your dry-cell battery. Notice it has a terminal (connector) in the center and one near the outside edge. Unless otherwise marked, the center terminal is called positive (+) and the outer terminal is called negative (−). If you connect a wire from the negative terminal of one battery to the positive terminal of another, you have wired the batteries in series and increased the voltage to the sum total of the voltage of both batteries. The wires from the circuit are attached to the other terminal of each battery.
4. Use the 10-cm. wire to connect a second battery in series. Now, when you use your electromagnet, the wire will be carrying three volts.
5. Connect your electromagnet as shown in Figure 164-1 and pick up as many clips as you can. Record the results.
6. What do you think would happen if you used two batteries and 20 coils of wire? Try it.

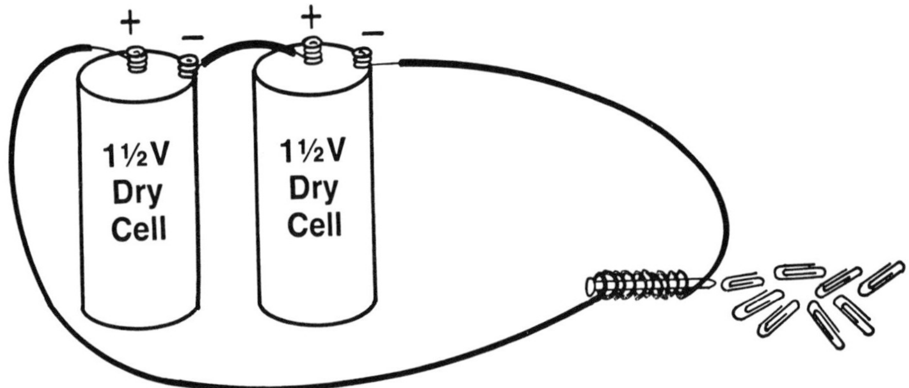

FIGURE 164-1. Electromagnet with two batteries and paper clips.

TEACHER INFORMATION

Series wiring is commonly used to increase the voltage of dry-cell batteries. Six- and nine-volt batteries contain four and six cells. Each cell produces 1½ volts connected in series. More about batteries and how they work is developed later in this section.

ACTIVITY 165: What Happens When Current Flowing Through a Wire Changes Direction?

MATERIALS NEEDED

- 50-cm. (20 in.) length of insulated single-strand copper wire stripped at both ends
- Flashlight battery
- Compass

PROCEDURE

1. Place the center of the wire over the compass as you did in Activity 160. Touch the ends of the wire to the terminals of the battery and watch the needle.
2. Now touch the ends of the wire to the opposite terminals of the battery. Since electricity flows *from* the negative (−) terminal *to* the positive (+) you have reversed the flow of current through the wire.
3. Switch the ends of the wires several times. What happens to the compass needle?

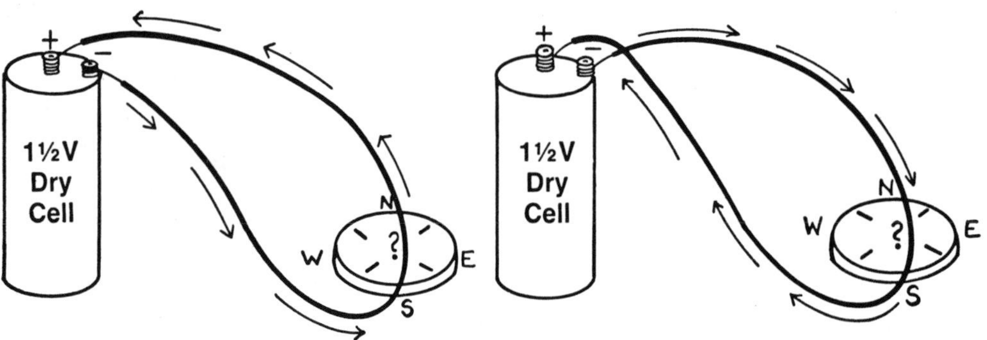

FIGURE 165-1. Compasses near wires with current flowing in opposite directions.

TEACHER INFORMATION

The direction of flow of electric current has not been used until now. At this point you should emphasize that electricity produced in this manner flows in one direction through the wire. It flows from the negative to the positive terminals of the battery when a path is provided. We will discover later that some current moves back and forth, or *alternates,* within a wire.

Each time the direction of the flow of current changes in this activity, the compass needle will reverse, indicating that the poles of the electromagnetic field switch when the direction of the flow of current is reversed.

ACTIVITY 166: How Does the Direction of the Flow of Current Affect an Electromagnet?

MATERIALS NEEDED

- Electromagnet used in Activity 164
- 1½-volt dry-cell battery
- Compass
- Two bar magnets
- String 20 cm. (8 in.) long

PROCEDURE

1. Place the compass flat on the table. Connect your electromagnet to the battery and bring it near the compass. Observe which end of the needle points to the electromagnet.
2. Switch the ends of the wires leading to the battery terminals as you did in Activity 165. What happens to the compass needle?
3. Suspend one bar magnet from the piece of string. Bring each end of the other bar magnet near it. What happened? This should help you remember a characteristic of magnets that you learned when you were studying magnetism.
4. Bring your nail and coil of wire near both ends of the suspended bar magnet (don't connect it to the battery yet). What happened?
5. Connect the wires to the battery and bring the pointed end of the electromagnet near the bar magnet. Now turn your electromagnet around so the flat end comes near the bar magnet. What happened?
6. Keep the flat end near the suspended bar magnet and reverse the flow of current through your electromagnet by switching the wires on the battery terminals. Do this several times and observe the behavior of the bar magnet (don't move the electromagnet). What can you say about this characteristic of an electromagnet?

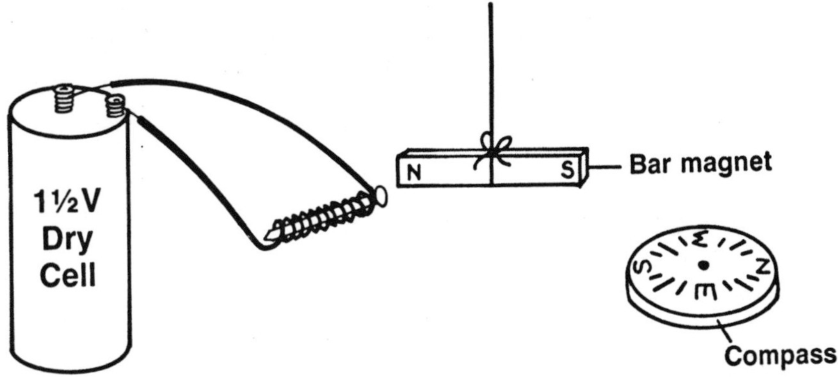

FIGURE 166-1. Electromagnet, compass, and suspended magnet.

TEACHER INFORMATION

Electromagnets have poles. When the direction of the flow of current is reversed (in this case by switching wires on the terminals), the poles of the electromagnet reverse. This is a characteristic of electromagnets that is not found in permanent magnets. Because of this phenomenon, electric motors and generators are possible. To demonstrate this try the following:

Have one student hold the electromagnet near the suspended bar magnet. Have another student touch the wires to the battery. As soon as the poles of the two magnets come close to each other, switch the wires on the terminals of the battery. The pole of the electromagnet, which was attracting a pole of the bar magnet, will reverse and repel the same pole of the bar magnet (remember opposites attract, likes repel). With practice, the students can make the bar magnet spin around by reversing the poles of the electromagnet. Now all that is needed is a device to switch the direction of current automatically and you have a simple electric motor.

ACTIVITY 167: How Can You Tell If Electric Current Is Flowing Through a Wire?

MATERIALS NEEDED

- 10 m. (11 yds.) of 22-gauge insulated copper wire stripped at both ends
- Three 10-cm. (4-in.) lengths of wire
- One 30-cm. (12-in.) length of wire
- Steel needle
- One 20-cm. (8-in.) strip of wood lath
- Dry-cell battery
- Thread
- Paper clip
- Bar magnet

PROCEDURE

1. Make a coil of your long piece of wire by winding it around a dry-cell battery. Don't coil about 50 cm. (20 in.) at each end.
2. Remove the coil from the battery and use the 10-cm. (4-in.) pieces of wire to hold it together in three places.
3. Use the 30-cm. (12-in.) wire to secure it in an upright position on the lath.
4. Magnetize the needle by rubbing it 30 times in the same direction with a bar magnet. It should now pick up a paper clip.
5. Use thread to hang the needle balanced in the middle of the coil. Compare your finished product with Figure 167-1.
6. We have learned that electric current flowing through a wire causes a magnetic field to form around the wire. We found that when the wire is coiled, the magnetic field is stronger. The needle is a magnet. If an electric current flows through the coil of wire, what do you predict will happen?
7. Touch the bare ends of your coil of wire to the dry cell. Was your prediction correct?

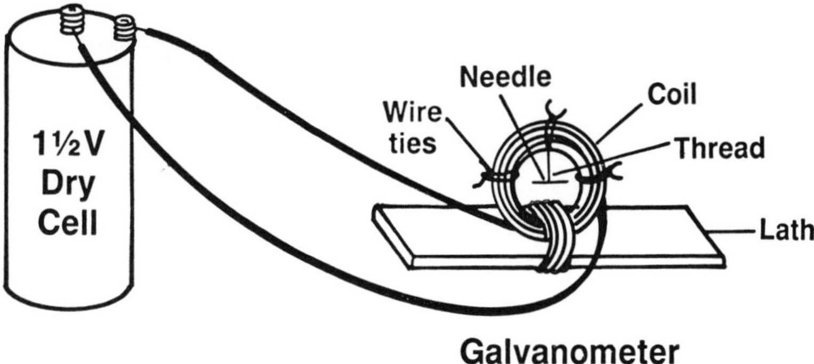

FIGURE 167-1. Coil of wire with suspended needle.

8. This is a simple galvanometer used to detect the direction and flow of electric current. Touch the wires to a battery and notice the direction the needle points. Now, switch the wires on the terminals of the battery. This device can be used to detect the flow of even small amounts of electric current.

TEACHER INFORMATION

Ideally, each child should construct a galvanometer. Groups of three or four should be maximum. If a middle-grader is able to construct, explain, and predict the behavior of a galvanometer, it will indicate that he or she understands some of the important ideas about magnetism and electricity.

Several galvanometers will be needed in the following activities. If cost is a limiting factor, a somewhat higher-gauge (thinner) wire could be substituted, but there is increased danger of heat.

ACTIVITY 168: How Is Electricity Produced by Chemical Means?

MATERIALS NEEDED

- Wide-mouthed glass cup or jar
- 8-cm. (3-in.) zinc strip
- 8-cm. (3-in.) copper strip
- 8-cm. (3-in.) carbon rod
- Salt
- Lemon juice
- Vinegar
- Water
- Galvanometer

PROCEDURE

1. Add water to the jar or cup until it is three-fourths full.
2. Dissolve two teaspoons of salt in the water.
3. Tightly connect one end of your galvanometer to the copper strip and put it in the glass. Bend your zinc strip into a hook on one end and hang it inside the glass.
4. Wait a few seconds. Observe the needle of your galvanometer as you firmly touch the other wire to the zinc strip.
5. What happened? Wait a few seconds and try again.
6. Replace the copper strip with the carbon rod and repeat the activity.
7. Try lemon juice in place of salt water. Try vinegar. (Be sure to rinse the jar or cup thoroughly after each investigation.)
8. When you have tested all the materials, ask your teacher to explain what is happening.

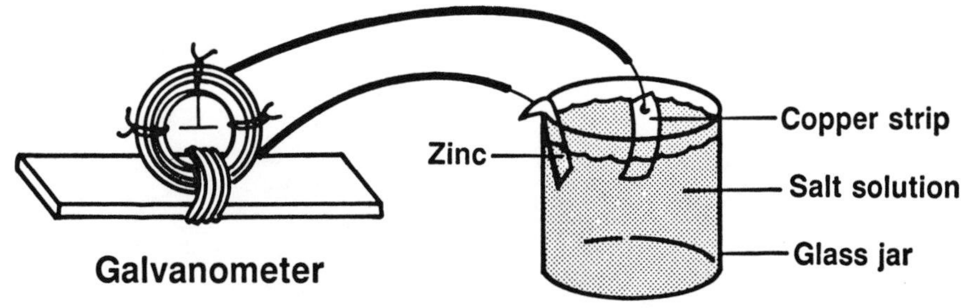

FIGURE 168-1. Homemade cell galvanometer.

TEACHER INFORMATION

When placed in an acid or base (alkaline) solution, some materials give up or take on electrons readily through a chemical process called ionization. Zinc metal changes into ions, and furnishes electrons to the negative terminal. When a low-resistance-path copper wire is provided from a negative material to a positive one, electrons will flow along the path (galvanometer) from the zinc to the copper or carbon. You can explain this using the diagram in Figure 168-1 by adding plus (+) along the side of the copper or carbon rod and minus (−) along the zinc strip. The reason the children are asked to wait a few seconds before touching the wire to the zinc is to allow time for the electrons to build opposite charges on the copper and zinc strips. Carbon rods and zinc strips may be obtained from old dry-cell or flashlight batteries. A carbon core runs through the center. The case is made of zinc.

ACTIVITY 169: How Does a Dry-Cell or Flashlight Battery Work?

(Teacher-supervised activity or teacher demonstration)

MATERIALS NEEDED

- Flashlight and dry-cell batteries cut in half
- Paper and pencil
- Illustration from Activity 168 (for comparison)

PROCEDURE

1. Compare the half flashlight or dry-cell battery with the diagram from Activity 168.
2. Except for the galvanometer, all the types of materials used in Activity 168 can be identified in the batteries. Can you find them?
3. Draw a picture of a battery cut in half. Label the parts. Compare your picture with those made by other members of the group. Can you explain how you think it works?
4. Have you ever seen a battery leak and damage a flashlight? Batteries contain a weak acid or alkaline solution usually in a tightly packed absorbent material. Since your battery is old, this solution has probably dried up.

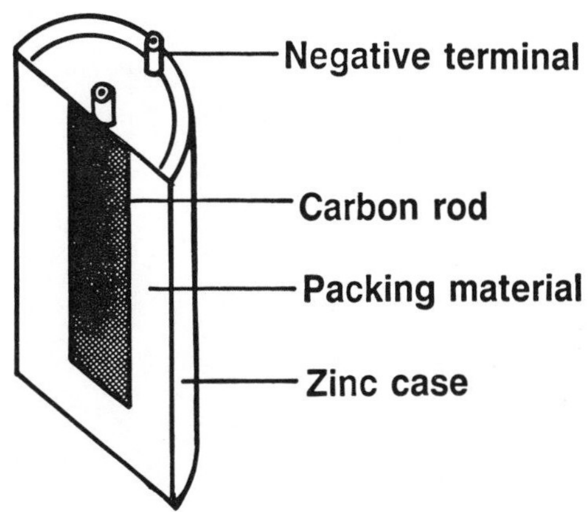

FIGURE 169-1. Cross section of dry cell.

TEACHER INFORMATION

By the end of this experience, students should be able to explain in general terms how electricity is produced by chemical means. Ionization is a relatively sophisticated concept, with several theories that are still being investigated.

Elementary school students should understand that certain materials will develop a positive or negative charge in the presence of an acid or a base (salt), and that chemically produced electricity flows in one direction, from negative to positive, in a conductor (wire).

Note: Batteries should be cut with a metal saw. Parents might do this. Be sure both terminals are on the batteries you use.

CAUTION: This activity involves the use of cut-open flashlight cells, exposing acid substances. Close supervision is very important to keep the acid from getting in eyes, or on skin, clothing, or other materials that might be damaged by the acid. Wash hands thoroughly after handling the cells.

ACTIVITY 170: How Can Electricity Be Produced by a Lemon?

MATERIALS NEEDED

- Large, fresh lemon
- Zinc and copper strips
- Galvanometer

PROCEDURE

1. Just for fun, let's try to turn a lemon into part of a battery.
2. Attach the copper strip to one wire of the galvanometer and stick it into the lemon.
3. Push the zinc strip into the lemon.
4. Wait a few seconds, then observe the needle on the galvanometer as you firmly touch the wire to the zinc strip. What happened? Wait a few seconds more and try again.
5. Using information you learned in Activities 168 and 169, explain what is happening.
6. Could you use another fruit such as a grapefruit or a tomato? Try it.

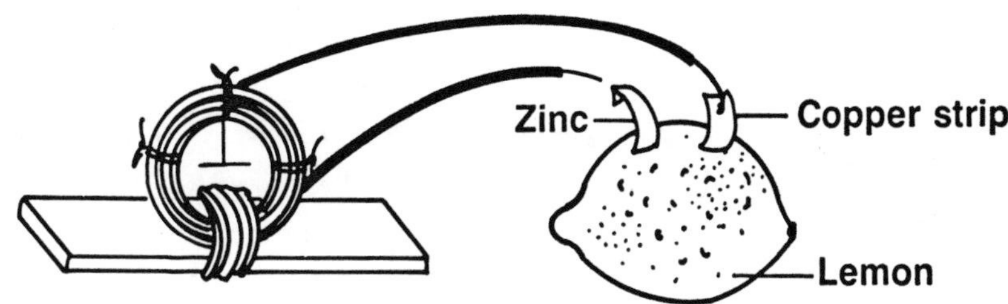

FIGURE 170-1. Lemon cell with coil of wire and suspended needle.

TEACHER INFORMATION

The lemon contains citric acid, which will cause the same reaction as other weak acids. Tomatoes and citrus fruits usually contain enough acid to affect the galvanometer.

If you have enough galvanometers, this is recommended as a "take-home-and-talk-about-it" activity.

ACTIVITY 171: How Can Mechanical Energy Produce Electricity?

MATERIALS NEEDED

- Galvanometer
- Galvanometer coil without needle
- Strong magnet

PROCEDURE

1. Securely attach the wires from one galvanometer to the other.
2. Hold the galvanometer without the needle in one hand and move the strong magnet back and forth through the center or around the coil.
3. Observe the needle on the other galvanometer. Can you see a relationship in what is happening?
4. Think of some words to describe the behavior of the needle. Discuss this with your teacher and other students.

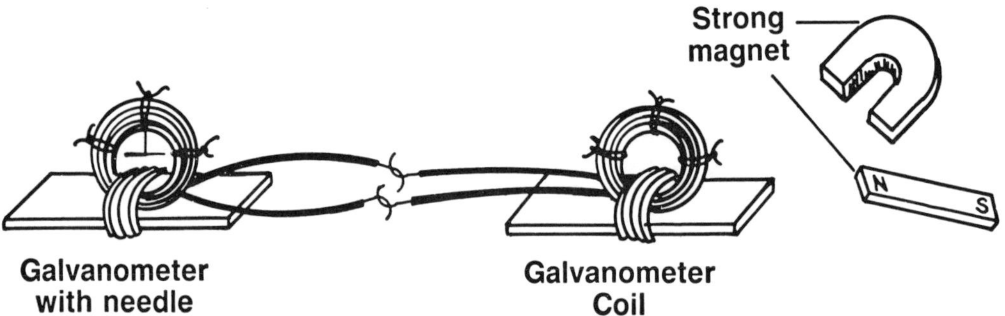

FIGURE 171-1. Two coils, suspended needle,and two magnets.

TEACHER INFORMATION

Remember, when electric current flows through a coil of wire, a magnetic field is created around the wire. In this case, the opposite is happening. A strong magnetic field is going through the coil of wire and creating an electric current. If you observe the needle closely as the magnet goes through the coil, it will reverse the direction in which it is pointing each time the magnet moves back and forth. Instead of flowing in one direction through the wire, the moving magnetic field causes the electrons to move back and forth or *alternate* their direction within the wire. Step 4 asks children to think of some words to describe the behavior of the needle. Electricity produced in this manner is called *alternating current.*

Because of this phenomenon, the generator, which is a powerful magnetic field passing through large coils of wire, has made electricity relatively inexpensive and plentiful in our lives.

If you can locate a small hand generator (crank type) you will notice it nothing more than a coil of wire turned mechanically in a strong magnetic fiela. Commercial electricity is usually produced by water or steam. A turbine, which is an enclosed water wheel with curved blades, spins rapidly when water or steam under great pressure is directed into it. This provides the mechanical energy to turn huge generators. Atomic energy is used in place of coal to heat the water and create steam to turn the turbines. See your encyclopedia for further information.

Use very thin insulated wire, if available, to make the coil for this activity.

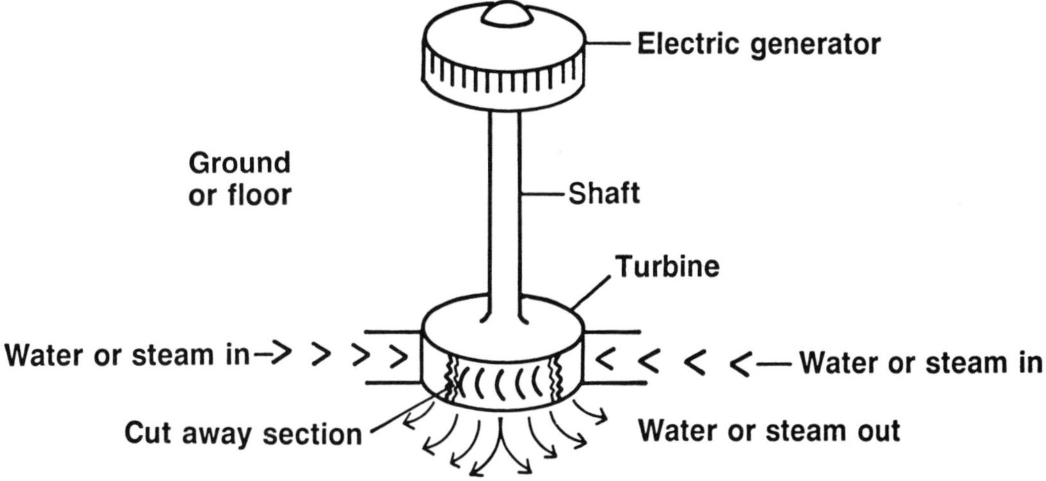

FIGURE 171-2. Generator.

ACTIVITY 172: What Is a New, Important Source of Electric Power?

MATERIALS NEEDED

- Solar cells
- Galvanometer
- Light source

PROCEDURE

1. In recent years scientists have been trying to find new sources of electricity to replace our rapidly diminishing fossil fuel resources (coal and oil). A most promising source is solar (sun) energy. Look at your solar cell. When light strikes this cell, a very small amount of electrical energy is produced.
2. Connect your cell to the galvanometer and shine a bright light on it. As you turn the light on and off, observe the needle on the galvanometer. What happens to the needle? Can you tell if the current is flowing in one direction or alternating?

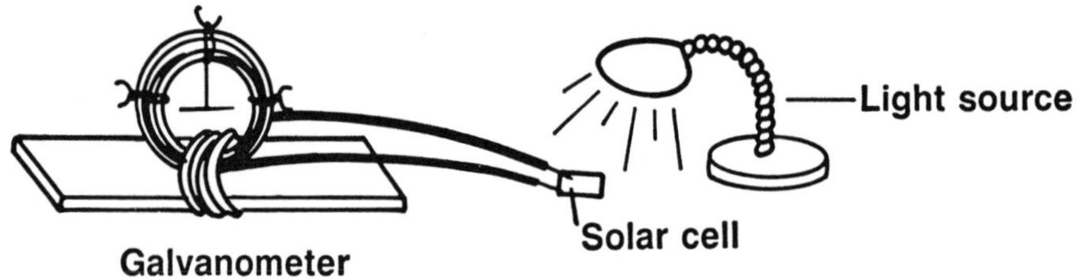

FIGURE 172-1. Solar cell in suspended needle circuit and light source.

TEACHER INFORMATION

Solar energy is becoming increasingly important and common in our lives. Most children have seen solar cells used in calculators, cameras, and other devices that require small amounts of electricity.

The space program has rapidly expanded the development of this energy source. Space vehicles and satellites use electricity produced in this manner to recharge the batteries that provide electrical power.

A major obstacle to wide use of solar power is the limited amount of electric current each cell can produce. Huge areas of solar cells are required to produce significant amounts of electrical energy. The current produced flows in one direction, just as in flashlight batteries. Also, on the earth, solar cells as primary producers of electrical energy are limited to daylight hours.

As with Activities 170 and 171 you need to construct the galvanometer for this activity using very thin insulated wire because of the small amounts of electric current that are generated.

Solar cells (often connected in series) can be obtained from many electrical or electronic stores.

ACTIVITY 173: How Can Electricity Help Us Communicate?

MATERIALS NEEDED

- Two small light sockets with bulbs
- Two switches (similar to those used in Activity 155)
- Dry-cell battery
- Six 1-m. (39-in.) lengths of insulated copper wire

PROCEDURE

1. Use your materials to construct a circuit like the one in Figure 173-1.
2. Press one switch. What happened?
3. Release the first switch and press the second one. What happened?
4. Press both switches at once.
5. Can you think of some use for a device like this?
6. If it is available, you could splice more wire into the circuit and take one switch and light into another room.

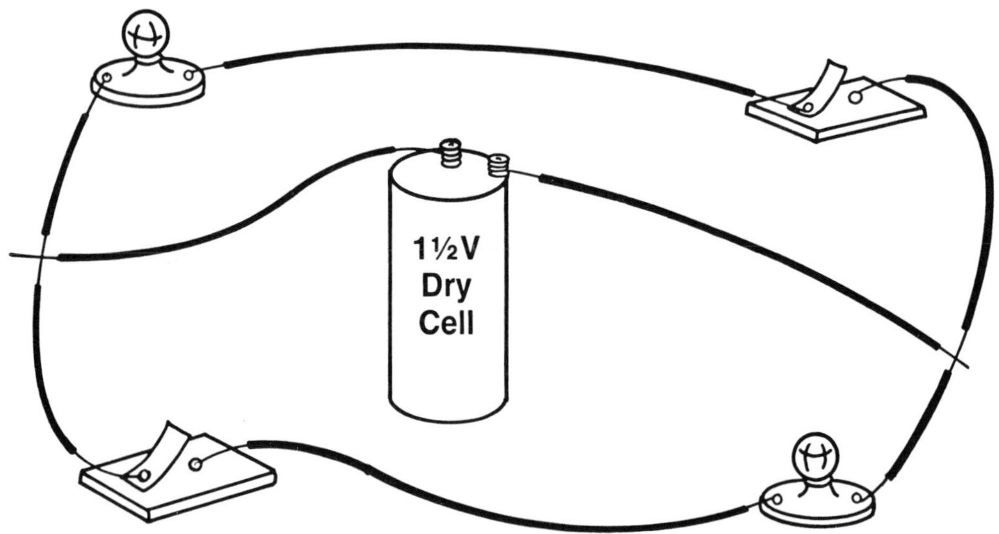

FIGURE 173-1. Two telegraphs wired to one battery.

TEACHER INFORMATION

This is a variation of the telegraph. There are several ways to wire the circuit. This is parallel. The original telegraph sets were wired in series so all keys but one had to be closed and all messages went through all the *sounders* in the circuit. Telegraph offices often followed the railroads and needed only one wire on the poles. The iron rails were used as the second or *ground* wire. The original telegraph, patented by Morse, used an electromagnet to attract a magnetic material (soft iron) and make a loud clicking sound. Telegraphers were trained to hear combinations of long and short "dots and dashes" to represent letters of the alphabet. This is called the Morse Code.

The completion of the transcontinental telegraph near the end of the Civil War was extremely significant. For the first time, a message could travel across the nation in seconds rather than weeks. The circuit above uses the electric light, which was not invented until much later. For enrichment, children might enjoy designing a telegraph using electromagnets.

BIBLIOGRAPHY

Selected Professional Texts

BLOUGH, GLENN O., AND JULIUS SCHWARTZ. *Elementary School Science and How to Teach It* (7th ed.). New York: Holt, Rinehart & Winston, 1984.

CARIN, ARTHUR A., AND ROBERT B. SUND. *Teaching Science Through Discovery* (5th ed.). Columbus, OH: Charles E. Merrill Pub. Co., 1985.

ESLER, WILLIAM K., AND MARY K. ESLER. *Teaching Elementary Science* (4th ed.). Belmont, CA: Wadsworth Pub. Co., 1984.

GEGA, PETER C. *Science in Elementary Education* (4th ed.). New York: John Wiley & Sons, Inc., 1982.

JACOBSEN, WILLARD J., AND ABBY BARRY BERGMAN. *Science for Children*. Englewood Cliffs, New Jersey: Prentice-Hall, 1980.

KAUCHAK, DONALD, AND PAUL EGGEN. *Exploring Science in Elementary Schools.* Chicago: Rand McNally, 1980.

ROWE, MARY BUDD. *Teaching Science as Continuous Inquiry: A Basic* (2d ed.). New York: McGraw-Hill, 1978.

VICTOR, EDWARD. *Science for the Elementary School* (5th ed.). New York: MacMillan Publishing Company, 1985.

Periodicals

Astronomy. AstroMedia Corp., 625 E. St. Paul Ave., Milwaukee, Wisconsin 53202

Audubon. National Audubon Society. 950 Third Ave., New York, NY 10022

Discover. Time Inc. 3435 Wilshire Blvd., Los Angeles, CA 90010

National Geographic. National Geographic Society, 17th and M Sts. N.W., Washington, DC 20036

Natural History. American Museum of Natural History, Central Park West at 79th St., New York, NY 10024

*Ranger Rick's Nature Magazine**. National Wildlife Federation, 1412 16th St. N.W., Washington, DC 20036

Science. American Association for the Advancement of Science, 1515 Massachusetts Ave. N.W., Washington, DC 20005

Science and Children. National Science Teachers Association, 1742 Connecticut Ave. N.W., Washington, DC 20009

Smithsonian. Smithsonian Associates, 900 Jefferson Dr., Washington, DC 20560

*World**. National Geographic Society, 17th and M Sts., Washington, DC 20036

*Zoo Books**. Wildlife Education Ltd., 930 West Washington St., San Diego, CA 92103

*For Elementary Age Students

Check on subscription addresses. Many periodicals are now using the National Data Center in Boulder, Colorado, rather than National Headquarters.

Sources of Free and Inexpensive Materials for the Physical Sciences

Before requesting free and inexpensive materials, consider the following:

1. Use school stationery whenever possible. Most suppliers prefer it; some require it.
2. When requesting free materials, it is an act of courtesy to include a self-addressed, stamped envelope.
3. Do not ask for excessive amounts of free materials. Remember, the suppliers are generously paying the costs.
4. Be specific in your requests.
5. A word of thanks is in order at the time of your request and upon receipt and use of the materials.

American Chemical Society
1155 Sixteenth Street, N.W.
Washington, DC 20036
(pamphlets entitled "Chemistry Brainteasers" and "A Chemistry Project from Start to Finish" available in free single copies, nominal charge for classroom sets)

American Indian Archaelogical Institute
Route 199, P.O. Box 260
Washington, CT 06793
(pamphlets about ancient Indian sites and common tools used)

American Iron and Steel Institute
1000 Sixteenth Street, N.W.
Washington, DC 20036
(booklet and filmstrip entitled "From Supernovas to Scientists" to You")

Chemical Manufacturers Association
2501 M Street, N.W.
Washington, DC 20037
(booklet about food additives; pamphlet entitled "Chemicals in Normal Everyday Foods"; a guide and glossary entitled "Consumers Chemistry")

Concern, Inc.
1794 Columbia Road, N.W.
Washington, DC 20009
(pamphlets about ecology, water, air, wetlands, etc., available at small charge)

General Motors
3044 West Grand Boulevard
Detroit, MI 48202
(catalog of teaching aids about cars and manufacturing)

International Oceanographic Foundation
3979 Rickenbacker Causeway
Miami, FL 33149
(booklets about careers in oceanography)

National Audubon Society
1130 Fifth Avenue
New York, NY 10001
(catalog of materials dealing with birds, wildlife, energy, etc., with prices)

National Coal Association
Coal Building
1130 Seventeenth Street, N.W.
Washington, DC 20036
(publications about coal, including an activity program for grades K–3 entitled "Discovering Coal")

National Science Teachers Association
1742 Connecticut Avenue, N.W.
Washington, DC 20009
(catalog of science publications, posters, and other learning aids, with prices)

Phillips Petroleum Company
Bartlesville, OK 74004
(information about various types of energy, the energy crisis, and solutions)

Union Carbide Consumer Products Co.
Old Ridgebury Road
Danbury, CT 06817
(pamphlet entitled "See How They Run" explains science experiments with batteries)

U.S. Committee for Energy Awareness (USCEA)
1735 First Street, N.W., Suite 500
Washington, DC 20036
(list of publications and audiovisuals about various types of energy, 1–25 copies free, larger quantities available for nominal charge with discount for educational services)

United States Department of Commerce
Weather Bureau
Washington, DC 20036
(posters, pamphlets, and booklets regarding weather, storms and warnings; booklets entitled "Amateur Weather Forecaster" and "Owlie Skywarns Weather Book")

Science Supply Houses

Carolina Biological Supply Co.
2700 York Rd.
Burlington, NC 27215

Central Scientific Company
2600 South Kostner Avenue
Chicago, IL 60623

Edmund Scientific
101 E. Gloucester Pike
Barrington, NJ 08007
(Catalog for industry and education)

Fisher Scientific Company
4901 West Lemoyne
Chicago, IL 60651

Flight Systems, Inc.
9300 East 68th Street
Raytown, MO 64133
(Model rocketry)

Frey Scientific
905 Hickory Lane
Mansfield, OH 44905
(General science catalog)

Markson Science, Inc.
7815 S. 46th St.
Phoenix, AZ 85040
(Similar to Edmund)

MMI Space Science Corp.
2950 Wyman Parkway
P.O. Box 19907
Baltimore, MD 21211
(Astronomy and space science, teaching materials reference catalog)

Sargent-Welch Scientific Co.
7300 N. Linder Ave.
P.O. Box 1026
Skokie, IL 60077
(General science supply, similar to Frey)

Ward's Natural Science Establishment
3000 Ridge Road East
Rochester, NY 14622